GROWTH
OF THE
BLACK
POPULATION

GROWTH
OF THE
BLACK
POPULATION
a study of demographic trends

REYNOLDS FARLEY

University of Michigan

MARKHAM PUBLISHING COMPANY / CHICAGO

MARKHAM SOCIOLOGY SERIES

Robert W. Hodge, Editor

ADAMS, *Kinship in an Urban Setting*
FARLEY, *Growth of the Black Population: A Study of Demographic Trends*
FILSTEAD, ed., *Qualitative Methodology: Firsthand Involvement in the Social World*
LAUMANN, SIEGEL and HODGE, eds., *The Logic of Social Hierarchies*
ZEITLIN, ed., *American Society, Inc.: Studies of the Social Structure and Political Economy of the United States*

ACKNOWLEDGMENTS

Professor Donald Bogue of the University of Chicago first encouraged me to study trends in the fertility of blacks in the United States. For a long time, I was convinced that the difficulties of conducting research on this topic far outweighed any merits that such a study might have. However, I had the very good fortune to spend two summers working for Wilson Grabill at the Bureau of the Census on fertility research. Discussions with him and observations of his ability to detect fertility trends from seemingly chaotic data eventually led me to believe that a study of these fertility trends was possible. As a result, I completed a dissertation describing Negro cohort fertility. Chapters 4 and 10 of this monograph are revised and up-dated versions of that dissertation.

Professor Philip Hauser, Judah Matras, and Karl Taeuber of the University of Chicago were insistent that I not only describe the trend of fertility but account for the observed changes. This challenge led to investigations of fluctuations in mortality, migration, economic status, and health conditions in order to explain why the fertility rates of blacks fell before World War II and increased thereafter.

Many of my teachers and colleagues at the University of Chicago, Duke University and the University of Michigan frequently provided advice and intellectual stimulation as well as answers to factual questions. Among these were Nathan Keyfitz, Hal Winsborough, Dudley Duncan, Albert Hermalin, William Hodge, and James Palmore. Ronald Freedman and David Goldberg of the University of Michigan commented upon earlier drafts of this monograph. Paul Glick, of the Bureau of the Census and Arthur Campbell, then with the National Center for Health Statistics, were helpful in providing the necessary data and pointing out possible deficiencies.

Financial support for this investigation was obtained from two major sources. The Rockefeller Foundation provided assistance for most of the computations reported in this study as well as clerical and secretarial help. The Cooperative Research and Demonstration Grants Program of the Social and Rehabilitation Service of the Department of Health, Education, and Welfare, Grant Number CRD-458-C1-9, "Urbanization and Its Effects on the Negro Family," supported the investigations reported in Chapters 6 and 7. A Duke University Faculty Research Grant was also of assistance in this study.

CONTENTS

1. THE GROWTH OF THE BLACK
    POPULATION: Introduction and Summary
    of Findings   1

2. THE GROWTH OF THE BLACK
    POPULATION BEFORE THE CIVIL WAR   15

3. THE DEVELOPMENT OF A NATIONAL
    NEGRO POPULATION   41

4. RECENT CHANGES IN NEGRO FERTILITY   76

5. DIFFERENTIALS IN NEGRO FERTILITY   101

6. TRENDS IN MARITAL STATUS AND
    THEIR EFFECT UPON FERTILITY   121

7. THE PROCESS OF FAMILY FORMATION   166

8. THE USE OF BIRTH CONTROL   192

9. THE EFFECTS OF CHANGES IN HEALTH
    CONDITIONS AND STANDARDS OF
    LIVING   206

10. APPENDIX: The Construction of Negro
    Cohort Fertility Rates   246

    Subject Index   279

    Author Index   284

Chapter 1

THE GROWTH OF THE BLACK POPULATION: INTRODUCTION AND SUMMARY OF FINDINGS

The black population of the area now known as the United States grew from an estimated sixty persons in 1630 to over twenty-three million in mid-1969.[1] During the early seventeenth century, merchants in the colonial ports needed manual laborers. It was difficult to obtain workers from European countries and they began importing Negro slaves. One important advantage of this source of labor was that slaves reproduced and thereby insured a continuing supply of workers. During the eighteenth century, planters in the southern colonies discovered a burgeoning market for their prime crops: tobacco and rice. They too needed additional laborers and imported slaves in large numbers. As a result, the black population grew rapidly; by the time of the American Revolution there were almost three-quarters of a million Negroes in the thirteen states. They composed about one-fifth of the nation's population.

Since the Revolution, the Negro population has continued to grow. This growth has occurred primarily through natural increase, not immigration. This monograph is concerned with the demographic expansion of the American Negro population. The first aim is to describe the varying rates of population growth. This is done by analyzing trends in fertility and trends in mortality. The second aim is to account for changes in these demographic rates. Sociological factors, such as changes in the family system; ecological factors, such as rural to urban population

---

[1] A number of statistics are mentioned in this chapter. Methods of computation and sources of information are discussed and documented in the substantive chapters which follow.

1

shifts; and economic and health conditions are examined to explain the growth of the black population.

Changes in Negro Fertility Rates

It is very difficult to learn much about the childbearing of blacks in the pre-Revolutionary period. None of the colonies had reliable birth registration systems and there were no regular censuses. We can do no more than determine that the Negro population must have grown by 4 percent each year from 1700 to 1790. This population growth was a consequence of both natural increase and the importing of slaves.

It is easier to describe population growth since 1790 for censuses have been taken every ten years. Between the time of the Revolution and the Civil War, the Negro population continued to grow rapidly at a rate in excess of 2 percent each year. The population doubled between 1790 and 1820; and then doubled again in the next thirty year interval. Some historians have argued that the continued importing of slaves explains this growth. However, an examination of historical and demographic evidence indicates that while some slaves entered during this period, they must have been few in number. The primary reason for population growth since the Revolution has been natural increase: births have been more numerous than deaths.

It is impossible to ascertain exactly how high the birth rates were at the beginning of the nineteenth century. The United States censuses did not ask blacks their age or tabulate Negroes by sex until 1820. But there is a more extensive collection of census data for blacks for the period from 1830 to 1850. Techniques of demographic analysis, particularly the quasi-stable population techniques, were used to derive vital rates for this span.

In the pre-Civil War period, the crude birth rate was about 55 per 1,000 and the general fertility rate, that is, births per 1,000 women in the childbearing age range of 15 to 44, was about 250, indicating that each year one-quarter of the women of childbearing age bore a child.

Data from the Census of 1910 provide some additional information about family size during the last century. Negro women who began their childbearing in the decade prior to the Civil War and who survived to menopause, bore an average of almost seven children. Fewer than 10 percent had no children and upwards of 30 percent had ten or more children. The fertility rates of blacks must have reached a biological maximum before the Civil War. Chapter 2 explores these matters in greater detail.

Apparently, the black population continued to grow rapidly for a decade or so after the Civil War. We cannot be certain of this for the post-Civil War censuses were particularly deficient, and many people were omitted in the enumerations of 1870 and 1890. The Negro growth rate began to slacken after 1880, and for a long time the growth rate decreased. Reduction in fertility was the major reason why the black population switched from rapid to slow growth.

We cannot trace in detail the declines in fertility for we know little about birth rates during the latter decades of the last century or the early decades of this century. The stable population methodology cannot be used to estimate fertility rates and the vital registration system was incomplete. However, we know that the crude birth rate sunk to a level of about 20 per 1,000 by the 1930s and the general fertility rate was approximately 100, indicating that about one out of ten women in the childbearing ages had a child each year.

This monograph describes the calculation of cohort fertility rates for blacks. These rates allow us to know how rapidly women born in a given period formed their families, and how many children they eventually had. In addition, they permit us to analyze how different age groups of women contributed to the fertility rate of a particular year.

The cohort fertility analysis indicates that Negro women who were born between 1900 and 1910 were most affected by the very low fertility rates of the Depression years—the 1930s. These cohorts bore fewer children than either the women who preceded them or the women born more recently. They completed their childbearing with an average of two and one-half children. An important reason for the lower fertility was an increase in the proportion of women who never bore a child. Approximately 30 percent of the women born during the early years of the twentieth century never had children. There was also a decrease in the proportion of women who had many children. Between the Civil War and the Depression, Negro fertility rates were cut in half or, perhaps even more, and the average family size reduced by about four children.

A resurgence of rapid population growth among blacks began around 1940. The growth rate during the 1940s was two times the growth rate of the 1930s. From 1950 to 1960, the black population increased by over 2 percent each year. A sharp upturn in fertility accounts for these recent changes in growth. The crude birth rate climbed to 35 per 1,000 in the late 1950s and the general fertility rate increased to 160, reaching a peak in the 1955–59 period.

Many of the women who began their families after World War II are still young enough to bear additional children. For this reason, we cannot be certain of the full effects which the baby boom will have upon family size. The peak fertility performance will probably belong either to the women born between 1930 and 1934 or to the women born between 1935 and 1939. Considering their fertility up to 1966, we can conjecture that the women born in the years 1930–34 will complete childbearing with an average of at least four children. Black women born in 1935–39 got off to an even faster start in their family formation. It is possible that they may complete their families with an even larger number of children.

Childlessness has been greatly reduced and few of the women born during the 1930s will reach menopause without becoming mothers. Among whites, there has been a consistent shift away from large families but this has not happened among Negroes; rather, the proportion of black women bearing six, seven or more children increased during the post-World War II years. Chapter 4 discusses these recent changes in black fertility. Figure 1–1 illustrates the changes in family size and fertility, showing estimates of the completed family size for cohorts of black women born between 1835 and 1939.

Negro fertility rates, which were at a very high level before the Civil War, fell to a low level during the Depression but increased rapidly during and following World War II. Chapter 5 investigates whether this pattern of change characterized all groups of blacks or whether it was limited to certain groups. This chapter focuses upon differentials in childbearing.

This study finds that there have always been regional, rural-urban, and socio-economic differences in the fertility of blacks. For example, in 1880, as in 1967, Negro women who lived in the North had lower fertility rates than women who lived in the South. In 1910, as in 1960, women in cities, whether the cities were located in the North or South, bore fewer children than rural women. The wives of men with white collar jobs have consistently borne fewer children than the wives of men who worked as laborers. Extensively educated women have had smaller families than women who attended school for only a few years.

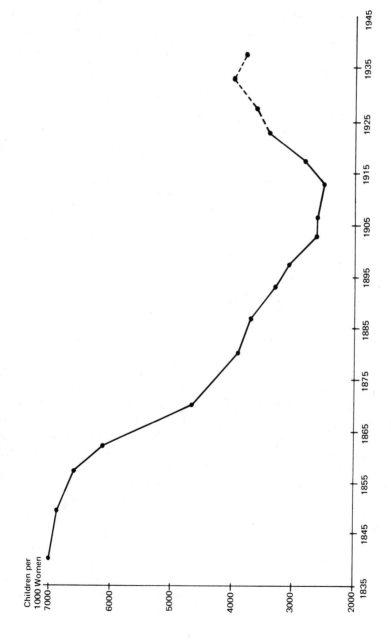

Figure 1-1
Estimates of Numbers of Children Ever-Born to Cohorts of Black Women

Between 1910 and 1940 similar fertility trends characterized all groups of black women. Among both urban and rural women and among women at all socio-economic levels, fertility decreased and childlessness became more common. In particular, the pre-1940 decline in childbearing cannot be attributed simply to the urbanization of blacks. Rural fertility rates fell rapidly, even more rapidly that those in cities, during the thirty-year period before 1940.

The years since 1940 have witnessed increases in fertility and decreases in childlessness among all groups of black women. Fertility went up among urban women, among college educated women as well as among women on southern farms and among women who did not even complete elementary school. There is evidence, however, that in the 1940 to 1960 period, increases in fertility were somewhat greater among rural women and among women with the characteristics of lower socio-economic status than among urban women or among higher status women. Thus, although there was a rise in fertility for all groups, differentials in fertility widened during this time span.

Trends in Mortality

It is even more problematic to study long run trends in death rates among blacks than it is to analyze trends in fertility. The censuses have asked no mortality question comparable to the query about the number of children ever born, which provides some information about fertility and which has been asked since 1890. There have also been fluctuations in the completeness of the census counts of blacks and changes in the accuracy with which age is reported. This makes it difficult to infer mortality rates from the census age distributions.

The national vital statistics figures indicate that since the 1930s death rates have fallen, and Negro life expectation at birth has gone up from about 48 years in 1930 to 64 years in 1966. What happened before 1930 is quite mysterious. We do know that death rates among urban blacks were very high early in this century. In 1900, for cities in the Death Registration Area, the infant mortality rate among blacks exceeded 300 deaths per 1,000 births. Life expectation at birth for Negroes in Washington, D.C. was thirty years for the period 1901–1910. There was a gradual shift of blacks away from rural areas into urban areas, and this may have limited improvements in health conditions since reported death rates were typically higher in cities than elsewhere.

The quasi-stable population techniques can be used with data for the pre-Civil War era. These suggest that the crude death rate must have been about 30 per 1,000 and that there were 250 to 300 infant deaths per 1,000 live births each year. A Negro, who survived to age ten during the period 1830 to 1850, could have expected to live approximately 41 additional years. The national life table for blacks in 1930 indicated an expectation of life at age ten of 45 years. This suggests that, with the exception of a possible reduction in infant and childhood mortality, there may have been minimal gains in life expectation during the seven decades following the Emancipation.

Contemporary accounts indicate that the death rate among blacks went up sharply during and after the Civil War. Regular food supplies were interrupted and contagious diseases spread among the camps occupied by many of the freedmen. Unfortunately, it is not possible to obtain demographic measures of these changes in mortality.

Between the end of Reconstruction and the Depression decade, certain major diseases, among them malaria, cholera, yellow fever, and typhoid fever, ceased to be important causes of death. In some cities, health activities were initiated, infectious and contagious diseases controlled, and infant mortality rates were reduced after 1900. However, it is difficult to find evidence that there was a general improvement in the health and vitality of the black population. Most blacks lived in the rural South throughout this period, an area of the country which became overpopulated and impoverished. One result of this may have been a decline in the standard of living and a deterioration in diets. Accounts of rural living conditions stress the difficulties most blacks faced in keeping themselves alive. They note the shortages of food, the prevalence of disease, and the lack of medical services in rural areas.

Beginning in 1935, the federal government provided large sums of money to state and local health agencies to improve their health services. This had the effect of greatly increasing public health facilities throughout the nation, particularly in those areas which had previously been too impoverished to afford such health care. During World War II, the income and purchasing power of blacks rose, leading to improved standards of living. This change, along with the development of public health services, reduced the death rate and extended the life span. Declines in the death rate after 1940, combined with the increases in fertility to produce very rapid population growth and as a result during the 1950s, the black population grew as rapidly as during the pre-Civil War period.

Reasons for Changes in the Growth Rate

To account for changes in the growth rate, we must explain why fertility rates consistently declined from about 1880 to 1940 and then rose sharply. Three hypotheses were tested to determine why childbearing rates fluctuated as they did. These hypotheses were: first, that change in fertility could be explained by changes in the age at which women married, the proportion who married, or the stability of marriages; second, that changes in fertility are explicable by changes in the use of birth control; third, that changes in fertility result from changes in health conditions, particularly the health conditions that affect the capability of women to bear children.

The Influence of Changes in Marital Status

Chapter 6 describes changes in marital status and attempts to measure the effect these changes have had on fertility rates. It is very difficult to determine trends in marital status for neither the censuses nor studies of Negro life provide much reliable information concerning marital and family relationships.

Apparently, most blacks who came to this country were unable to bring strong traditions of African family life with them. The mixing of slaves from different tribes on the trip across the Atlantic and during their stay in the West Indian isles, a stay which often involved several generations, insured that few African mores or marriage customs were brought into the American colonies.

There was no such thing as legal marriage among most blacks during the years of slavery, for masters could always sell their slaves whenever they wished. Most descriptions of the family life of slaves were strongly influenced by the pro- and anti-slavery feelings of their authors. Supposedly, the family system which emerged was that of serial monogamy. At an early age, black women began living with a spouse. Sometimes these were enduring relationships, but in other cases, partners were frequently changed.

Franklin Frazier, who wrote most extensively about the black family, claimed that after Emancipation two types of families became common. One type was a matriarchal family often involving impoverished blacks. This was a continuation of the serial monogamy system. The family size was large, many children were illegitimate, and frequently one woman cared not only for her own children but also for those of her relatives and friends.

Frazier argued that other blacks in the post-Civil War period purchased land or secured steady jobs in the cities of the South. He contended that these more economically secure blacks rapidly adopted the values of the white majority. They tried to maintain stable, patriarchal families and disapproved of illegitimacy and desertion.

Frazier believed that the proportion of blacks in stable families rose during and after Reconstruction. Later, however, black landowners found it difficult to retain their property and moved into cities or onto somebody else's land to become sharecroppers. With World War I there came a major migration of many Negroes into northern cities. The rapid urbanization of rural blacks, in Frazier's view, was incompatible with marital stability. Once the migrants arrived in cities, the black men discovered they could not obtain adequate homes for their families nor could they find steady and well-paying jobs once the World War I boom collapsed. Desertion and high rates of illegitimacy were, in Frazier's judgment, inevitable consequences of this shift in population.

Census data can be used to validate only some of Frazier's contentions. Data about marital stability are available only for dates since 1910. Since that time marital disruption has become somewhat more common among Negroes, although changes in marital status are quite small. There has been an increase in the proportion of women who report they are married yet do not live with a husband—but this has been partially offset by a decline in the proportion who are widows. This apparent trend toward greater marital disruption was operative during the period from 1910 to 1940 which included the severe years of the Depression and also during the more prosperous period from 1940 to 1967. Chapter 6 points out that the increase in desertion and divorce was not simply the result of blacks moving into cities. Rather, marital disruption became more common among both women in rural areas and those in urban areas; among both women in the South and those in the North.

A further investigation of census data suggests there have been no major changes in the age at which blacks marry or the proportion who marry since 1890. However, as a consequence of increasing marital disruption, the proportion of black women of childbearing age who lived with a spouse declined from 1910 to 1965; and the average number of years black women spent living with a husband has gradually decreased throughout this century.

The hypothesis that fluctuations in black fertility result from changes in marital status can neither be completely rejected nor accepted. Between 1910 and 1940, fertility rates declined and some part of this fall may be attributable to marital disruptions becoming more common. However, after 1940, fertility rates went up very rapidly despite a decrease in the proportion of black women who lived with a husband. Thus, the post-1940 rise in fertility cannot be attributed to changes in marital status.

The Use of Birth Control

We know little about the history of birth control among blacks for there are no reports, covering a sufficient time-span, on this topic. During the 1930s, some investigations were carried out with particular groups of Negro women. They revealed that few women had ever used any technique to limit or space their childbearing. In addition, women who used birth control often used ineffective methods, such as douching, and thus their fertility was little affected by the use of birth control. If a national study had been conducted during the Depression decade, it probably would have discovered that as few as 10 or 15 percent of the black married women of childbearing age had ever used contraceptives. This suggests that the long term decline in black fertility occurred despite the fact that few black women used birth control.

In 1960, and again in 1965, national surveys were conducted. Non-white or Negro women were asked about their fertility and their use of family planning. By 1960, about three-fifths of the married women of childbearing age reported that they had used some method of birth control; by 1965, this proportion increased to three-quarters. The 1965 study found that during the previous five year period, birth control became increasingly popular with the groups of women, such as rural women or those who had only a grade school education, who reported very low rates of use in

1960. In addition, during the 1960s, many black women apparently began using the new and more reliable contraceptive techniques.

These studies indicate that between the 1930s and the 1960s the practice of birth control by blacks became much more common. However, during this period, fertility rates increased, indicating that fluctuations in black fertility are not a simple function of changes in the use of birth control and suggesting that birth rates in the post-World War II period would have been even higher if the use of birth control had not become so common.

The Effects of Changing Health Conditions

It is impossible to state precisely how various diseases affect the childbearing capacity of a population. We have indicated that until recently, few black women effectively used birth control. Yet childlessness increased. Approximately 10 percent of the women born from 1835 to 1844 reached age 45 without becoming mothers but almost one-third of the women born from 1905 to 1909 remained childless throughout their lives. The prevalence of disease may account for this change in childlessness and the reduction in fertility. Two diseases and their consequences are discussed in Chapter 9.

After the Civil War, many blacks in the rural South depended upon cotton crops for their livelihood. Beginning about 1890, a number of changes adversely affected southern agriculture, particularly cotton farming. First, there was boll weevil infestation; later, there was a precipitous fall in cotton prices during and after World War I. Many black farmers were forced into tenant or peonage arrangements with the owners of large holdings. These arrangements typically limited the ability of rural blacks to keep their own animals or to grow their own fruits or vegetables. They also insured that sharecroppers or tenant farmers had no cash income for much of the year. This absence of cash meant that fresh meats, fruits, and milk could not be purchased. As a result of their unvaried and restricted diet, many rural blacks developed pellagra, a vitamin B deficiency disease. This disease seemingly became more common during the early decades of this century as southern agriculture became more depressed. While this ailment does not have a direct effect upon fecundity, it is a generally debilitating disease which disrupts the operations of the central nervous system and it afflicted proportionally more women than men. The increasing incidence of this disease is indicative of the health problems rural blacks faced and may be related to the decline in fertility.

Little is known about the history of venereal disease among blacks. However, by the 1930s, syphilis and gonorrhea were apparently quite widespread. Various studies discovered that about 20 percent of the adult black population had such diseases during the Depression years. The gradual urbanization of the black population and the absence of venereal disease control programs or expedient treatment procedures implies that the prevalence of these diseases may have increased prior to and during the 1930s.

Venereal disease has direct effects on fertility. Gonorrhea will eventually produce sterility, if it is untreated, and syphilis reduces fertility; a pregnant woman who has this disease is quite likely to have a stillbirth or abort a fetus unless she receives treatment. The incidence of childlessness among blacks may be, in part, a consequence of an increase in venereal disease.

After 1935, there were major changes in public health programs. The Social Security Act began this by providing maternal and child health programs and supported venereal disease control programs by local health agencies. Later, much larger appropriations for maternal and child health were made when the extent of the problems became known. Special bills were enacted to enable the Public Health Service to eliminate syphilis and gonorrhea and technical innovations, such as the use of penicillin, made it easier to control these ailments. During the World War II years, special acts provided aid to mothers and their infants. After the war, the government's activities in the health field continued to grow through increased support for hospitals and greater aid for medical services for the impoverished. Before World War II, no more than one-quarter of the Negro births were hospitalized, but by 1955, more than three-quarters were hospitalized.

The maternal mortality rate among blacks, the fetal death ratio, and the mortality rate of black infants from syphilis did not decline significantly before the public health programs were expanded. From about 1937 to 1955, these death rates plummeted to lower levels. Interestingly enough, the incidence of childlessness also decreased during this period.

In conclusion, between the time of the Emancipation and the Depression, only limited improvements were made in health conditions among blacks. Certain fertility inhibiting diseases probably became more common and helped to cut the birth rate. Since the 1930s, health conditions have improved. Births have been hospitalized, maternal and infant death rates have fallen, the effects of venereal disease have been minimized, and childlessness has been reduced. These changes have influenced the childbearing ability of blacks. They are the important reasons for the decline in fertility which occurred before the Depression, and the more recent rise in fertility.

The Future Course of Negro Fertility

Since 1960, fertility rates have declined. Is this a temporary change or is this the beginning of a trend toward lower fertility and slower population growth? To answer such questions, we need to know how variables influence the number of children that black women bear. In Chapter 5, differentials in fertility are discussed, and in Chapter 7 data from the Census of 1960 are analyzed to develop analytic models of family formation.

Four variables are described which have independent and significant effects upon childbearing. Age at marriage is related to fertility, for the older a woman is when she marries, the fewer children she has. Educational attainment has two effects upon fertility. There is a direct effect, for educational attainment has the effect of reducing fertility, apart from the effects of the other variables considered in the model. Education also has an indirect effect, for the more years a woman remains in school, the older she is likely to be when she marries, and this decreases fertility.

Demographers have often pointed out that women from rural backgrounds typically bear more children than do women raised in cities. For purposes of analysis, black women were divided into two groups; those born in the South and those born outside this region. Almost all northern black women were born, and presumably raised, in cities while the majority of southern born women of childbearing age in 1960 came from rural backgrounds. Region of birth (that is, coming from a rural background), was found to be an important variable. Northern born women had significantly fewer children than did women from the South. Apparently, being born and raised in a northern city had the consequence of lowering fertility rates. But this same variable, region of birth, had no independent effect upon the age at which women married or the stability of their marriages.

To measure the effect marital disruptions have upon fertility, women were again divided into two groups. The first group in-

cluded women who had married only once and who lived with
their husbands at the time of the census in 1960. The second group
included women who had been married more than once as well as
deserted, divorced and widowed women (that is, women who experienced some marital disruption). This variable was found to
have a significant independent effect upon fertility because the
women in unbroken marriages had larger numbers of children
than the women whose marriages had been disrupted.

The black population of the United States has experienced a
demographic transition, although it is different from the typical
transitions many populations have undergone. Before the Civil
War, death rates were high but the fertility rate was even higher
and the population grew rapidly. Toward the end of the nineteenth century and during the first one-third of the twentieth
century, the growth rate slackened mainly because fertility rates
fell while the mortality rate remained at a high level. Rather than
resulting from the deliberate and intentional control of family
size, the slowdown of growth resulted from changes in health
conditions. Once these conditions were changed by higher standards of living and the elimination of diseases, fertility rates increased rapidly and the growth rate rose. This happened despite
the urbanization of blacks and substantial increases in their educational attainment and income.

It is likely that the high birth rates and growth rates of the
post-World War II era will be but one stage, and a temporary
stage, in the demographic transition of the black population. Surveys of fertility expectations indicate that most black women
would like to have small families; in fact, their fertility desires
may be even smaller than those of white women. In the future,
an increasing proportion of the women of childbearing age will
come from urban backgrounds and have extensive educations, two
factors which this monograph shows will lead to lower fertility.
The increasing use of contraceptives by black women at all socio-
economic levels, combined with the desire for smaller families,
implies that there will be further declines in fertility and a slowing of population growth.

Chapter 2

THE GROWTH OF THE BLACK POPULATION BEFORE THE CIVIL WAR

Pre-Revolutionary Growth of the Black Population

The earliest settlements in what is now the United States—Boston on Massachusetts Bay, Newport on Narragansett Bay, New Amsterdam and Philadelphia along major rivers and Charles Town on the Carolina coast—all developed into trading centers during the seventeenth century.[1] Each was a port which obtained products from an interior hinterland and traded for items coming from Europe, the West Indies, or Africa. At an early date, a need arose for manual labor. In both northern and southern colonies, attempts were made to enslave Indians, but the American Indians were not very docile and could easily elude white men to drift back to their tribes.[2] Indentured servants were another source of labor, but, since mercantilism was popular in Europe, these servants were difficult to obtain and would work for only a specified number of years.[3] Indentured servants also had legal rights and could sue their masters if they believed they were not treated fairly.[4]

Black slaves were a third source of labor and they possessed distinct advantages. They could be obtained cheaply; they were held perpetually; and their skin color identified their status and

---

[1] Carl Bridenbaugh, *Cities in the Wilderness* (New York: Capricorn Books, 1955), pp. 468–469.

[2] George H. Moore, *History of Slavery in Massachusetts* (New York: Appleton, 1866), p. 2 and Chap. III; Samuel McKee, *Labor in Colonial New York: 1664–1766* (New York: Columbia University Press, 1935), p. 311.

[3] McKee, *op. cit.*, p. 89.

[4] Marcus W. Jernegan, *Laboring and Dependent Classes in Colonial America: 1607–1783* (New York: Frederick Ungar, 1931), p. 54.

discouraged them from running away. Finally, and very important, slaves provided their own replacements. Thus, the reproductive capability of blacks helps to explain their presence and popularity in the early American colonies.[5]

The Northern Colonies

The importing of black slaves began early in the 1600s. Negroes arrived in New Amsterdam as early as 1626 and Boston received its first blacks in 1638.[6] The black population of the northern colonies grew slowly during the seventeenth century. Many of the slaves were brought into New Amsterdam where they were used chiefly as stevedores, although some were employed on Dutch farms in the Hudson Valley.[7] A smaller number of slaves were found in New England ports during this period.[8]

Prior to 1697, the Royal African Company had a monopoly on slave trading, but after that date any British subject could engage in the business.[9] New England merchants quickly discovered the profit to be made in the sale of blacks. Local items, such as rum, dried fish, and dairy products were taken to Africa where they were traded for slaves. These slaves were then carried to the West Indies where they were exchanged for molasses which was returned to New England and used to make rum.[10] As these commercial activities flourished, so did the need for workers. The continental wars and their American counterparts made it difficult to obtain European immigrants. Increasing numbers of slaves were brought in and the black population of the northern colonies grew more rapidly during the first half of the eighteenth century than during any later period. Blacks performed much of the labor in northern cities and some learned skilled trades such as barbering, fishing or cooperage.[11]

---

[5] Abbot E. Smith, *Colonists in Bondage* (Chapel Hill: University of North Carolina Press, 1947), p. 29.

[6] Lorenzo J. Greene, *The Negro in Colonial New England: 1620–1776* (New York: Columbia University Press, 1942), p. 17; James E. Allen, *The Negro in New York* (New York: Exposition Press, 1964), p. 17.

[7] Edgar J. Manus, *A History of Negro Slavery in New York* (Syracuse: Syracuse University Press, 1966), Chaps. I and III.

[8] John H. Franklin, *From Slavery to Freedom*, 3rd ed. (New York: Alfred A. Knopf, 1967), p. 104.

[9] Oliver P. Chitwood, *A History of Colonial America*, 3rd ed. (New York: Harper & Row, 1961), p. 345.

[10] *Ibid.*, p. 346.

[11] Carl Bridenbaugh, *Cities in Revolt* (New York: Capricorn Books, 1955), p. 88.

Many censuses were taken throughout the seventeenth century in the northern colonies. It is impossible to ascertain the accuracy of these enumerations but they describe two trends. First, the color composition of the colonies changed between 1700 and 1750, for the black population grew more rapidly than the white. By 1750, blacks comprised about 5 percent of the population.[12] They were concentrated in a few cities, some of which had an even greater proportion of blacks in 1750 than in 1960. For instance, more than one-fifth of New York City's population was black in 1746, and in 1755 Negroes made up one-quarter of the population of Newport and one-seventh of the population of all Rhode Island.[13]

Second, the number of blacks in northern colonies reached a peak sometime around 1750 and grew very slowly, if at all, thereafter. The first national census, taken in 1790, enumerated fewer blacks in Connecticut and Rhode Island than were counted by colonial censuses some forty years earlier. In New York, Pennsylvania, and Massachusetts, the black population grew very slowly from 1750 to 1790.[14]

Various reasons account for the low growth rates. First was the availability of white workers, for after the Treaty of Paris was signed, it became easier to obtain immigrants from Europe. White workers were preferred because it was believed they could more easily learn skilled trades and would work more diligently. A second reason was fear that the black population would grow too rapidly. There were race riots and slave uprisings in the colonies. A revolt of slaves in New York City in 1712, resulted in the deaths of nine whites and 27 slaves; a suspected Negro conspiracy in the same city in 1741 led to the execution of 23 people.[15] These racial difficulties raised questions about the wisdom of importing additional blacks. A third reason was the growing indignation about the holding of slaves. Quakers in Pennsylvania campaigned against the slave trade and succeeded in getting restrictions placed upon it.[16] Similar sentiment in New York, Connecticut and Rhode

[12] U. S., Bureau of the Census, *Historical Statistics of the United States: Colonial Times to 1957* (Washington: Government Printing Office, 1960), Series Z 1–19.

[13] U. S., Bureau of the Census, *A Century of Population Growth* (Washington: Government Printing Office, 1909), Table 95.

[14] Evarts B. Greene and Virginia D. Harrington, *American Population before the Federal Census of 1790* (New York: Columbia University Press, 1932), pp. 17–19, 50, 63–64, 91–92, 115 and 116.

[15] Franklin, *op. cit.*, pp. 92–93.

[16] Ulrich B. Phillips, *American Negro Slavery* (Magnolia, Mass.: Peter Smith, 1940), p. 112.

Island led to the passage of laws forbidding the importing of slaves. In Massachusetts, slavery was abolished by a court decision at the time of the Revolution.[17] Finally, slave traders found it more profitable to sell their cargoes in the South than in the North.

The Southern Colonies

Ecological conditions in the South encouraged the growth of black population. During the 1600s, the British purchased their tobacco from Spanish isles in the West Indies.[18] It was economically more desirable that a British colony supply this tobacco. Colonists in Virginia and Maryland experimented with tobacco and found that it could be grown. Toward the end of the seventeenth century, planters wished to increase their output and cut costs but they faced a labor shortage. Tobacco growing demanded —and still demands—much effort.[19] Early in the year seeds must be planted; the seedlings must then be cared for and transplanted. The fields must be hoed and weeded, and tobacco plants must be checked for worms. Leaves must be harvested at the appropriate time and then cured. Finally, leaves are stripped from their stems and prepared for shipping. To obtain workers to perform these tasks, tobacco growers began importing slaves in large numbers in the late 1600s. As tobacco plantations extended through the Tidewater area, so did the number of slaves.

South Carolina and the southern coast grew less rapidly than other colonial areas during the seventeenth century, for it was not as agriculturally productive until the introduction of new crops. Rice was first successfully grown in the Carolina lowlands, in 1694, and soon became the chief product exported through Charles Town.[20] The growing of rice, in addition to normal care, required the draining and periodic reflooding of swampy areas. Blacks were believed to be biologically suited for this work. Swampy areas bred malaria-carrying mosquitoes and whites who worked in rice fields were afflicted by this disease. Negroes

---

[17] W. E. Burghardt DuBois, *The Suppression of the African Slave Trade to the United States: 1638–1870* (New York: Longmans, Green, 1896), pp. 30–38.

[18] Phillips, *op. cit.*, p. 69.

[19] Herbert S. Klein, *Slavery in the Americas: A Comparative Study of Virginia and Cuba,* (Chicago: University of Chicago Press, 1967), pp. 178–179.

[20] U. S., Bureau of the Census, *Historical Statistics . . .* , Series Z 262–280; Bridenbaugh, *Cities in the Wilderness*, p. 178.

were assumed to be immune and thus were highly valued workers.[21]

The development of rice farming led to a rapid increase in the number of blacks in South Carolina and, by 1700, at least half of the population was black.[22] The colonial assembly worried about a possible insurrection and enacted duties on incoming slaves or insisted that planters bring in white workers as well as slaves.[23] The British abrogated these laws since they threatened to reduce the profits of British firms, and the slave population continued to increase.

In the 1740s, indigo was first grown in South Carolina, and soon thereafter the British Navy began paying a bounty for Carolina indigo.[24] This crop increased the need for slaves, for it also required intensive labor. In addition, its growing season complemented that of rice and one group of slaves could be used for both crops.

Southern colonies took few censuses before the Revolution, but estimates of population were made occasionally and lists of taxables were compiled. These meager sources indicate that the black population grew during the eighteenth century and became more dispersed geographically. At the beginning of the century, slaves were concentrated in the Tidewater area around Chesapeake Bay and near the southern port, Charles Town. By the Revolution, they were spread throughout Virginia, Maryland, the Carolinas and Georgia. Almost all the blacks lived in rural areas and performed unskilled jobs. Charles Town was the only southern town of any size, and here blacks were employed in both manual and skilled jobs. Some masters taught their slaves trades and encouraged them to become artisans. One group of white skilled tradesmen, the shipwrights, protested they were being driven out of business by slaves.[25]

In 1790, 35 percent of the population of the South were Negroes. In South Carolina, the black proportion was the highest— about 45 percent—and in Tennessee it was the lowest—10 percent.[26]

---

[21] Phillips, *op. cit.*, p. 91.

[22] Greene and Harrington, *op. cit.*, pp. 172–173.

[23] Chitwood, *op. cit.*, p. 346.

[24] Curtis P. Nettles, *The Roots of American Civilization*, 2nd ed., (New York: Appleton-Century-Crofts, 1963), p. 232.

[25] Bridenbaugh, *Cities in Revolt*, p. 88.

[26] U. S., Bureau of the Census, *Negro Population in the United States: 1790–1915* (Washington: Government Printing Office, 1918), p. 45.

Components of Pre-Revolutionary Growth

It is impossible to know precisely how rapidly the black population grew before the Revolution. Attempts have been made to assemble all demographic data concerning the colonies.[27] These data include censuses of some areas, reports of colonial administrators and estimates made by European travelers. They indicate that in 1700, 250,000 inhabited the colony; about 30,000 of them were black. In 1750, the colonies had a population of 1.2 million including 250,000 Negroes.[28] This implies the black population grew in excess of 4 percent per annum from 1700 to 1750 while the white population expanded by 3 percent each year. The first federal census, taken in 1790, counted 3.9 million Americans, 750,000 of whom were black.[29] From 1750 to 1790, the growth rate was approximately three percent for each race. These eighteenth century growth rates are very high. For instance, from 1950 to 1960, when the national population was growing rapidly, the annual increase was only 1.7 percent.

Two components contributed to the growth of the black population during this period: slaving and the surplus of births over deaths. Different estimates of these components have been made. For instance, Louis Dublin argued that rates of natural increase among Negroes were very high and that natural increase accounted for most of the growth. He believed that a maximum of 175,000 slaves were imported between 1700 and the Revolution.[30] William Rossiter, in his monograph, *A Century of Population Growth*, believed that rates of natural increase were lower and that 275,000 slaves were imported between 1700 and 1776.[31]

Each of these estimates is based on conjectures about the levels of mortality and fertility, but there is no evidence which permits us to establish accurately what these levels were. Writers in this period paid very little attention to health conditions other

---

[27] Greene and Harrington, *op. cit.*; Stella H. Sutherland, *Population Distribution in Colonial America* (New York: Columbia University Press, 1936); U. S., Bureau of the Census, *A Century of Population Growth;* J. Potter, "The Growth of Population in America, 1700–1860," *Population in History*, D. V. Glass and D. E. C. Eversley, eds. (Chicago: Aldine Publishing, 1965), 631–687.

[28] U. S., Bureau of the Census, *Historical Statistics . . .* , Series Z 1–19.

[29] *Ibid.*, Series A 45–46.

[30] Louis I. Dublin, *Health and Wealth* (New York: Harper & Bros., 1928), p. 250.

[31] U. S., Bureau of the Census, *A Century of Population Growth*, p. 36.

than to note that plagues seemed less common and less devastating in America than in Europe. Some authors lamented the death of many slaves during Middle Passage—that is, the crossing from Africa to America—and in clearing the swamps of the South, but this provides no information about the overall death rate.

It is no easier to determine how frequently Negro women bore children. A few Pre-Revolutionary censuses enumerated blacks by age and they found that a very large percentage of the population was young; for instance, 30 percent or more of the Negroes were under age 10.[32] This suggests very high fertility for childbearing would have to occur frequently to produce such a youthful age structure.

There apparently was no family or marriage system which restricted childbearing among slaves. African traditions and mores were probably destroyed as slaves from many different tribes were mixed together in America. In parts of the West Indies, the Catholic Church attempted to institutionalize a marriage system and insisted that masters respect the marital wishes of their slaves, but in the North American colonies, slaves were defined as property and were unable to enter into any contracts including marriage.[33] Thus a social system emerged which probably encouraged early and frequent sexual intercourse.[34] Miscegenation was apparently very common in the eighteenth century. At least, in the South, there was a widespread belief that black women were particularly lascivious.[35] The offspring of these unions were classed, almost without exception, as Negroes. It is likely, then, that the birth rates of the black population were high during this period for there appear to be few factors which discouraged childbearing.

Post-Revolutionary Growth of the Black Population

National Growth Trends

It is easier to describe population growth since the founding of the country, for censuses have been taken every ten years.

---

[32] Greene and Harrington, *op. cit.*, pp. 97–98.

[33] Klein, *op. cit.*

[34] Winthrop D. Jordan, *White Over Black: American Attitudes Toward the Negro, 1550–1812* (Chapel Hill: University of North Carolina Press, 1968), p. 160.

[35] *Ibid.*, pp. 150–163.

TABLE 2–1
National Population and Annual Growth Rates 1790–1969

Dates	Population (000) White	Population (000) Negro	Average Annual Growth Rates for Interdecennial Period White	Average Annual Growth Rates for Interdecennial Period Negro	Proportion of Total Population Negro
1790	3,172	757	–	–	19%
1800	4,306	1,002	3.06%	2.80%	19
1810	5,862	1,378	3.08	3.19	19
1820	7,867	1,772	2.94	2.51	18
1830	10,537	2,329	2.92	2.73	18
1840	14,196	2,874	2.98	2.10	17
1850	19,553	3,639	3.20	2.36	16
1860	26,923	4,442	3.20	2.00	14
1870	33,589	4,880	2.22	.94	13
1880	43,403	6,581	2.56	2.99	13
1890	55,101	7,389	2.39	1.25	12
1900	66,809	8,834	1.92	1.79	12
1910	81,732	9,828	2.01	1.07	11
1920	94,821	10,463	1.48	.63	10
1930	110,287	11,891	1.51	1.28	10
1940	118,215	12,866	.70	.79	10
1950	134,942	15,042	1.33	1.56	10
1960	159,467	18,916	1.67	2.29	11
1969	178,225	22,727	1.14	1.88	11

Sources:

U. S., Bureau of the Census, *Historical Statistics of the United States: Colonial Times to 1957* (Washington: Government Printing Office, 1960) Series A 95–122; *Current Population Reports,* "Estimates of the Population of the United States by Age, Race, and Sex: July 1, 1969," Series P-25, No. 428 (August 19, 1969), Table 2.

Table 2–1 shows the number of whites and Negroes at each census date and average annual growth rates. The black population grew rapidly for many decades following the Revolution, although not quite as rapidly as in the colonial era. Up to 1850, the black population expanded by 2 to 3 percent each year. An annual growth rate of 2.5 percent doubles a population in less than thirty years. Since the Negro growth rates approached or exceeded this figure, the black population doubled every generation prior to the Civil War.

Following the Civil War, the growth rate of the black population decreased. It appears that growth from 1860 to 1870 was much slower than in the previous decade, but this growth rate is based on data from the census of 1870, a notoriously inaccurate enumeration. In any event, the growth rate declined for many decades after the end of slavery. The Depression decade was one of very slow growth. At growth rates of the 1930s, it would have taken ninety years for the Negro population to double. The eighteenth century and much of the nineteenth witnessed a very vigorous growth of blacks, but this came to an end during the early decades of this century.

A trend toward more rapid growth emerged during World War II and accelerated after that war, and from 1950 to 1960 the black population grew as rapidly as in some pre-Civil War periods. Fertility rates have fallen since 1959, and the growth rate of the most recent period, although high in an historical context, represents a decline from the peak rates of the 1950s.

The growth of the black population slackened before many Negroes moved North and into cities. Prior to World War I, few Negroes migrated away from the South. The Census of 1910, for instance, found that 90 percent of the blacks lived in the Southern states.[36] Similarly, the first sharp increase in the proportion of Negroes who lived in cities occurred between 1910 and 1920.[37] Yet, before World War I, the growth rate declined, indicating that urbanization and northern living did not precipitate the slowing of population growth.

Growth rates of the Negro and white populations may be easily compared. From 1750 to about 1820, the two races grew at about the same rate. For the long period extending from 1820 to the Depression, the white population grew more rapidly than the Negro, reflecting immigration from Europe. As a consequence, the proportion of the nation's population which was black, fell from 19 percent in 1820 to 10 percent in 1930. Since the Depression, the black population has grown more rapidly than the white and the proportion of blacks has gradually increased, attaining 11 percent in 1969.[38]

The Quality of Census Data

There is an important question which must be asked: how accurate is the information about Negroes provided by the cen-

---

[36] U. S., Bureau of the Census, *Negro Population of the United States: 1790–1915*, p. 33.

[37] U. S., Bureau of the Census, *Fifteenth Census of the United States: 1930*, Population, II, pp. 62–64.

[38] U. S., Bureau of the Census, "Estimates of the Population of the United States by Age, Race, and Sex: July 1, 1969," *Current Population Reports*, Series P-25, No. 428 (August 19, 1969), Table 2.

suses? Perhaps some of the fluctuations in growth rates principally reflect changes in census procedures or census completeness. Three topics must be discussed: the overall accuracy of the
censuses; the procedures used to define a person as a Negro; and,
finally, changes in the geographic areas included in the various
censuses.

For a very long time, there has been suspicion about the
count of blacks. Until 1880, United States marshals and their
appointees gathered census data. Many of these men were chosen
for political reasons and lacked the talent needed to enumerate
the population. Frederick Olmstead, who traveled extensively in
the South, visited South Carolina during the mid-1850s. He believed census reports for that state were very unreliable. He described the marshals as "generally excessively lazy, and neglectful
of their duty, among that class which was most ignorant. . . ."[39]
He continued:

> I have seen an advertisement of a deputy census mar-
> shal in Alabama or Georgia announcing that he would be
> at a certain tavern in his district, on a certain day, for
> the purpose of receiving from the people of the vicinity
> —who were requested to call upon him—the information
> it was his duty to obtain from them.[40]

The Census of 1870, the first taken after the Civil War, was
thought to be particularly erroneous in its count of the southern
population. During Reconstruction, many of the marshals and
their appointees in the South were carpetbaggers or scalawags
who were ignorant of the local terrain and incapable of satisfactorily counting the population. The Census Office had no control
over enumerators or enumeration districts and little control over
enumeration procedures.[41] Francis Walker, superintendent of this
census, termed the count, ". . . inadequate, partial and inaccurate,
often in a shameful degree."[42]

The Census of 1890 was also believed to have undercounted
the black population. Tallies from that census did not seem reasonable in comparison with tallies from the 1880 and 1900 enu-

[39] Frederick L. Olmsted, *A Journey in the Seaboard Slave States* (New
York: G. P. Putnam's Sons, 1904), II, p. 150.

[40] *Ibid.*, pp. 150–151.

[41] Francis A. Walker, "Statistics of the Colored Race in the United
States," *Publications of the American Statistical Association*, II (September-
December, 1890), 97.

[42] *Ibid.*

merations. Eventually, the Census Bureau attempted to correct the 1870 and 1890 censuses by assuming that the censuses of 1860, 1880 and 1900 were accurate and then interpolating to estimate the Negro population in 1870 and 1890.[43]

The validity of the 1920 census has also been questioned, for this census was taken as of January 1, while earlier censuses were taken in August, June or April. Inclemencies of winter weather impeded enumerators in rural areas in 1920. Since most blacks lived in rural places, this may have produced a serious undercount. One analyst has presented data indicating that this did happen.[44]

Since 1935, the United States has had a nationwide system for registering births. Information about mortality rates can be used to survive the number of individuals born each year to the dates of the 1940, 1950 and 1960 censuses. The estimated number of survivors can then be compared to the enumerated population to assess how accurately these censuses counted people born since 1934. Additional assumptions about the pattern of census errors can be made in order to judge the overall accuracy of recent censuses.[45] Studies which have utilized this methodology indicate the black population was underenumerated by about 10 percent in 1960 and by a slightly larger amount in 1940 and in 1950.[46]

Changes in the accuracy of the censuses do not affect the long-term trends in population growth which are indicated in Table 2–1, but the growth rates for particular decades are not correct. From 1860 to 1870, the black population grew more rapidly than indicated by the censuses and in the following decade it grew less rapidly than indicated. Similarly, the growth rate

---

[43] U. S., Bureau of the Census, *Negro Population in the United States: 1790–1915*, pp. 26–30.

[44] Kelly Miller, "Enumeration Errors in Negro Population," *Scientific Monthly*, XIV (February, 1922), 168–187.

[45] Ansley J. Coale, "The Population of the United States in 1950 Classified by Age, Sex and Color—A Revision of Census Figures", *Journal of the American Statistical Association*, L (March, 1955), 16–54.

[46] U. S., Bureau of the Census, *Current Population Reports*, "Estimates of the Population of the United States and Components of Change, by Age, Color, and Sex 1950 to 1960," Series P-25, No. 310 (June 30, 1965), Table C-2; Jacob S. Siegel and Melvin Zelnik, "An Evaluation of Coverage in the 1960 Census of Population by Techniques of Demographic Analysis and Composite Methods," *American Statistical Association, Proceedings of the Social Statistics Section, 1966*, p. 82; Jacob S. Siegel, "Completeness of Coverage of the Nonwhite Population in the 1960 Census and Current Estimates and Some Implications," *Social Statistics and the City*, ed. David M. Heer (Cambridge, Mass.: Joint Center for Urban Studies, 1967), pp. 13–54; Coale, *loc. cit.*, p. 29.

shown for 1910 to 1920 is too small and that for 1920 to 1930 is too large. It is impossible to determine exactly what the growth rates were in these decennial periods. For the other intercensal periods, the consecutive censuses were taken using similar techniques and the growth rates computed from these censuses are not seriously deficient.

The Definition of Race

Every national census has classified the population by color or race, but there have been changes in the definitions and procedures used to obtain this information. When the first censuses were taken, the Secretary of State provided neither forms nor instructions to the marshals who did the enumerating. Enumerators must have made their own judgments about race or color. In 1830, enumeration schedules were supplied for the first time. These provided a space for the race of each person, but no information was given as to how race was defined.[47]

Dissatisfaction with the Census of 1840, particularly with data which implied that many free Negroes were insane, led to attempts to improve the next census.[48] Detailed instructions were provided the marshals along with enumeration schedules. Each person was assumed to be white if the enumerator left a given space blank. A person was classed as a Negro if the enumerator wrote a B or an M in the appropriate column indicating the person was black or mulatto. These terms were not defined until 1870. In that year, the meaning of black was not specified, but enumerators were told that *mulattoes* ". . . includes quadroons, octoroons and all persons having any perceptible trace of African blood . . ." and that "important scientific results depend upon the correct determination of this class. . . ."[49] Identical instructions were given in 1880.

---

[47] Carroll D. Wright, *The History and Growth of the United States Census* (Washington: Government Printing Office, 1900), pp. 16–31.

[48] The Census of 1840 reported that among free Negroes, 1 in 162 was insane, but among slaves only 1 in 1558 was insane. Southern protagonists claimed that this demonstrated that freedom incapacitated Negroes. Edward Jarvis, one of the nation's first vital statisticians, discovered numerous errors in these tabulations and John Quincy Adams, then serving in the House, alleged that southerners in the State Department falsified the census. Eventually, two congressional committees investigated census accuracy. William Stanton, *The Leopard's Spots: Scientific Attitudes Toward Race in America: 1815–59* (Chicago: University of Chicago Press, 1960), pp. 58–61; Wright, *op. cit.*, pp. 39–40.

[49] Wright, *op. cit.*, p. 157.

In 1890, enumerators had to indicate the race of each person, and a blank space was no longer assumed to indicate that a person was white.[50] In addition, the enumerators had to assess blood content:

> Be particularly careful to distiguish between blacks, mulattoes, quadroons, and octoroons. The word "black" should be used to describe those persons who have three-fourths or more black blood; "mulatto," those persons who have three-eights to five-eights black blood; "quadroon," those persons who have one-fourth black blood; and "octoroon," those persons who have one-eighth or any trace of black blood.[51]

Data concerning quadroons and octoroons proved useless, and, in 1900, enumerators were instructed to use the term black for full blooded Negroes and mulatto for all other persons with some trace of Negro blood. After 1910, the term mulatto was dropped and, until 1960, census takers had to use their own judgment of a person's race. Individuals of mixed white-Negro or Indian-Negro ancestry were classed as Negro.[52]

It is unlikely that these changes in census procedure resulted in serious errors in the count of Negroes. Racial characteristics have been salient throughout the nation's history, and racial segregation has been persistent, indicating that in most places local customs have clearly defined racial status, a status which enumerators could readily identify.

The method of obtaining racial information was changed in 1960 when self-administered questionnaires were used. The head of each household was asked to indicate the race of each member of his household. Enumerators obtained racial information only from respondents who did not list their own race. There is no evidence that this self-reporting procedure either improved or impeded the identification of Negroes, although it did improve the identification of Orientals and American Indians.[53]

---

[50] *Ibid.*, p. 187.

[51] *Ibid.*

[52] U. S., Bureau of the Census, *Sixteenth Census of the United States: 1940;* Instructions to Enumerators, Population and Agriculture, 1940, p. 43; *Census of Population: 1950*, Enumerator's Reference Manual, pp. 33–34.

[53] U. S., Bureau of the Census, *Censuses of Population and Housing: 1960*, Procedural History, p. 190; *Census of Population: 1960*, PC(2)–1C, p. xi.

Changes in the Land Area

From 1800 to the Civil War, midwestern states, from Ohio in the East to South Dakota in the West, were added to the Union. This had little effect on Negro population growth, for each state contained no more than a few hundred blacks when it was admitted to the Union. Similarly, when California and the other western states were added, they contained very small Negro populations.[54]

In 1803, the United States completed the Louisiana Purchase, and the Census of 1810 was the first to enumerate Louisiana, an area which contained about 40,000 blacks.[55] However, many of these blacks had been enumerated in other states in 1800. They were brought to Louisiana after 1803, for this area was suitable for cotton growing and was rapidly settled by southern planters and their slaves.[56]

The censuses of the last century showed that the black population grew more rapidly during the 1840s than during the 1830s. A popular explanation was that, in the 1830s, enterprising slave owners took slaves and established cotton plantations in eastern Texas. Texas was not included in the Census of 1840 but was enumerated in 1850, and this pattern of migration would produce the observed fluctuation in the growth rate.[57]

However, the black population of Texas in 1850 was small— about 60,000 or a little over 1 percent of the nation's total.[58] Regardless of what assumptions are made about Negro population growth in Texas, the national growth rates for the 1830 to 1850 period would not be significantly changed.[59]

The states which were added to the Union since the middle of the nineteenth century had very small Negro populations when they entered. For instance, Alaska and Hawaii contained a total of only 11,000 blacks when they were first included in a decennial census in 1960.[60] We conclude that the addition of new areas to

---

[54] U. S., Bureau of the Census, *Negro Population: 1790–1915*, p. 45.

[55] *Ibid.*

[56] Joe Gray Taylor, *Negro Slavery in Louisiana* (Baton Rouge: Louisiana Historical Association, 1963), pp. xi and 35.

[57] George Tucker, *Progress of the United States in Population and Wealth in Fifty Years* (New York: Hunt's Merchant's Magazine, 1855), p. 94.

[58] U. S., Bureau of the Census, *Negro Population: 1790–1915*, p. 45.

[59] J. D. B. DeBow, *The Industrial Resources of the Southern and Western States*, I (New Orleans: DeBow's Review, 1852), 305.

[60] U. S., Bureau of the Census, *Census of Population: 1960*, PC(1)–3B and 13B, Table 15.

the United States accounts for very little of the change in population growth rates.

The Role of Slaving in Population Growth

The black population grew rapidly prior to the Civil War. Some writers claim that many slaves were imported up to 1860 and that this accounts for the growth. Herskovitz, for instance, claimed that two and one-half million slaves were imported between the Revolutionary and Civil Wars.[61] However, both demographic and historical evidence indicates that natural increase, rather than the slave trade, accounted for the population growth.

Before 1790, each of the states enacted laws which either forbade the importing of slaves or placed prohibitive tariffs on this trade.[62] In the North, these laws resulted from opposition to slavery and fear of too large a black population. In the South, there was an economic problem. By the time of the Revolution, the area east of the Appalachians had been almost completely cultivated, leaving little room for new plantations. In addition, markets for southern agricultural products waned after the Revolution, obviating the need for more slaves. At the time of the Revolution, slaves were as numerous as whites in many areas of the South. Slave uprisings occurred throughout the West Indies during the eighteenth century and fear of such uprisings led Southerners to prohibit the importing of additional slaves.

During the 1790s, technological changes increased the South's need for labor. Faced with declining markets for rice and indigo, Carolina planters attempted to grow cotton. The lowlands proved to be fertile for long staple sea-island cotton, but this was not a hardy crop and would thrive only along the coast line. Short staple cotton could be grown in the interior, but so much labor was required to separate the lint that it was not a profitable crop.[63] Many men tried to invent machines to separate the lint; finally, in 1793, Eli Whitney invented a practical gin, making possible the cotton economy which persisted for over a century. Southern planters began growing cotton and found that British merchants would buy this crop almost as rapidly as they could grow it. Large areas of South Carolina and Georgia were quickly converted to

---

[61] Melvin J. Herskovitz, "Social History of the Negro," *A Handbook of Social Psychology*, ed. Carl Murchison (Worcester, Mass.: Clark University Press, 1935), p. 236.

[62] DuBois, *op. cit.*, pp. 70–74.

[63] Phillips, *op. cit.*, Chap. ix.

cotton production and the Louisiana Purchase opened up the Gulf Coast area.

The booming cotton economy created a demand for more slaves. For some time the demand was met by purchasing surplus slaves from the tobacco region. Later, southern legislators discussed the opening of ports to the international slave trade. South Carolina was the only state which permitted this trade. The legislature opened the port of Charleston in 1804.[64] The legal importing of slaves ended in 1807 with the passage of a federal law. During the span 1804 to 1807, 202 slaving vessels landed 39,000 slaves in Charleston.[65] It is likely that during this period some other slaves entered illegally from the Spanish colony of Florida.

Between 1800 and 1810, the black population grew by 400,000. Slaving and the addition of Louisiana probably account for no more than one-fifth of this increase, indicating that during this early period, the surplus of births over deaths was the major reason for population growth.

Census returns fail to substantiate the claim that many blacks were illegally imported after 1807. Male slaves, that is, prime field hands, had market value in excess of that of female slaves[66] and the typical slave ship was fitted to carry twice as many men as women.[67] If slaving continued after 1807, the censuses should have enumerated a predominance of black men. The census of 1820 was the first to tabulate Negroes by sex. This census found 103 males per 100 females.[68] This is a low sex ratio. It is lower, for instance, than the sex ratio for whites in 1910—107 males per 100 females—a population which was heavily influenced by immigration.[69] From 1820 to 1860, the female black population grew more rapidly than the male and the sex ratio declined, suggesting that few slaves entered the country.

During the 1850s, the international demand for cotton rose and production that decade far exceeded production in earlier decades.[70] It might be expected that more slaves were imported

---

[64] Daniel P. Mannix and Malcom Cowley, *Black Cargoes* (New York: Viking Press, 1962), pp. 187–188.

[65] *Ibid.*, pp. 188–189; DuBois, *op. cit.*, p. 111.

[66] Frederic Bancroft, *Slave Trading in the Old South* (Baltimore: J. H. Furst, 1931), Chap. xvi; Phillips, *op. cit.*, p. 370.

[67] George F. Dow, *Slave Ships and Slaving* (Salem, Mass.: Marine Research Society, 1927), p. 148.

[68] U. S., Bureau of the Census, *Negro Population: 1790–1915*, p. 147.

[69] *Ibid.*, p. 43.

[70] U. S., Bureau of the Census, *Historical Statistics . . .* , Series K-302.

during this decade, for the price of slaves also rose to unprecedented heights.[71] However, the growth rate of Negro population from 1850 to 1860 was lower than that of any of the preceding six decades and the Census of 1860 failed to find a surplus of young black males.

Few Negroes have emigrated from the United States. The idea of sending blacks back to Africa originated in the 1700s and the return of free Negroes to Africa began as early as 1815.[72] However, the African Colonization Society settled only 15,000 American Negroes in Africa during the years 1817 to 1899.[73] The underground railroad may have led some blacks to Canada, but few remained there, for the Canadian census of 1871 found only 22,000 Negroes in the entire nation.[74]

These data indicate that while migration has had an effect on population growth rates, it has had a minor effect when compared to natural increase.

Fertility and Mortality Rates of Negroes in the Pre-Civil War Period

Techniques of Analysis

Having established that the black population grew because of natural increase, we need to ascertain the level of fertility and mortality rates. Unfortunately, there was no registration of Negro births and only a few cities registered deaths during this period. The only information which can be used to determine the vital rates is data concerning the growth rate and age structure of the population.

Lotka demonstrated that if a population has constant fertility and mortality rates, it will eventually grow at a fixed rate and attain an age structure which does not change. The population is then said to be in a stable state. If a population has attained stability, it is possible to determine its vital rates merely by knowing its growth rate and some rudiments of its age composition. In recent years, there has emerged a very extensive literature

---

[71] Phillips, *op. cit.*, p. 370.

[72] Benjamin Quarles, *The Negro in the Making of America* (New York: Collier Books, 1964), p. 96; Jordan, *op. cit.*, pp. 546–569.

[73] Philip J. Staudenraus, *The African Colonization Movement: 1816–1865* (New York: Columbia University Press, 1961), p. 251.

[74] Canada, Dominion Bureau of Statistics, *Ninth Census of Canada: 1951*, Population, I, 30–31.

concerning stable population analysis. This literature has widely discussed the assumptions and techniques involved in stable population analysis and has provided many data which facilitate the analysis such as model life tables and model stable populations.[75] In addition, investigations have been conducted to determine how estimates of vital rates can be made if a population, instead of having constant fertility and mortality rates, has vital rates which have undergone change.[76]

The black population approximated stability for much of the pre-Civil War period.[77] The age structure was nearly constant and the growth rate changed very little from one decade to the next. This suggests that the techniques based on stable population analysis can be used to estimate fertility and mortality rates.

The Census of 1850 was the first to tabulate blacks by detailed ages; thus, the decade of the 1840s was the first for which demographic rates were calculated.[78] To compute these rates, three pieces of information were used: first, the growth rate of the black population from 1840 to 1850; second, the distribution of population by age in 1850; and third, information about a possible change in the birth rate. Between 1820 and 1850, the growth rate declined by a small amount. This most likely reflected a decrease in fertility since there are indications that the percentage of population at young ages fell during this period.

These data were used with the techniques of stable population analysis to calculate the crude death rate, the crude birth rate, the expectation of life and the general fertility rate; that is, the ratio

---

[75] Ansley J. Coale and Paul Demeny, *Regional Model Life Tables and Stable Populations* (Princeton: Princeton University Press, 1966); United Nations, Department of Economic and Social Affairs, Population Studies, No. 42, Manual IV, *Methods of Estimating Basic Demographic Measures from Incomplete Data* (1967); Alvaro Lopez, *Problems in Stable Population Theory* (Princeton: Office of Population Research, 1961).

[76] Ansley J. Coale and Melvin Zelnik, *New Estimates of Fertility and Population in the United States* (Princeton: Princeton University Press, 1963), pp. 82–89; United Nations, *op. cit.*, pp. 25–29.

[77] Melvin Zelnik, "Fertility of the American Negro in 1830 and 1850," *Population Studies*, XX, No. 1 (July, 1966), 77–83; Reynolds Farley, "The Demographic Rates and Social Institutions of the Nineteenth Century Negro Population: A Stable Population Analysis," *Demography*, II (1965), 386–398.

[78] The Census of 1850 tabulated blacks by fourteen age categories; the Censuses of 1840 and 1830 used six age categories while the Census of 1820 used only four age groups. U. S., Bureau of the Census, *Negro Population in the United States: 1790–1915*, p. 158.

TABLE 2-2
Demographic Rates of the Black Population 1840-1860

	1840–1850	1850–1860
Rate of Natural Increase	24 per 1000	20 per 1000
Crude Birth Rate	53 per 1000	49 per 1000
Crude Death Rate	29 per 1000	29 per 1000
Infant Mortality Rate	274 per 1000	302 per 1000
General Fertility Rate	240 per 1000	221 per 1000
Life Expectation		
At Birth		
Males	33 years	30 years
Females	35 years	33 years
At Age 10 Years		
Males	42 years	40 years
Females	43 years	42 years

Source:

U. S. Bureau of the Census, *Negro Population in the United States: 1790–1915* (Washington: Government Printing Office, 1918), p. 166. See text for methods of computation.

of births in a year to women ages 15 to 44. These rates are shown in Table 2–2.

The most tenuous assumption for these calculations is the one concerning the fertility decrease.[79] The vital rates shown in Table 2–2 were estimated by making various other assumptions: namely, that there had been no fertility decline, that the decline began in 1830 rather than 1820, and that the rate of decline was at different levels. In each case, the estimated vital rates were very close to those which are shown in Table 2–2. Different assumptions about the timing and rapidity of fertility change would change the crude birth rate by no more than two or three points.

A different technique was employed to estimate demographic rates for the decade 1850 to 1860. The mortality rates from various model life tables were used to survive the Negro population by age in 1850 for ten years.[80] This produced a series of estimates of the Negro population in 1860. These estimates were compared to the population enumerated by the Census of 1860 to determine which schedule of mortality rates best reflected the experience of the black population. In this fashion, a life table was chosen.

[79] Zelnik, *loc. cit.*, p. 80.

[80] These mortality rates were obtained from the "West" model life tables contained in the Coale and Demeny volume, *Regional Model Life Tables and Stable Populations*.

Death rates from this life table were applied to an estimate of the population in 1855 to determine the crude death rate.[81] The crude death rate was then subtracted from the rate of natural increase for the decade to obtain the crude birth rate. These vital rates are also shown in Table 2–2.

Fertility Patterns

The figures in Table 2–2 indicate that Negro women in the pre-Civil War period were very prolific, for crude birth rates exceeded 50 per 1000. The general fertility rate of over 200 implies that each year more than one-fifth of the women ages 15 to 44 bore a child. Women who survived for the entire childbearing span must have borne an average of almost seven children. These rates are so very high that we must ask if they are really plausible. The answer is yes. The black population of the pre-Civil War period was a youthful population; more than 45 percent were under age 15.[82] Such a young population can have these high fertility rates. In fact, in the early 1960s birth rates in some African countries approached or exceeded this level.[83]

There were no accounts, written in the pre-Civil War period, which accurately described the fertility or family status of blacks. A few travelers noted the abundance of black children and the early ages at which Negro females became mothers but these comments do not describe fertility trends. Even though southern writers participated heatedly in the Malthusian controversy, they were not aware of the demographic rates of the black population and made no effort to ascertain what they were.[84]

Prior to the Emancipation, 90 percent of the blacks were enslaved.[85] Apparently, there were no social institutions or mores which limited the childbearing of slaves. There was no legal marriage between slaves in the United States.[86] Male and female slaves apparently lived together whenever they wished and for as

---

[81] The population in 1855 was estimated by averaging the population in 1850 and 1860.

[82] U. S., Bureau of the Census, *Negro Population: 1790–1915*, p. 166.

[83] United Nations, *Demographic Yearbook: 1966*, Table 7.

[84] Edmond Cooks, "The Malthusian Theory in Pre-Civil War America," *Population Studies*, XX, No. 3 (March, 1967), 354–358; E. P. Hutchinson, *The Population Debate* (Boston: Houghton-Mifflin, 1967), Chap. x.

[85] U. S., Bureau of the Census, *A Century of Population Growth in the United States: 1790–1900*, Table 17.

[86] Kenneth M. Stampp, *The Peculiar Institution* (New York: Vintage Books, 1956), p. 198.

long as they wished, the principal constraint being the availability of partners. Some masters, perhaps many, made a point of deliberately keeping married slaves together. However, as historians have noted, the economic interests of slave owners opposed the development of stable families among blacks.[87] Every slave was a chattel who could be sold whenever his master wished. In the absence of mores or legal restraints, there emerged a marital system which, for most blacks, must have involved a series of consecutive matings beginning about the age of puberty. This pattern led to the high fertility rates.

It has been asserted that slave breeding was commonly practiced by slave owners.[88] One historian, Ulrich Phillips, who examined materials pertaining to this topic concluded there was no evidence of slave breeding.[89] Some owners, who needed cash, did sell young slaves when they attained prime working ages and young women whose fertility had been proven brought greater prices than childless women, although not as great a price as a male slave brought.[90] However, this is hardly evidence of slave breeding. A more important question to ask is what owners might have done to raise or lower the fertility of blacks. It was possible for slave owners to punish their chattels who did not cohabit and to reward females slaves after they had borne or raised a large number of children. Accounts of slave life, however, fail to mention any such practices. Rather, they indicate that since most blacks lived near many other blacks, matings were frequent and children were numerous.

Health Conditions

The mortality rates shown in Table 2–2 indicate that in the pre-Civil War period, blacks, at birth, could expect to live about thirty years. This is a very brief life span. Non-whites in the United States in 1967 had a life expectation of 64 years,[91] and even in the

---

[87] Klein, op. cit., p. 49; E. Franklin Frazier, The Negro Family in the United States (Chicago: University of Chicago Press, 1939), Part 1; Stanley M. Elkins, Slavery, 2nd ed. (Chicago: University of Chicago Press, 1968), p. 53.

[88] Franklin, op. cit., p. 178; Bancroft, op. cit., Chap. iv; Stampp, op. cit., pp. 245–251.

[89] Phillips, op. cit., p. 361.

[90] Ibid.

[91] U. S., National Center for Health Statistics, Vital Statistics of the United States: 1967, II, Part A, Table 5–2.

less developed world, life spans are presently close to 50 years.[92] The life span of blacks before 1860 was apparently shorter than that of other groups living about the same time. The earliest life tables constructed for a population within the United States referred to the State of Massachusetts for the period 1850 and 1855. These showed a life span of 39 years.[93] Life tables computed in conjunction with the 1841 Census of England indicated a life expectation of 41 years.[94]

It is difficult to learn about mortality among blacks during the last century. Many essays reported on the health conditions of slaves, but typically, they were heavily influenced by the views of their authors towards slavery. Defenders of the system argued that slaves represented highly valued capital investments. Consequently, masters took great care to preserve slaves in peak physical condition, providing medical care and even hospitalization for their ailing slaves. For dangerous occupations such as draining swamps or building railroads, hired labor—often Irish immigrants—were employed to avoid possible injuries to slaves. In addition, it was argued that more than 60 percent of all slaves were held by masters who owned fewer than twenty slaves.[95] These masters would come into daily contact with their slaves and would provide humane care.

Abolitionists contended that slaves did not receive satisfactory food and were often forced to live in miserable conditions. They charged that planters commonly worked their slaves to death in order to save crops or cut costs.[96]

Some information is available concerning the diet and health practices of slaves. Descriptions of the plantation system indicate that food was generally plentiful but monotonous. An unchanging diet of a peck of corn or beans, three or four pounds of pork and some molasses provided the basic subsistence for most slaves.[97] Such a diet provides sufficient quantity, but to be healthful, a diet should include additional items of fresh food. Some travelers

[92] United Nations, op. cit., Table 21.

[93] Louis I. Dublin, Alfred J. Lotka and Mortimer Spiegelman, Length of Life, rev. ed. (New York: Ronald Press, 1949), p. 41.

[94] Ibid., pp. 324 and 326.

[95] U. S., Bureau of the Census, A Century of Population Growth in the United States: 1790–1900, p. 136.

[96] Phillips, op. cit., Chap. xv.

[97] Stampp, op. cit., p. 282; Orville W. Taylor, Negro Slavery in Arkansas (Durham, N.C.: Duke University Press, 1958), Chap. viii; William D. Postell, The Health of Slaves on Southern Plantations (Baton Rouge: Louisiana State University Press, 1951), Chap. iii.

mentioned that slaves obtained milk, fruit and vegetables and frequently fished or hunted game when it was in season.[98] Manuals for slave owners recommended these items.[99] However, there were times when fresh foods had to be purchased and some owners must have resisted such expenses. Other owners, instead of providing variety foods, allowed slaves to keep small gardens, but this practice was often condemned since slaves had little time or energy for gardening.[100] On most plantations, slaves prepared their own foods, but some owners believed that slaves did such a poor job of cooking their own meals, particularly cooking meat, that they set up cook houses.[101] It is impossible to assess the nutritional value of the typical slave's diet, but it did provide bulk. One estimate is that slaves typically consumed 4000 to 5000 calories each day.[102]

The housing conditions of most blacks were rustic. They usually lived in some type of log cabin similar to the housing of whites in rural areas.[103] A few planters realized that dirty living conditions were related to diseases and insisted that slave quarters be periodically cleaned and painted, but this was exceptional.[104] The housing of urban blacks, both free and enslaved, was generally of even lower quality than on plantations. A few lived with white families, but most lived in shanties, in basements, around warehouses or places abandoned by whites.[105]

It is impossible to know how prevalent contagious diseases were among blacks. To obtain information about diseases, the censuses from 1850 to 1900 attempted to ascertain how many died in the year prior to the enumeration and what the cause of death was. The results were unsatisfactory. The superintendent of the Census of 1850 believed that deaths were seriously undercounted and that only a death registration system would provide the needed data.[106] The superintendent of the Census of 1860 con-

---

[98] J. G. Taylor, op. cit., pp. 108 ff.

[99] Postell, op. cit., pp. 31–38.

[100] James B. Sellers, Slavery in Alabama (University, Ala.: University of Alabama Press, 1950), pp. 92–98.

[101] Ibid., p. 96.

[102] U. S., Bureau of the Census, Historical Statistics . . . , Series Z-388.

[103] Charles S. Sydnor, Slavery in Mississippi (New York: D. Appleton-Century, 1933), pp. 39–44; Stampp, op. cit., pp. 293–295.

[104] Stampp, op. cit., p. 294.

[105] Richard C. Wade, Slavery in Cities (New York: Oxford University Press, 1964), pp. 112–117.

[106] U. S., Census Office, Mortality Statistics of the Seventh Census of the United States: 1850, p. 8; U. S., Bureau of the Census, Negro Population in the United States: 1790–1915, p. 298.

tended that a life table for Britain represented the mortality experience of the United States better than the death statistics collected by the Census of 1860.[107]

Descriptions of life in the South indicate that malaria was the most common disease and that this disease affected both whites and Negroes. In most areas, malaria was common immediately following settlement, but after marshes were drained and ponds filled, the incidence typically decreased.[108] Throughout the South, planters expected and planned for periods of time during the fall in which few of their slaves could work because of the prevalence of malaria.[109] Malaria generally did not kill its victims but did debilitate them. The use of quinine to treat this disease was known but not widely used in the South.[110]

Epidemics of yellow fever occurred frequently. Most descriptions of this disease describe its awful consequences for urban populations, but it also ravaged rural areas.[111] Blacks were better able to withstand this disease than whites, for the disease was endemic in West Africa and some Negroes inherited an immunity.[112] However, it still took a toll of Negroes, for the immunity was not universal and there was no effective treatment.

Cholera was introduced into the South in the 1830s and proved to be more fatal to Negroes than to whites.[113] This disease spread rapidly in both rural and urban areas and led to a great loss of life. The cause of this disease and methods for treating it were unknown in the pre-Civil War South. A few planters did perceive its connection with the water supply and either moved their slaves or changed the water supply when the disease spread.[114] Contemporary accounts suggest that cholera was a very common cause of slave deaths. Tuberculosis, dietary diseases and various types of fevers were less frequently mentioned as causes of death.[115]

Infant and maternal death rates were very high. Many deliveries took place without any medical supervision. Most midwives did not realize the importance of cleanliness, so many in-

---

[107] U. S., Census Office, *Preliminary Report on the Eighth Census: 1860*, p. 30.

[108] Postell, *op. cit.*, p. 7.

[109] Stampp, *op. cit.*, p. 300; O. W. Taylor, *op. cit.*, pp. 153–155.

[110] J. G. Taylor, *op. cit.*, p. 116; O. W. Taylor, *op. cit.*, p. 162.

[111] Postell, *op. cit.*, p. 6.

[112] Jordan, *op. cit.*, p. 529.

[113] Postell, *op. cit.*, p. 6; J. G. Taylor, *op. cit.*, p. 119; Dublin, *Health and Wealth*, p. 259.

[114] Postell, *op. cit.*, pp. 94–95; Stampp, *op. cit.*, p. 120.

[115] Postell, *op. cit.*, pp. 79–81; Stampp, *op. cit.*, p. 300.

fants must have died, often of tetanus, shortly after they were born.[116]

Many of the large and some of the smaller cities had hospitals for slaves, and, on some plantations, there were special buildings used as infirmaries.[117] Many doctors made a regular practice of treating slaves, and the account books of some plantations indicate that sizable medical expenses for slaves were regularly incurred.[118] However, the state of medical knowledge was not very advanced. Most southern doctors had not graduated from a medical school; rather they learned by observing other doctors practice. Licensing regulations were not strict so the field of medicine included unskilled practitioners and quacks. Causes of contagious diseases were generally unknown and most treatments were based on folk lore.[119] It is impossible to believe that medical practice significantly lowered the death rate or controlled diseases.

In summary, in the pre-Civil War period, there were few influences which reduced either mortality or fertility rates. The crude birth rate must have exceeded 50, and the typical woman must have borne seven or more children by the time she reached menopause. Crude death rates must have been approximately 30 and probably would have been higher had not the food supply been so regular and plentiful. The death rates for particular areas probably fluctuated widely from year to year, depending upon the presence or absence of contagious disease.

Summary

Blacks entered the American colonies early in the seventeenth century, shortly after the first white settlers arrived. The population, both white and Negro, grew slowly during the 1600s. In the next century, the northern colonies engaged in a prosperous trade while the southern colonies exported several profitable crops. A need arose for additional workers and blacks were brought into the colonies in large numbers. As a result, the Negro population grew very rapidly from about 1700 to 1760 due both to the slave trade and natural increase.

The importing of slaves slackened just before the Revolution and after the Revolution relatively few slaves were imported.

---

116 Stampp, *op. cit.*, p. 304.
117 Postell, *op. cit.*, Chap. xiii.
118 Sydnor, *op. cit.*, pp. 46–53; O. W. Taylor, *op. cit.*, p. 167.
119 Postell, *op. cit.*, Chap. vi.

This reduced the growth rate; nevertheless, the black population continued to grow at a high rate, doubling every twenty-five years or so.

During the period from 1820 to 1860, the growth rate of the black population seemingly declined, and this cannot be attributed to a gradual elimination of the slave trade. Neither demographic data nor contemporary accounts of living conditions satisfactorily explain why the growth rate tapered off. We speculate that both fertility and mortality rates fluctuated widely from year to year and were not subject to deliberate intervention. There is no reason to believe that black couples controlled their childbearing or that medical science or public health activities effectively limited diseases. The decline in growth rates must have been a consequence of general changes in health condition, changes in the prevalence of infectious diseases and changes in the ability of women to bear children and keep them alive.

Chapter 3

THE DEVELOPMENT
OF A NATIONAL NEGRO POPULATION

The growth rate of the black population slackened during the seventy years between the Civil War and the Depression, but the population became widely distributed across the entire country. The first section of this chapter discusses shifts in the geographic location of Negroes. The next section discusses the changing fertility trends, and the final section analyzes the fluctuations of mortality rates which occurred during this period.

The Changing Location of Blacks

Regional Changes

For a long time, the Negro population of the United States was concentrated in the South. Figure 3–1, which shows the regional distribution of blacks, indicates that until after the turn of the twentieth century more than 90 percent of all blacks lived in the South. Table 3–1 contains average annual growth rates for the Negro population in each of the four regions of the country.

Throughout the nation's history there has been an out-migration of Negroes from the South. Prior to the Civil War, the midwestern states were the destination of many of the departing Negroes. The Northwest Ordinance declared there would be no slavery in any of the new midwestern states. The early settlers and founders of these states, however, feared a large black population and wrote laws to discourage any Negroes who considered moving into one of these states. Indiana and Illinois, for instance, ratified constitutions which forbade blacks—free or slave—from coming into the state, and Ohio adopted Black Laws which speci-

TABLE 3–1
Average Annual Growth Rates of the Black Population by Region: 1790–1968*

Period	Total Population	North East	North Central	South	West
1790–1800	2.8%	2.1%	–	2.9%	–
1800–1810	3.2	2.1	–	3.2	–
1810–1820	2.5	.8	–	2.6	–
1820–1830	2.7	1.2	–	2.8	–
1830–1840	2.1	1.3	7.7%	2.0	–
1840–1850	2.4	.5	4.2	2.4	–
1850–1860	2.0	.4	3.1	2.0	–
1860–1870	.9	1.4	3.9	.8	–
1870–1880	3.0	2.4	3.5	3.0	–
1880–1890	1.3	1.6	1.1	1.3	–
1890–1900	1.8	3.6	1.4	1.6	–
1900–1910	1.1	2.3	.9	1.0	5.2%
1910–1920	.6	3.4	3.8	.2	4.4
1920–1930	1.3	5.2	4.7	.5	4.3
1930–1940	.8	1.8	1.2	.6	3.5
1940–1950	1.6	3.9	4.5	.3	12.1
1950–1960	2.3	4.1	4.4	1.0	6.4
1960–1968	2.1	3.4	3.7	.5	6.1

* Growth rates were not computed for regions in which the Negro population at the beginning of a decade was less than 30,000.

Sources:

U. S., Bureau of the Census, *Historical Statistics* . . . , Series A 99–120, *Current Population Reports*, "Estimates of the Population of the United States by Age, Race, and Sex: July 1, 1968", Table 2; "Recent Trends in Social and Economic Conditions of Negroes in the United States," Series P-23, No. 26 (July, 1968), p. 3.

fied that if a Negro wished to enter the state he had to post a $500 bond and present court papers indicating that he was indeed free and not an escaped slave.[1] These laws were not particularly effective, for by the 1820s Negro communities existed in Cincinnati, Columbus and Portsmouth, Ohio.[2] By 1833, Detroit had a large enough black population that the militia had to be called out to put down racial strife; by the 1840s blacks were to be found in rural areas of southern Michigan.[3] The development of manu-

---

[1] Leon F. Litwack, *North of Slavery* (Chicago: University of Chicago Press, 1961), pp. 70–73.

[2] Richard C. Wade, *The Urban Frontier* (Chicago: University of Chicago Press, 1959), p. 221; Frank U. Quillin, *The Color Line in Ohio* (Ann Arbor: George Wahr, 1913), pp. 32 and 46.

[3] George N. Fuller, *Economic and Social Beginnings of Michigan* (Lansing: Wynkoop Hallenbeck Cranford, 1916), p. 147; George K. Hesslink, *Black Neighbors* (Indianapolis: Bobbs-Merrill, 1968), pp. 40–44.

43

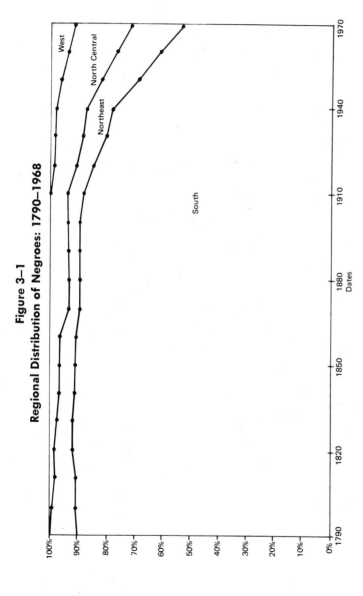

Figure 3–1

Regional Distribution of Negroes: 1790–1968

Sources:

U. S., Bureau of the Census, *Historical Statistics of the United States, Colonial Times to 1957* (Washington: Government Printing Office, 1960), Series A95–122; "Recent Trends in Social and Economic Conditions of Negroes in the United States," *Current Population Reports*, Series P-23, No. 26 (July, 1968).

facturing and commerce in such places as Cincinnati created the need for many laborers, and blacks filled some of these jobs.[4] In Michigan, the Quakers encouraged both fugitive slaves and free blacks to leave the South and populate the unsettled rural areas.[5]

During the pre-Civil War years, the Negro population grew least rapidly in the northeastern states. In the major cities of this section of the nation—Boston, New York and Philadelphia—the black population increased by small numbers each decade until 1840 and then remained constant or declined.[6] The reasons for this were changes in the economic opportunities available to blacks. Early in the century, many of the laborers and some of the artisans in Philadelphia were Negroes. As the city grew, more freedmen left the South for the opportunities of Philadelphia.[7] In New York City, early in the last century, blacks performed much of the common labor and occupied most of the personal service jobs.[8] Gradually, European immigrants began to drive blacks from these jobs and by the time of the Civil War, occupations that once had been dominated by black workers were dominated by the Irish.[9] In Philadelphia and Pittsburgh, there were a number of bloody riots between 1833 and 1842 in which white workers attempted to drive Negroes from the city.[10] These riots and the lack of job opportunities must have discouraged free Negroes from moving into these areas, and the very high mortality rates of the cities insured that the indigenous black population would grow slowly, if at all.

There was little migration of blacks away from the South in the period immediately following the Civil War. In the northeast, European immigrants continued to fill the need for unskilled

---

[4] Wade, *op. cit.*, pp. 223–224.

[5] George N. Fuller, *Michigan: A Centennial History of the State and its People* (Chicago: Lewis Publishing, 1939), p. 357; Hesslink, *op. cit.*

[6] John Daniels, *In Freedom's Birthplace* (Boston: Houghton Mifflin, 1914), p. 457; George Edmund Haynes, *The Negro at Work in New York City* reprint ed. (New York: Arno Press, 1968), p. 47; W. E. Burghardt DuBois, *The Philadelphia Negro*, reprint ed. (New York: Benjamin Blom, 1967), p. 36.

[7] DuBois, *The Philadelphia Negro*, p. 25.

[8] Sterling D. Spero and Abram L. Harris, *The Black Worker*, reprint ed. (New York: Atheneum, 1968), p. 13.

[9] Litwack, *op. cit.*, pp. 153–168; DuBois, *The Philadelphia Negro*, pp. 26–27; Spero and Harris, *op. cit.*, pp. 12–14.

[10] Edward R. Turner, *The Negro in Pennsylvania* (Washington: American Historical Association, 1911), pp. 160–164; Sam Bass Warner, Jr., *The Private City* (Philadelphia: University of Pennsylvania Press, 1968), Chap. vii.

labor. The Midwest received migrants from Europe and also from the eastern United States.

The era of Reconstruction ended with the inauguration of President Hayes in 1877. Gradually, one southern state after another ended Negro suffrage and reestablished white supremist governments controlled by the Democrats.[11] Mississippi was among the first states to put the integrated Republican government out of office, a change which was accompanied by much violence directed at blacks.[12] Later, cotton crops in Mississippi were extremely unsuccessful and the state was plagued by yellow fever.[13] These factors, combined with the efforts of railroad and land agents, led to a movement of blacks from Mississippi to Kansas. The number who moved was quite small and many quickly returned to Mississippi when they found that living conditions in Kansas were harsh.[14] There were similar efforts to encourage Negroes in North Carolina, Alabama and Louisiana to leave the South, but they met with little response.[15] In 1880, a Congressional investigation of the supposed exodus was begun, for the Democrats accused the Republicans of encouraging Negro migration so that black votes could be used to maintain Republican control of the northern and midwestern states.[16]

The first movement of large numbers of blacks away from the South coincided with World War I, but the pattern of northward migration began much earlier when economic opportunities attracted southern Negroes. Northern employers knew that the real or threatened presence of black workers was an effective instrument for ending strikes and keeping wages low. Consequently, black workers were used as strike breakers as early as 1855 in New York City.[17] After the Civil War, the importing of black workers from the South for this purpose became more common. In the 1870s Negro iron and steel workers were brought from Richmond to Pittsburgh[18] and, in the 1880s, black workers

[11] C. Vann Woodward, *The Strange Career of Jim Crow* (New York: Oxford University Press, 1957), Chap. ii.

[12] Vernon Lane Wharton, *The Negro in Mississippi: 1865–1890* (New York: Harper & Row, 1965), Chap. xiii.

[13] *Ibid.*, p. 112.

[14] Arna Bontemps and Jack Conroy, *Anyplace but Here* (New York: Hill and Wang, 1966), pp. 62–66.

[15] August Meier, *Negro Thought in America: 1880–1915* (Ann Arbor: University of Michigan Press, 1966), pp. 60–61.

[16] Bontemps and Conroy, *op. cit.*, p. 54.

[17] Spero and Harris, *op. cit.*, p. 131.

[18] R. R. Wright, Jr., "One Hundred Negro Steel Workers," in *Wage Earning Pittsburgh*, ed. Paul Underwood Kellogg (New York: Survey Associates, Inc., 1914), p. 106.

were brought into the Illinois coal fields.[19] In 1894 and again in 1904, stockyard workers in Chicago struck; management then went into the South to obtain Negro workers. The following year, the city's leading merchants responded in a similar manner when the Teamster's Union struck.[20]

There is less evidence that Negroes were imported as strike breakers to the cities along the East coast. Rather, some southern blacks, most often young men, realized there were employment opportunities in Philadelphia and New York, and left the South, particularly as agricultural production and farm income declined.[21] When the Democrats reestablished their control of the southern legislatures, toward the end of the last century, they instituted Jim Crowism and restricted opportunities for black teachers, businessmen, and professionals.[22] Anti-Negro riots occurred in such cities as Atlanta, Georgia and Wilmington, North Carolina, and the lynching of blacks reached a peak around the turn of the century.[23] These factors hastened an out-migration of Negroes from the South, particularly of the "talented tenth."[24]

A combination of push and pull factors led to a much greater out-migration of blacks from the South, between 1915 and 1920. Chiefly because of boll weevil infestation, cotton production fell by more than one-third from 1914 to 1915, and thereafter remained at a low level.[25] Reductions in income effected by this change not only impoverished rural Negroes, but led to unemployment and wage cuts for the many blacks in southern cities who worked at jobs dependent upon the cotton economy.[26] The cost of living, however, rose with the outbreak of the international war.[27]

---

[19] Bontemps and Conroy, op. cit., pp. 140–144.

[20] Allen H. Spear, Black Chicago: The Making of a Negro Ghetto, 1890–1920 (Chicago: University of Chicago Press, 1967), pp. 39–40; Spero and Harris, op. cit., p. 264.

[21] DuBois, The Philadelphia Negro, p. 80.

[22] Woodward, op. cit., pp. 81–87.

[23] U.S., Bureau of the Census, Historical Statistics . . . , Series H-454; Ray Stannard Baker, Following the Color Line (New York: Harper & Row, 1964), Chap. i; Woodward, op. cit., p. 70.

[24] Gilbert Osofsky, Harlem: The Making of a Ghetto (New York: Harper & Row, 1963), p. 20.

[25] U. S., Department of Agriculture, Agricultural Statistics: 1967, Table 85; Chicago Commission on Race Relations, The Negro in Chicago (Chicago: University of Chicago Press, 1922), p. 81.

[26] Chicago Commission on Race Relations, op. cit., p. 80.

[27] U. S., Bureau of the Census, Historical Statistics . . . , Series E-113, E-159, and E-161–176.

During World War I, the gross national product and manufacturing employment increased by about one-quarter.[28] Immigration to the United States had averaged more than one million persons per year from 1910 to 1914, but this ended in 1915 and large numbers of immigrants did not again enter the country until the 1920s[29]. This meant that northern firms had to expand their production and employment, but were unable to tap a labor reserve of European immigrants. Instead, they hired Negroes from the southern states. Many firms sent labor recruiters into the South and put willing workers on northbound trains. The Pennsylvania Railroad alone brought 12,000 Negro men north to maintain their tracks and equipment.[30] In Chicago, 50,000 Negroes were counted arriving from the South in an eighteen month span in 1917 and 1918.[31]

It is impossible to ascertain exactly how many blacks moved north during the World War I period. Contemporary accounts typically overestimated the numbers of migrants.[32] It is likely the total number of Negroes leaving the South during the entire World War I period was much less than the number of Europeans who entered the United States each year prior to the war, for the census of 1920 found there had been a net out-migration of only one-half million blacks from the South between 1910 and 1920.[33] Of course, the number who left the South but then returned before the census was taken is unknown. The manufacturing cities of the North Central states were the most frequent destinations of the migrants.[34] Smaller numbers went to the cities along the East Coast and few moved into the western states.[35]

The out-migration from the South of large numbers of Negroes continued after World War I. During the 1920s, the number of blacks who left was greater than during the previous decade.

---

[28] U. S., Bureau of the Census, *Long Term Economic Growth: 1860–1965* (Washington: Government Printing Office, 1966), Series A7, A8, and A9.

[29] U. S., Bureau of the Census, *Historical Statistics* . . . , Series C-88.

[30] Franklin, *op. cit.*, p. 472.

[31] Chicago Commission on Race Relations, *op. cit.*, p. 79.

[32] Elliot M. Rudwick, *Race Riot at East St. Louis: July 2, 1917* (Cleveland: World Publishing, 1966), Chap. xii.

[32a] Karl E. and Alma F. Taeuber, "The Negro Population of the United States," *The American Negro Reference Book*, ed. John P. Davis (Englewood Cliffs, N.J.: Prentice-Hall, 1966), p. 111.

[33] Conrad and Irene B. Taeuber, *The Changing Population of the United States* (New York: John Wiley, 1958), p. 110.

[34] *Ibid.*, p. 110.

[35] *Ibid.*

The factors responsible for the migration were much the same. The postwar boom in agriculture was short lived and cotton production fell during the early 1920s to very low levels.[36] The gross national product and manufacturing employment expanded and new immigration laws limited the flow of immigrants, particularly the influx of unskilled immigrants from eastern and southern Europe.[37] As a result, the black population of most northern cities and states increased more during the 1920s than during the World War I period.

In the 1930s there was continued out-migration from the South, albeit a migration stream which included fewer people than the migration stream of the previous decade.[38] "Push" factors, rather than economic opportunities in the North, must have been the major reason for the migration. For many years, declines in cotton production, depletion of soils, and the boll weevil encouraged southern Negroes to leave rural areas. However, Gunnar Myrdal argues that these factors had less effect than changes which occurred during the Depression decade. One important factor was the decreased national and international demand for the South's three major cash crops—cotton, sugar, and tobacco.[39] Of even greater significance was the Agricultural Adjustment Program introduced in 1933. This act called for acreage limitations in order to cut back surpluses and boost prices. In many areas of the South, landlords, encouraged by this act, reduced or eliminated their sharecroppers and tenant farmers.[40] In addition, the Agricultural Adjustment Program included payments to farmers who modernized and mechanized their farming, which reduced the number of blacks who could work in southern agriculture. These programs hastened the exodus of Negroes from the rural South even though their chances of finding work in the cities were not good.[41]

During World War II, many more blacks left the South than during World War I.[42] Again, the manufacturing cities of the North were the most common destinations. A new development was the movement of large numbers of Negroes to West Coast

---

[36] U. S., Department of Agriculture, op. cit., Table 85.

[37] U. S., Bureau of the Census, Historical Statistics . . . , Series C 88–100.

[38] C. Taeuber and I. B. Taeuber, op. cit., p. 110.

[39] Gunnar Myrdal, An American Dilemma, I (New York: McGraw-Hill, 1964), 251–252.

[40] Ibid., pp. 253–258.

[41] Ibid., p. 260.

[42] C. Taeuber and I. B. Taeuber, op. cit., p. 110.

cities where the expanding defense industries offered employment to many workers.

Agricultural productivity, that is output per farm worker,
increased more during the 1950s than during the 1940s, both
nationwide and in the South.[43] This, combined with the growth of
manufacturing, brought about a continued out-migration of Negroes from the South. This pattern of out-migration has continued to the present, for Table 3–1 indicates that the southern
Negro population is growing less rapidly than the Negro population in other regions. Despite many decades of large scale out-
migration, rates of natural increase among Negroes in the South
have been high and the number of blacks in the South, instead of
declining, has increased from nine million in 1910 to 12 million
in 1968.

Urbanization

Before the Civil War, there was little rural to urban migration by blacks. The Negro populations in many northern cities increased by small amounts, and in many southern cities the black
population actually declined before the war.[44] Slavery was not
compatible with an urban environment. In the city, slaves could
easily escape from their masters, hire themselves out or congre-
gate with other slaves or free blacks.[45] Since it was impossible to
control these urban slaves, many southern states and cities
adopted laws which discouraged the keeping of either slaves or
freedmen in cities.[46]

During and after the Civil War, the black population of
southern cities rose rapidly. Many slaves, upon learning of the
Emancipation Proclamation, left their plantations and flocked to
southern cities, to Union Army camps or to the offices to the
Freedman's Bureau.[47] This movement was symbolic of freedom to
many Negroes. Shanty towns appeared on the outskirts of most
southern cities, and the Census of 1870 showed that southern
towns had a much larger black population than in 1860.[48]

---

[43] U. S., Department of Agriculture, op. cit., Tables 662, 670, and 671.
[44] Richard C. Wade, *Slavery in Cities* (New York: Oxford University
Press, 1964), pp. 329–330.
[45] *Ibid.*, Chap. iv.
[46] *Ibid.*, Chap. ix.
[47] James M. McPherson, *The Negro's Civil War* (New York: Random
House, 1967), p. 65; Constance McLaughlin Green, *The Secret City* (Princeton: Princeton University Press, 1967), pp. 61–65.
[48] Reynolds Farley, "The Urbanization of Negroes in the United
States," *Journal of Social History*, II (Spring, 1968), 247.

TABLE 3–2
Proportion of Negroes Living in Urban and Rural Areas: 1890–1960

	Total United States		South		North and West	
	Urban	Rural	Urban	Rural	Urban	Rural
1890	20%	80%	15%	85%	62%	38%
1900	23	77	17	83	70	30
1910	27	73	21	79	77	23
1920	34	66	25	75	84	16
1930	44	56	32	68	88	12
1940	49	51	37	64	89	11
1950—old def.*	59	41	–	–	–	–
1950—new def.*	62	38	48	52	93	7
1960	73	27	58	42	95	5

* In 1950, the definition of urban residence was changed to include as urban those individuals who lived in places of less than 2500 but within the suburbs of central cities.
Sources:
> U. S., Bureau of the Census, Negro Population . . . 1790–1915, p. 92; Fifteenth Census of the United States: 1930, Population, II, pp. 62–64 and 72; Sixteenth Census of the United States: 1940, Population, Characteristics of the Non-White Population Race, Table 3; Census of Population: 1950, P-E, 3B, Table 2; Census of Population: 1960, PC(2)–1C, Table 1.

The gradual urbanization of blacks has continued since 1870.[49] We can be more certain of these trends for the period after 1890, for that was the first decennial census to provide specific tabulations of the urban and rural population. Table 3–2 indicates the rural-urban distribution of Negroes in the entire United States, in the South, the North, and West. Table 3–3 shows annual growth rates for the urban and rural population in each area.

The changes in employment and agriculture, discussed in the previous section, were also responsible for the urbanization of blacks. Since 1890, in both the South and North, the urban population has grown more rapidly than the rural. Nevertheless, it was not until World War II that the urban Negro population exceeded the rural. Among whites, this occurred thirty years earlier during World War I.[50]

The rural Negro population declined from a peak of seven million, in 1910, to five million, in 1960. This drop has undoubt-

---

[49] Meier, op. cit., p. 59.
[50] U. S., Bureau of the Census, Fourteenth Census of the United States: 1920, Population, II, p. 79.

TABLE 3–3
Average Annual Growth Rates for the Negro Population
in Urban and Rural Areas, 1890–1960

	Total United States		South		North and West	
Period	Urban	Rural	Urban	Rural	Urban	Rural
1890–1900	+3.0%	+1.3%	+2.9%	+3.3%	+3.3%	− .4%
1900–1910	+2.9	+ .4	+3.1	+ .5	+2.6	−1.0
1910–1920	+2.8	− .3	+1.9	+ .3	+4.5	− .1
1920–1930	+3.8	− .3	+2.8	− .4	+5.3	+2.2
1930–1940	+1.9	− .1	+2.0	− .2	+1.7	+ .7
1940–1950 *	+3.5	− .7	na	na	na	na
1950–1960 *	+3.9	−1.1	+3.0	−1.3	+4.7	+1.3

* In 1950, the definition of urban residence was changed to include as urban those people who lived in places of less than 2500 but within the suburban area of large cities. The 1940 to 1950 growth rates were calculated using the old definition of urban residence. The 1950 to 1960 growth rates were based on the new definition of urban residence.
Source:
  See Figure 3–1.

edly continued during the 1960s, for a recent Bureau of the Census survey found that the non-white farm population in 1968 was less than half as numerous as in 1960.[51]

There are regional differences in the distribution of rural or urban population. Outside the South, the black population has lived principally in cities. As early as 1890, two-thirds of the Negroes in the North and West were city dwellers. Within the South, a much smaller proportion lived in urban areas. On the eve of World War II, only one-third of the southern Negroes lived in cities and, until the mid-1950s, the majority of southern Negroes lived in rural areas.

Fertility Trends

Ratios of Children to Women

Between the Civil War and the Depression, the black population switched from very rapid growth to slow growth. The chief reason for this change was a decrease in the rate at which Negro women had babies. For at least sixty years, Negro birth

---

[51] U. S., Bureau of the Census, "Farm Population of the United States: 1968," *Current Population Reports*, Series Census-ERS P-27, No. 40 (July 31, 1969), Table 2.

rates declined. It is difficult to determine exactly when the decline started or how rapidly fertility decreased because there was no national system for registering births until the mid-1930s. Much of our knowledge of childbearing trends for this long period must be derived from information about the age distribution of the population. If a census tabulated a population by age and sex, it is possible to compute a ratio of children 0 to 4 to women ages 15 to 44. This is a fairly sensitive indicator of fertility because births in the five year interval preceding the census are repre-sented in the numerator and the women eligible to bear these children are included in the denominator.

Figure 3–2 shows ratios of children 0 to 4 per 1,000 women 15 to 44 for the period 1850 to 1968. Fertility rates among blacks may have fallen by a small amount before and during the Civil War. A more pronounced and uninterrupted decline occurred be-tween 1880 and 1940. Each census revealed a smaller ratio of chil-dren to women than the previous census. Finally, a minimum was reached in 1940 when the ratio was less than one-half as large as in 1880.

Since 1940, fertility rates have increased reflecting the post-war baby boom. A peak was attained in 1960 when the fertility ratio was almost as high as in 1880. Since 1960, fertility rates among Negroes have fallen and the ratio of children to women has decreased. The causes and components of these changes are discussed in following chapters.

Identical general trends characterize both white and Negro fertility rates. However, in the nineteenth century, white fertility was at a lower level and then declined less rapidly, but for a longer span, than did Negro fertility. During the 1920s and 1930s, fertility rates of the two racial groups were at about the same level. The post-World War II rise in childbearing was greater among Negroes than among whites. The recent declines in fertility were sharper among whites and, as a result, Negro and white fertility ratios have become increasingly different in recent years.

Gross Reproduction Rates

Although the ratio of children to women is a useful measure, it does have liabilities.[52] Changes from one period to another in

---

[52] For a discussion, see Bernard Okun, *Trends in Birth Rates in the United States since 1870* (Baltimore: Johns Hopkins Press, 1958).

Figure 3–2
Ratios of Children 0–4 to Women 15–44, 1850–1968

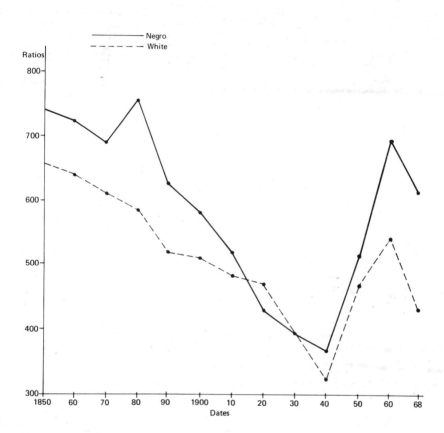

Sources:

U. S., Bureau of the Census, "Estimates of the Population of the United States by Age, Race, and Sex: July 1, 1968," *Current Population Reports*, Series P-25 No. 416 (February 17, 1969), Table 1; *Census of Population: 1950*, P-E, No. 3B Table 1; *Sixteenth Census of the United States: 1940*, Population, Characteristics of the Non-white Population by Race, Table 3; *Negroes in the United States: 1920–32* (Washington: Government Printing Office, 1935), p. 90; *Negro Population in the United States: 1790–1915* (Washington: Government Printing Office, 1918), p. 166.

U. S., Secretary of the Interior, *Ninth Census: 1890*, Vital Statistics of the United States, pp. 551–558.

infant mortality rates affect the proportion who survive from birth to be enumerated by a census. Also, changes in the completeness of census enumeration influence ratios of children to women. To overcome these difficulties, gross reproduction rates for the Negro population were estimated. This rate is a valuable indicator of fertility trends, for it shows the number of daughters a woman would bear if she lived to the end of her childbearing period and if fertility rates remained constant.

Since it is impossible to be certain about mortality trends or undercount prior to 1940, gross reproduction rates for this period were estimated making different assumptions about mortality and undercount.[53] First, they were computed without a correction for census undercount of children 0 to 4 or women ages 15 to 49 and, then, with the assumption that undercount rates, estimated for the non-white population in 1940, applied at every earlier census date.[54] The first mortality assumption was the official life tables, calculated from death rates for the population in the Death Registration Area, applied to the total black population. The second mortality assumption was that life tables derived by surviving the population from one census date to the next—described later in this chapter—represented the mortality experience of the black population. These latter life tables have much higher infant mortality rates than the official life tables, and thus produced much higher estimates of the births occurring in the five-year period before the census.

For 1940 and later years, two estimates of the gross reproduction rate were calculated. One was derived from the registered number of births and the number of women enumerated by the census or Current Population Survey. The second was calculated from birth data corrected for the under-registration of births and from estimates of the population corrected for census undercount. The methods used to make these corrections are discussed in Chapters 4 and 10.

---

[53] For a description of this methodology see: Bernard D. Karpinos, "The Differential True Rates of Growth of the White Population in the United States and their Probable Effects on the General Growth of the Population," *American Journal of Sociology* (September, 1938), 270–271; Wilson H. Grabill and Lee Jay Cho, "Methodology for Measurement of Current Fertility from Population Data on Young Children," *Demography*, II (1965), 50–73; U. S., Bureau of the Census, *Sixteenth Census of the United States: 1940*, Differential Fertility: 1940 and 1910, Standardized Fertility Rates and Reproduction Rates, Appendix D.

[54] Coale, *loc. cit.*, p. 29.

TABLE 3-4
Estimates of the Gross Reproduction Rates for Negroes: 1880-1966

Date	Uncorrected for Undercount		Corrected for Undercount	
	Assumes Higher Childhood Mortality	Assumes Lower Childhood Mortality	Assumes Higher Childhood Morality	Assumes Lower Childhood Morality
1880	3.21	2.73	3.55	2.90
1890	2.46	2.08	2.70	2.28
1900	2.42	2.08	2.65	2.28
1910	2.18	1.82	2.39	2.00
1920	1.72	1.33	1.91	1.47
1930	1.48	1.20	1.66	1.32
1940	–	1.11	–	–	1.26	–
1950	–	1.79	–	–	1.75	–
1960	–	2.23	–	–	2.10	–
1967	–	1.67	–	–	1.58	–

Sources:

U. S., Census Office, *Compendium of the Tenth Census: 1880*, Part I, p. 637; *Abstract of the Eleventh Census: 1890*, pp. 58–61.

U. S., Bureau of the Census, *Negro Population of the United States: 1790–1915* (Washington, Government Printing Office, 1918), *Sixteenth Census of the United States: 1940, Characteristics of the Non-white Population by Race*, Table 3; *Census of Population: 1950*, P-C1, Table 104; *Census of Population: 1960*, PC (2)–1C, Table 1, "Estimates of the Population of the United States and Components of Change, by Age, Color, and Sex 1950 to 1960", *Current Population Reports*, Series P-25, No. 310 (June 30, 1965) Table C-2; "Estimates of the Negro Population of the United States, by Age and Sex: July 1, 1960 to 1966," *Current Population Reports*, Series P-25, No. 367 (June 1, 1967) Table 1.

U. S., National Center for Health Statistics, *United States Life Tables: 1959–61*, I, Table II; *Vital Statistics of the United States: 1967*, I, Tables 1–19 and 1–50.

Ansley J. Coale, "The Population of the United States in 1950 Classified by Age, Sex, and Color-A Revision of Census Figures," *Journal of the American Statistical Association*, L, (March, 1955), 29.

Table 3–4 contains the estimated gross reproduction rates for 1880 to 1967. The different assumptions about infant mortality make very substantial differences in the estimated levels of these rates. One must be cautious in specifying what were the gross reproduction rates before 1940. Nevertheless, it is clear that changes in the gross reproduction rates show the same trend as the ratios of children to women: Fertility declined for many decades. If the childbearing rates of 1880 had persisted, each woman who survived for the entire childbearing span would have borne about three daughters. During the last twenty years of the nineteenth century—while most blacks remained in the rural

TABLE 3–5

Fertility of Cohorts of Ever-Married Negro Women Born During the Nineteenth Century

Years Women Born—	Children per 1000 Women	Women by Number of Children Ever Born						
		Total	0	1	2–4	5–6	7–9	10+
		Data from Census of 1910						
1835–44	7000	100%	6%	8%	21%	13%	20%	32%
1845–54	6897	100	7	8	21	13	20	31
1855–59	6580	100	8	8	22	14	19	29
1860–64	6162	100	9	9	24	14	19	25
		Data from Census of 1940						
1865–74	4678	100	11	11	33	17	16	12
1875–84	3985	100	16	12	35	16	12	9
1885–89	3688	100	18	13	36	15	11	7
1890–94	3340	100	22	15	34	13	10	6
1895–99	3091	100	24	16	33	12	10	5

Source:

     U. S., Bureau of the Census, *Sixteenth Census of the United States: 1940*, Population Differential Fertility: 1940 and 1910, Women by Number of Children Ever Born, Tables 3 and 6.

South—fertility declined; by 1900, the gross reproduction rate was in the neighborhood of two or two and one-half. The decline continued and the childbearing rates of 1940 implied that black women would average just over one daughter. This changed in the post-World War II era and the gross reproduction rate in the late 1950s was apparently at a higher level than it had been for fifty years.

Changes in Family Size

     The decline in Negro fertility rates resulted from changes in the size of families. Once, many black women had extremely large families—that is, ten or more children. Over time, this changed as small families and childlessness became common. These fluctuations can be observed by analyzing the figures contained in Table 3–5. Each line of this table indicates completed family size for women born during a specific period of the last century. These data were obtained from the censuses of 1910 and 1940 which asked women who had ever been married how many live children they had borne.[55]

---

[55] These data are available only for Negro women who survived to, and were enumerated by, the Census of 1910 or 1940. It is possible, but un-

The oldest women for which data are available were born between 1835 and 1844. They began their childbearing before the Civil War. Among this group, very few married women remained childless and few had small families. Two-thirds of the women who survived to be enumerated, bore at least five children and, on the average, each had seven children. Such high numbers of children support the view that Negro fertility was near a biological maximum during much of the nineteenth century.

Childbearing patterns changed rapidly. Each cohort of women following those born 1835–1844 bore fewer and fewer children. Women born just prior to the turn of this century completed their childbearing with an average of just over three children.

Two basic changes in family structure produced the lower fertility rates. First, there was a substantial increase in the proportion of women who remained childless or who had only one child. Among the women born between 1890 and 1899, almost one-quarter of the married women reached menopause without bearing a child and another one-sixth of these women had just one child. Second, there was a great reduction in the proportion of women who had extremely large families. For instance, one-third of the women born from 1835 to 1844 had ten children, but among Negro women born sixty years later, only one out of twenty had such a large number of offspring.

Similar information is available concerning the fertility of native white women.[56] A comparison of data for the two races indicates, first, that the fertility of white women was never as high as that of Negroes; in particular, there never was a large proportion of white women who had very many children. Second, the fertility of whites decreased during the same period of time, but at a slower rate. Third, the fertility decline among whites was due chiefly to a reduction in the proportion of women with five or more children, and there was only a modest increase in the proportion of white women who remained childless.

The vital statistics system reported that, in 1940, the Negro crude birth rate was about 27 per 1,000 and the general fertility

likely, that women who died prior to these censuses had different fertility patterns. For a further discussion of the quality of these data see: U. S., Bureau of the Census, *Sixteenth Census of the United States: 1940*, Population, Differential Fertility: 1940 and 1910, Women by Number of Children Ever Born, pp. 5–6 and 408–410.

[56] U. S., Bureau of the Census, *Sixteenth Census of the United States: 1940*, Differential Fertility: 1940 and 1910, Women by Number of Children Ever Born, Tables 1 and 4.

rate—births per 1,000 women 15 to 44—was 100.[57] These compare to the crude birth rate of 55, and the general fertility rate of 225, for the pre-Civil War period. Thus, Negro fertility rates were reduced by at least one half, and perhaps even more, in the period between the Civil War and the Depression.

Mortality rates were the primary interest of demographers during this period, but a few observed the fertility decline and commented about its implications. After the Census of 1900, Walter Willcox noted that for twenty years fertility rates had fallen among both whites and non-whites in both urban and rural areas, but that the decline ". . . is steadier and far more marked among non-Caucasians than among whites."[58] He predicted that the black population would grow slowly if at all in the future because their mortality rates remained high while their fertility rates decreased. He speculated that this trend might indicate that blacks were losing out in a type of evolutionary competition with Caucasians.[59]

Following the Census of 1920, Warren Thompson analyzed ratios of children to women and observed that blacks in the rural South were having barely enough children to replace themselves. In urban areas, Negro birth rates were far below replacement levels. He believed this was indicative of an intentional race suicide, that Negroes realized they had few opportunities in American society and decided to have very few children.[60]

Mortality Trends

The years following Emancipation apparently witnessed a sharp rise in Negro mortality rates. The migration of many blacks from the rural South to cities and Union army camps led to shortages of food and serious medical problems. Unsanitary conditions aided the spread of contagious diseases, particularly smallpox and cholera.[61] The first year of freedom was one of hunger, disease, and death for many blacks.

---

[57] U. S., National Center for Health Statistics, *Vital Statistics of the United States: 1965*, Vol. I, Table 1–2.

[58] U. S., Bureau of the Census, *Twelfth Census of the United States: 1900*, Supplementary Analysis, p. 239.

[59] Walter F. Willcox, "The Probable Increase of the Negro Race in the United States," *Quarterly Journal of Economics*, XIX (August, 1905), 559–572.

[60] Warren S. Thompson, *Ratio of Children to Women: 1920*, Census Monograph XI (Washington: Government Printing Office, 1931), pp. 148–149.

[61] George R. Bentley, *A History of the Freedman's Bureau* (Philadel-

At first, the Federal Government expressed little interest in the ex-slaves. Some Union Army generals tried to feed or employ the blacks who followed them, but other generals sent them back to plantations.[62] Gradually, relief agencies and politicians in both the North and South realized that blacks were suffering a great deal and many were dying.[63] As a result, Congress established the Freedman's Bureau in 1865; its aim was to provide rations and shelter for the impoverished blacks.[64] Later, attempts were made at disease control by establishing sanitation standards. Eventually, forty-six hospitals were established and upwards of one million blacks received medical assistance by 1869.[65] In 1870, the activities of the Freedman's Bureau and federal programs of relief for ex-slaves ended.[66]

During the late nineteenth century, many commentators argued that Negro death rates were much higher after Emancipation than before. Frequently, they mentioned that insanity, tuberculosis and venereal diseases were almost unknown among slaves but afflicted many freed Negroes.[67] Some predicted that blacks would soon die out because of their inability to resist diseases. Social Darwinism was a popular philosophy at this time and many writers linked the high death rates to the supposed inferiority and immorality of Negroes. In 1877, the New York Times editorialized:

The causes which lead to this terrific death rate among the colored people need not long be sought after. They are only too apparent to those who are conversant with the modes of life of the Negroes of the cotton states. They neglect or starve their offspring, abandon the sick to their own resources, indulge every animal passion to excess, and, when they have money, spend their

---

phia: University of Pennsylvania Press, 1955), p. 16; Wharton, *op. cit.*, pp. 52–53; Green, *op. cit.*, p. 64.

[62] Franklin, *op. cit.*, pp. 272–273; McPherson, *op. cit.*, Chap. x.

[63] Green, *op. cit.*, p. 64; Franklin, *op. cit.*, p. 274; Bentley, *op. cit.*, Chap. ii.

[64] Bentley, *op. cit.*, p. 76.

[65] W. E. Burghardt DuBois, *Black Reconstruction in America*, Reprint Edition (Cleveland: World Publishing, 1964), p. 226.

[66] Bentley, *op. cit.*, p. 211.

[67] Thomas J. McKie, "A Brief History of Insanity and Tuberculosis in the Southern Negro," *Journal of the American Medical Association*, XXVIII (1897), 537–538; Theophilus O. Powell, "The Increase of Insanity and Tuberculosis in the Southern Negro since 1860, and its Alliance and some of the Supposed Causes," *Journal of the American Medical Association*, XXVIII (1896), 1185–1188.

nights in the most disgusting and debilitating de-
bauches.[68]

At the end of the century, Frederick Hoffman, a statistician
with Prudential Insurance, studied trends over time in Negro
mortality rates and concluded:

> . . . the Southern black man at the time of emancipation
> was healthy in body and cheerful in mind. He neither
> suffered inordinately from disease nor from impaired
> bodily vigor. His industrial capacities as a laborer were
> not of a low order, nor was the condition of servitude
> such as to produce in him morbid conditions favorable
> to mental disease, suicide or intemperance. What are the
> conditions thirty years after? The pages of this work
> give but one answer, an answer which is a most severe
> condemnation of modern attempts of superior races to
> lift inferior races to their own elevated position, an
> answer so full of meaning that it would seem criminal
> indifference on the part of a civilized people to ignore it.
> In the plain language of facts brought together, the
> colored race is shown to be on the downward grade,
> tending toward a condition in which matters will be
> worse than they are now, when diseases will be more
> destructive, vital resistance still lower, when the num-
> ber of births will fall below the deaths and the gradual
> extinction of the race take place. Neither religion nor
> education nor a higher degree of economic well being
> have been able to raise the race from a low and anti-
> social condition . . .[69]

It is difficult to determine whether these views of the incidence of disease among Negroes had any factual base for we have
few data which pertain to mortality rates for this period. There
were four southern cities which registered deaths throughout
the nineteenth century, but nothing is known of the completeness
or accuracy of this registration. In three cities—Charleston, Mobile, and Savannah—crude death rates for Negroes were higher
from 1880 to 1894 than from 1845 to 1860.[70] In New Orleans, this
pattern was reversed. Death rates for specific age groups of
blacks are available only for Charleston. In this city, mortality

---

[68] Quoted in: Henderson H. Donald, *The Negro Freedman* (New York:
Henry Schumen, 1952), p. 157.

[69] Frederick L. Hoffman, "Race Traits and Tendencies of the American
Negro," *Publications of the American Economic Association*, XI, Nos. 1, 2
and 3 (August, 1896), 312.

[70] *Ibid.*, pp. 53–54.

rates were higher during the 1890s than during the 1840s.[71] These data suggest that Negro mortality may have been higher after the Civil War than before, but they pertain to a few cities and are not a satisfactory base for making inferences about the entire population.

The Development of Negro Life Tables

There are no life tables which report mortality conditions among blacks during the years following the Civil War. The calculation of life tables depended upon the development of a system for registering deaths. A limited start upon a federal death registration system was made in 1890, but life tables for the black population of the registration area were not calculated until after 1900.[72] The tables for 1900 showed that Negro males, at birth, could expect to live 33 years and females could expect to live 35 years.[73] Life tables have been computed at each census date since 1900, and life expectations from these tables are shown in Table 3–6. They indicate there has been a general and consistent improvement in Negro health conditions from 1900 to 1960. The decades 1910 to 1920 and 1940 to 1950 stand out as ones of particularly rapid progress.

Life tables for years prior to 1930, however, were based not on the experience of the national Negro population, but upon the population which lived in the Death Registration Area. In 1900 and 1910, this area included ten northern states and the District of Columbia.[74] The black population of this area was almost exclusively an urban population. However, most Negroes—80 percent in 1900 and 77 percent in 1910—lived in rural areas.[75] At this time, reported death rates for rural areas were much lower than those reported for urban areas, presumably because

---

[71] *Ibid.*, p. 56.

[72] In the mid-1880s John Shaw Billings constructed life tables for the colored populations of Baltimore, New Orleans and Washington, D. C. These tables showed an expectation of life at birth of 22 years for males and 26 for females. I believe these were the earliest life tables computed for a black population. U. S., Census Office, *Tenth Census of the United States: 1880*, Report on the Mortality and Vital Statistics of the United States, Part II, pp. 771–788.

[73] U. S., National Center for Health Statistics, *Life Tables: 1959–61*, Vol. 1, Table 12.

[74] These states were Maine, New Hampshire, Vermont, Massachusetts, Rhode Island, Connecticut, New York, New Jersey, Indiana and Michigan.

[75] See Table 3–2.

TABLE 3–6

Life Expectation of Negroes Based on Data
from the Death Registration System

	Males			Females		
	At Birth	At Age 5	At Age 10	At Birth	At Age 5	At Age 10
1900–02[a]	32.5	45.1	41.9	35.0	46.0	43.0
1909–11[a]	34.1	44.3	40.7	37.7	46.4	42.8
1919–21[a]	47.1	50.2	46.0	46.9	48.7	44.5
1929–31	47.6	48.7	44.3	49.5	49.8	45.3
1939–41	52.3	53.0	48.3	55.6	55.4	50.8
1949–51[b]	58.9	57.9	53.0	62.7	60.9	56.2
1959–61[b]	61.5	60.0	55.2	66.5	64.5	59.7
1966[b]	60.7	58.8	54.0	67.4	65.2	60.4

[a] Data refer to population living within Death Registration States.
[b] Data refer to non-white population.
Source:
    U. S., National Center for Health Statistics, *Vital Statistics of the United States: 1966*, II, Part A, 5–4; *United States Life Tables: 1959–61*, 1, No. 1, 31.

diseases spread more rapidly among urban populations. In 1900, for instance, whites in rural parts of the Death Registration Area could expect to live about eight years longer than whites who lived in urban places.[76] In 1920, an investigation revealed that life expectancy among Negroes in states in which the population was principally rural was six years greater than life expectation in the northern states where almost all blacks lived in cities.[77]

As the Death Registration Area expanded, southern states with large rural populations and with relatively low mortality rates were added. This means that some of the rise in life expectation, indicated in Table 3–6, is attributable to changes in the registration area rather than to an improvement in health conditions.

Techniques Used to Estimate Mortality

A technique, mentioned in Chapter 2, can be used to make some inferences about the trends over time in Negro mortality rates.[78] Suppose we know the population at two census dates and

---

[76] Dublin, Lotka and Spiegelman, *op. cit.*, Table 20.
[77] U. S., Bureau of the Census, *United States Abridged Life Tables: 1910–20* (Washington: Government Printing Office, 1923).
[78] For a description and examples of this technique see: United Nations, Department of Economic and Social Affairs, "Methods of Estimating

we wish to calculate a life table for the intervening period. For example, we might consider the black female population and the period from 1900 to 1910. Since there was very little in-migration of foreign blacks to the United States, the women who were counted by the Census of 1910 were survivors of a somewhat larger group of women who should have been counted by the Census of 1900. Women at ages 20 to 24 in 1910, for instance, were survivors of the females who were ages 10 to 14 in 1900. These data from successive censuses can be used to estimate mortality levels.

One procedure would be to estimate mortality rates by directly comparing the same group of women counted at two census dates. However, this leads to erroneous estimates of mortality. Censuses are not equally inclusive in their enumerations of the population. The age group 0 to 4 is frequently undercounted by a substantial amount. This means that one census may enumerate more individuals at ages 10 to 14 than the previous census enumerated at ages 0 to 4 which would imply that no one dies.

Different techniques have been proposed to surmount this problem. We might consider the Negro female population by five-year age groups enumerated in 1900. These figures are shown in Table 3–7. Each of these groups of women was survived for ten years according to different mortality rates. These mortality rates came from life tables for females. These life tables had expectations of life at birth between 22.5 years and 32.5 years; they were selected from a larger collection of model life tables developed for purposes of demographic analysis.[79]

The next step was to compare estimates of the 1910 population developed by surviving 1900 population for ten years to the actual population enumerated by the Census of 1910. To eliminate problems arising from the miscount of particular age groups, the comparisons were made with cumulative data. First, the female population counted in 1910 was cumulated to deter-

---

Basic Demographic Measures from Incomplete Data," *Population Studies*, No. 42 (1967), pp. 7–12; Paul Demeny and Frederic C. Shorter, "Estimating Turkish Mortality, Fertility, and Age Structure: Applications of Some New Techniques," Publication No. 218, Faculty of Economics, University of Istanbul (Istanbul, 1968); Pravin M. Visaria, "Mortality and Fertility in India, 1951–1961," *Milbank Memorial Fund Quarterly*, XLVII (January, 1969), 91–116.

[79] The model life tables used in this analysis were the "West" model life tables from Coale and Demeny, *op. cit.*, pp. 3–8.

TABLE 3–7
The Female Negro Population in 1900 Projected to 1910
Assuming Different Mortality Levels

| | Enumerated Female Negroes in 1910 | Estimates of Female Negroes in 1900 | | | | |
| | | Assumed Expectation of Life at Birth | | | | |
		$e_0 = 22.5$	$e_0 = 25.0$	$e_0 = 27.5$	$e_0 = 30.0$	$e_0 = 32.5$
0–4	612	465	479	492	503	513
5–9	602	533	539	544	549	554
10–14	543	473	479	484	489	494
15–19	508	428	435	441	447	452
20–24	510	419	426	433	440	446
25–29	377	302	308	314	319	324
30–34	262	206	210	215	218	222
35–39	241	186	190	194	198	201
40+	768	430	447	462	476	489

Sources:
    U. S., Bureau of the Census, Negro Population in the United States: 1790–1915 (Washington: Government Printing Office, 1918), p. 166; Ansley J. Coale and Paul Demeny, Regional Model Life Tables and Stable Populations, (Princeton: Princeton University Press, 1966) pp. 3–7.

mine the number of women who were 10 and over, 15 and over and so forth. These figures are shown in Table 3–8. Then, these different estimates of the 1910 population were compared to the enumerated population to ascertain which set of mortality rates most accurately survived the 1900 population to 1910. Linear interpolation was used to determine what level of life tables would produce the 1910 populations. These are shown in the right hand columns of Table 3–8.

    This technique does not produce a unique estimate of mortality for a ten year period. The mortality level which best survives the population 10 and over in 1900, to ages 20 and over in 1910, may not be the same mortality level which best survives the population 25 and over in 1900, to ages 35 and over in 1910. To select a unique life table for a period, the different estimates of mortality were arrayed and their median value was used. In doing this, the mortality level estimated by surviving the total population in 1900, to ages 10 and over in 1910, was not used. Mortality levels estimated from these age groups were uniquely low, apparently reflecting the fact that women 10 to 14 in 1910 were much more completely enumerated than the women who were 0 to 4 years old in 1900.

TABLE 3-8
Procedure to Estimate Mortality Rates for Negro Females: 1900 to 1910

Ages	Enumerated Female Negroes at Specified Age and Over	Estimates of Female Negroes at Specified Age and Over in 1910 — Assumed Expectations of Life at Birth					Interpolated Estimates of Life Expectancy	
		$e_0 = 22.5$	$e_0 = 25.0$	$e_0 = 27.5$	$e_0 = 30.0$	$e_0 = 32.5$	e_0	e_5
10+	3,667	3,443	3,514	3,579	3,639	3,694	31.3	44.2
15+	3,089	2,977	3,035	3,087	3,136	3,181	27.6	41.8
20+	2,537	2,443	2,496	2,543	2,586	2,627	27.2	41.5
25+	1,988	1,972	2,017	2,059	2,097	2,133	23.4	38.9
30+	1,529	1,543	1,582	1,617	1,650	1,681	21.6	37.7
35+	1,193	1,124	1,156	1,184	1,211	1,236	28.3	42.3
40+	880	822	847	870	892	912	28.6	42.4
45+	654	616	637	656	674	690	27.3	41.6
50+	468	430	447	462	476	489	28.7	42.5

Source:

See Table 3–7.

It is possible to use this technique for periods of time other than ten years. For instance, the population enumerated in 1880 was survived to 1900 and compared to the Census of 1900 to determine the mortality level which typified the twenty year period between 1880 and 1900.

This census-survival procedure is sensitive to census accuracy. If one census did a much poorer job of enumerating the population than the census that preceded or the one that followed it, the estimates of life expectation will reflect the peculiarities of the deficient census.

This technique was used to estimate the Negro life span for the periods 1850 to 1860, 1880 to 1900 and for each ten year period since the turn of the century. Data from the Census of 1870 were not used because there is widespread agreement that this census was incomplete. An estimate was made of mortality for the period 1860 to 1880, but it was inconsistent with other estimates of the Negro life span in the nineteenth century. Undoubtedly, this is a result of census errors and inconsistencies, because the 1860 and 1880 censuses were taken in very different fashions.

Originally, data from the Census of 1890 were used, but they produced estimates of mortality from 1880 to 1890 which were extremely high and estimates for 1890 to 1900 which were very low. This confirms the belief that the Census of 1890 was inaccurate and missed many blacks. As an alternate procedure, mortality rates for the period 1880 to 1900 were estimated.

These computations used census data for females and estimated life spans for women only. Female blacks have been more completely enumerated by censuses than males.[80] There have been particularly serious undercounts of young adult Negro males. For instance, Coale estimated that about 20 percent of the nonwhite males 15 to 44 in 1950 were missed by the census.[81] This is not a new problem, for Willcox noted problems of undercount and age heaping among blacks in the censuses of 1890 to 1900.[82] Because of these undercount problems, the use of the survival technique produces estimates of the male life span which are

[80] Coale, loc. cit., p. 35; U. S., Bureau of the Census, "Estimates of the Population of the United States and Components of Change by Age, Color and Sex: 1950 to 1960," Table C-2; Siegel, loc. cit., p. 41.

[81] Coale, loc. cit., p. 44.

[82] Walter F. Willcox, "Negroes in the United States," U. S., Bureau of the Census, Twelfth Census of the United States: 1900, Bulletin 8 (Washington: Government Printing Office, 1904), pp. 209–211.

TABLE 3–9
Life Expectation of Negro Females Estimated from Decennial Census Data

Time Period	At Birth	At Age 5	At Age 10
1850–1860	27.8	41.9	40.9
1880–1900	25.0	40.0	37.4
1900–1910	27.5	41.7	39.0
1910–1920	25.0	40.0	37.4
1920–1930	34.4	46.2	43.4
1930–1940	36.7	47.7	44.5
1940–1950	55.6	59.1	54.9
1950–1960	66.6	65.7	61.0

Source:
    See text for method of computation.

longer than the female life span.[83] Attempts to overcome this problem by making assumptions about the pattern of census undercount of Negro men proved fruitless.

The results of this investigation are shown in Table 3–9 which contains estimates of life expectation at birth, at age 5 and at age 10. As a check upon the accuracy of this method, the estimates of life expectation developed by the census survival technique were compared to those derived from data of the vital registration system. The expectations of life for the period 1940 to 1950, shown in Table 3–9, are identical to those indicated by the national life table for non-white women in 1945,[84] Expectations shown for 1950 to 1960 are one year longer than the expectations indicated by the 1955 life table for non-whites.[85] This agreement suggests the validity of the census survival approach to the construction of life tables for the recent period.

For the decades before 1940, there is little agreement between the census survival estimates of the life span and those of the vital statistics life tables. For early dates, such as 1900 and

---

[83] Demeny and Gingrich used these techniques for ten year periods, between 1900 and 1940, and produced life tables which indicated that Negro males survived as much as four years longer than Negro females. Life tables for the Death Registration States for this period indicated that females had longer life spans than males. Paul Demeny and Paul Gingrich, "A Reconsideration of Negro-White Mortality Differences in the United States," *Demography*, IV, No. 2 (1967), 825.

[84] Thomas N. E. Greville, *United States Abridged Life Tables: 1945*, U. S., National Office of Vital Statistics, Special Reports, XXIII, No. 11 (April 15, 1947), 249.

[85] U. S., National Office of Vital Statistics, *Vital Statistics of the United States: 1955*, Vol. I. Table BA.

1910, this may not be surprising since the vital statistics life tables were based on data from just a few states. However, in 1930, all states but one provided mortality information, and in 1920, twenty-seven states provided mortality data.[86] For these periods, the census survival estimates of the life span are much shorter than those of the vital statistics life tables.

A comparison of the two types of life tables indicated that the census survival tables had much higher infant and childhood death rates than did the vital statistics life tables. In the older age groups, the death rates were more alike. This raised two possibilities.

First, the model life tables used to calculate the census survival life tables were based on the mortality patterns of western European nations and the total population of the United States.[87] It is possible that the mortality patterns of blacks in this country differed basically from that of these model life tables. This possibility was investigated by using a variety of model life tables derived from other populations; however, in each case the estimates of mortality were close to those indicated in Table 3–9. Another study, conducted by Zelnik, suggests that age patterns of mortality among United States blacks are different from those observed among other populations but that census undercount helps to account for this.[88]

Second, there may have been a substantial under-registration of infant and childhood deaths among blacks which would have the effect of reducing death rates at young ages as estimated by the vital statistics system. Some under-registration of infant deaths seems quite likely since few of the Negro births occurred in hospitals. For instance, in 1935, it was estimated that less than 20 percent of the black births took place in a hospital.[89] In many rural areas, Negro infants and children may have died and their deaths were not recorded.

After extensive investigation and much experimentation, no satisfactory way was discovered to determine exactly what were the infant and childhood mortality rates among blacks before 1940.[90] It is likely that the life tables based on vital statistics data

---

[86] Dublin, Lotka and Spiegelman, *op. cit.*, pp. 45–46.

[87] Coale and Demeny, *op. cit.*, p. 14.

[88] Melvin Zelnik, "Age Patterns of Mortality of American Negroes: 1900–02 to 1959–61," *Journal of the American Statistical Association*, LXIV (June, 1969), 433–451.

[89] U. S., National Office of Vital Statistics, *Vital Statistics of the United States: 1950*, I, 95.

[90] For further discussion see: Demeny and Gingrich, *loc. cit.*, pp. 826–834.

overestimate life expectation at birth, but it is impossible to measure the margin of error or to be certain that the estimates from the census survival life tables are more nearly accurate. As a result, we deemed it advisable to study general trends in mortality by analyzing changes in life expectation for females at age 5 as shown in Table 3–9.

Changes in Mortality and Health Conditions

A study of the figures in this table suggests there have been four periods in the history of Negro mortality in the United States. One period came to an end about the time of World War I, but when it began is much more difficult to ascertain. We can do no more than speculate that life expectation at age 5 must have been approximately 40 years throughout the span from the 1840s to the time of World War I.

The second period extended from just after World War I— perhaps from 1919—to the mid-1930s. During this period, there was apparently some improvement in health conditions and an increase in life expectancy although some evidence, discussed in the following pages, challenges this conclusion.

The period of most rapid improvement in mortality lasted from the Depression decade until the mid-1950s. D˙ ring a twenty year span, Negro life expectation increased by aᴜ least fifteen years.[91] We are certain that this was the period during which mortality declined most substantially.

The final period extends from about 1955 to the present. Although death rates from some diseases have decreased, there has been no general improvement in the level of mortality since the mid-1950s. Life expectations for both whites and non-whites, in the mid-1960s, were about same as those of a decade earlier.[92]

During the first period, contagious diseases were the most common causes of death. We know most about the situation in cities, for John Shaw Billings encouraged studies of deaths by cause during the 1880s.[93] About a decade later, DuBois and others began empirical studies of the living conditions of urban blacks.[94] These

[91] Thomas N. E. Greville, *loc. cit.*, U. S., National Office of Vital Statistics, *Vital Statistics of the United States: 1955*, Vol. I, Table BA; U. S., National Center for Health Statistics, *Vital Statistics of the United States: 1966*, Vol. II, Table 5–6.

[92] *Ibid.*

[93] U. S., Census Office, *Tenth Census: 1880*, Report on the Mortality and Vital Statistics of the United States, Part II.

[94] DuBois, *The Philadelphia Negro;* Atlanta University Publications, *Mortality Among Negroes in Cities*, Proceedings of the Conference for In-

investigations revealed that while there were some prosperous blacks, the majority of Negroes in cities, both in the North and South, were impoverished. Urban houses frequently were unheated hovels or shacks located on alleys, often without a water supply or a sewage system. Many blacks did not earned enough to purchase satisfactory food or sufficient clothing to protect themselves against the elements.[95] Southern Negroes who moved to northern cities were reported to be frequently unprepared for the harsh weather and suffered greatly in cold spells. These factors, combined with the lack of public health activity, produced a very high death rate among urban Negroes. Tuberculosis and pneumonia were, by far, the most common causes of death; diseases which were closely related to economic status. Diseases to the nervous system, diarrhea, and typhoid fever were the next most commonly reported causes of death among urban blacks.[96] The infant mortality rates, among blacks, were extremely high, reflecting poverty and disease. For instance, in Washington, D. C. in 1900, the infant mortality rate was 366; in Baltimore, 356 and in New York, 348.[97]

Less is known about conditions in rural areas, but census enumerators, in 1900, did attempt to ascertain the causes of death of each member of a household who died in the year ending May 31, 1900. Consumption, pneumonia, diseases of the nervous system, diarrhea, typhoid fever and malaria were the most frequent causes of death in rural areas.[98] These causes of death suggest that living standards were low and that many blacks depended upon unsanitary water supplies.

Prior to World War I, the development of public health programs and improvements in sanitary systems reduced urban death rates caused by typhoid fever and diarrhea,[99] although DuBois noted that public health benefits were not always ex-

---

vestigations of City Problems (Atlanta, 1896); *Social and Physical Condition of Negroes in Cities*, Proceedings of the Second Conference for the Negro City Life (Atlanta, 1897); *The Health and Physique of the Negro American*, A Social Study Made under the Direction of the Eleventh Atlanta Conference (Atlanta, 1906).

[95] These problems are also discussed in Green, *op. cit.*, p. 148, and in Chicago Commission on Race Relations, *The Negro in Chicago* (Chicago: University of Chicago Press, 1922), Chap. v.

[96] U. S., Census Office, *Twelfth Census of the United States: 1900*, Vital Statistics, Part 1, Table 19.

[97] *Ibid.*

[98] *Ibid.*

[99] Dublin, Lotka and Spiegelman, *op. cit.*, pp. 147–159.

tended to black ghettoes.[100] These improvements were offset by the gradual shift of black population from relatively healthy rural areas to relatively unhealthy cities. It seems likely there was no general imporvement in rural health conditions before World War I. In fact, the gradual spread of the boll weevil reduced the income and lowered the standard of living of rural blacks. These poor conditions had the effect of keeping rural morbidity and mortality rates at a high level.

In 1918, an epidemic of influenza spread across the United States. The crude death rate among non-whites for that year was 28 per thousand compared to a death rate of 23 for the prior year and 21 for the following year.[101] What happened to Negro mortality rates between 1919 and the mid-1930s is not altogether clear. Some evidence indicates the death rate fell and that contagious diseases became rarer. Estimates of the life span contained in Table 3–6 show that the 1920s were healthier years than the previous decade. The Death Registration Area for 1920 included thirty-four states and the District of Columbia.[102] The life table for females in this area, *for 1930*, showed an expectation of life two years greater than that for Negro females in the same area *in 1920*.[103] The Metropolitan Life Insurance Company held policies on the lives of almost one-fifth of the Negro population during the 1920s.[104] Mortality rates among these policy holders dropped sharply between 1919 and 1921.[105] Studies of infant mortality indicated that death rates were lower during the 1920s than before the war. In Baltimore, for instance, the infant mortality rate among Negroes fell from 219, in 1916, to 94, in 1930, and in Philadelphia the decrease, for the same period, was from 160 to 100.[106]

There is conflicting evidence. Although the life span of females in the Death Registration Area of 1920 increased between 1920 and 1930, the life span of males decreased by a small

[100] DuBois, *The Philadelphia Negro*, pp. 152–168.

[101] U. S., Bureau of the Census, *Historical Statistics . . .* , Series B-129. These are age adjusted death rates for the Death Registration Area.

[102] U. S., National Center for Health Statistics, *Vital Statistics of the United States: 1966*, Vol. II, Table 5–5.

[103] Dublin, Lotka and Spiegelman, *op. cit.*, Table 83.

[104] Dublin, *op. cit.*, p. 269.

[105] Louis I. Dublin and Alfred J. Lotka, *Twenty Five Years of Health Progress* (New York: Metropolitan Life Insurance, 1937), Appendix Table B.

[106] S. J. Holmes, *The Negroes' Struggle for Survival* (Berkeley: University of California Press, 1937), Table XXIV.

amount.[107] In Tennessee, an extensive study of mortality failed to detect any reduction of mortality rates among either rural or urban Negroes after 1921; indeed some of the death rates went up.[108] A study of mortality among Negroes in ten southern states found that, between 1921 and 1933, death rates for age groups under thirty decreased, but this was offset by a rise in the mortality of the older age groups.[109] Louise Kennedy studied Negro mortality rates in ten northern cities and concluded that, between 1919 and the mid-1920s, mortality decreased, but thereafter the trend was reversed and by the late 1920s, death rates were as high as in 1910.[110] The Metropolitan Life records failed to indicate any improvement between 1921 and 1931.[111]

It is difficult to summarize these conflicting studies. It seems clear that urban mortality from some diseases was reduced during the 1920s. Public health activities and higher standards of living reduced tuberculosis deaths, at least in urban areas. Deaths from such contagious diseases as diarrhea and typhoid fever were also cut, and, within the North, there was an unambiguous decline in infant mortality.[112]

The migration of blacks to urban areas and changes in death rates in rural areas may have offset decreases in urban mortality rates. It is impossible to be certain of the mortality trend in rural areas. To be sure, living standards of rural Negroes were low and contagious diseases were common. Carter Woodson began his monograph on the rural black population with a chapter entitled, "Keeping Alive in the Country."[113] He observed that most rural blacks had an unhealthy diet, drank untreated water which served as a medium for spreading disease, had little knowledge of how diseases were contracted and no access to medical care.[114] Charles Johnson studied rural Negroes who lived near Tuskegee

---

[107] Dublin, Lotka and Spiegelman, *op. cit.*

[108] Elbridge Sibley, *Differential Mortality in Tennessee: 1917–1928* (Nashville: Fisk University Press, 1930).

[109] Mary Gover, *Mortality Among Southern Negroes since 1920*, U. S., Public Health Service, Public Health Bulletin, No. 235 (June, 1937), p. 6.

[110] Louise V. Kennedy, *The Negro Peasant Turns Cityward* (New York: Columbia University Press, 1930), Chap. ix.

[111] Dublin and Lotka, *op. cit.*

[112] Gover, *op. cit.*; Mary Gover, *Mortality Among Negroes in the United States*, U. S., Public Health Service, Public Health Bulletin, No. 174 (1927); Holmes, *op. cit.*, Chaps. v and vi.

[113] Carter Woodson, *The Rural Negro* (Washington: Association for the Study of Negro Life and History, 1930).

[114] *Ibid.*, Chaps. iii and iv.

in 1930 and devoted a chapter to "Survival." He also observed the very poor diet, the ignorance of disease and the absence of medical care.[115]

While these studies indicate that disease was very common, they do not demonstrate that mortality rates were either improving or worsening. There may be reason for thinking that the situation was getting worse. These studies linked poverty to the lack of food and the high death rates. While there were wide variations in the price of cotton during the 1920s, this was a time of general depression for southern agriculture. Heer claimed that gross income per southern farm worker, in 1927, was only 58 percent as great as in 1919.[116] Mortality rates may have gone up as poverty increased during the 1920s.

It is easier to describe recent trends in mortality, for there has been a nationwide vital statistics system since 1933. Three developments explain the recent reductions in Negro death rates. One factor is the development of public health facilities. A few cities had public health agencies as early as the nineteenth century; after the turn of this century more cities and counties created such agencies.[117] By the beginning of the Depression, one-sixth of the nation's counties had some type of public health service.[118] After 1935, public health activities accelerated; that year, Congress appropriated large sums of federal monies for this purpose for the first time.[119] In the following years, the appropriations were increased, and a national interest in and support for public health developed in the late 1930s.

A second factor was the emergence, during the 1930s and the 1940s, of new techniques for diagnosing and treating contagious diseases. Particularly important was the appearance of the sulfa drugs, the antibiotics, and pneumonia serum therapy.[120]

A third factor was an improvement in the standard of living of blacks. Studies of both rural and urban Negroes in the 1930s,

---

[115] Charles S. Johnson, *Shadow of the Plantation* (Chicago: University of Chicago Press, 1966), Chap. viii.

[116] Clarence Heer, *Income and Wages in the South* (Chapel Hill: University of North Carolina Press, 1930), p. 18.

[117] John J. Hanlon, *Principles of Public Health Administration* (St. Louis: C. V. Mosby, 1950), p. 40.

[118] Frederick D. Mott and Milton I. Roemer, *Rural Health and Medical Care* (New York: McGraw-Hill, 1948), p. 239.

[119] Hanlon, *op. cit.*, pp. 50–52.

[120] Iwao M. Moriyama, *The Change in Mortality Trend in the United States*, U. S., National Center for Health Statistics, Vital and Health Statistics, Analytic Studies, Series 3, Number 1 (March, 1964), p. 38.

found that many lived on meager diets and this lack of food fostered high morbidity rates, particularly from tuberculosis.[121] During and after World War II, the income of blacks increased much faster than did the cost of living. For instance, between 1939 and 1955, the median wage and salary income of Negro men increased by a factor of five while consumer prices did not quite double.[122]

These changes in public health and standards of living cut the infant mortality rate in half, from 83 deaths per 1,000 births in 1937, to 42 in 1956.[123] Among adult Negroes, the death rates from infectious and parasitic diseases, particularly deaths from tuberculosis, influenza and syphilis, were reduced. In 1937, infectious diseases caused 20 percent of the Negro deaths.[124] By 1955, the same causes accounted for less than 2 percent of the deaths,[125] and the death rate, adjusted for changes in age composition, decreased from 19 per 1,000 to 10.[126]

Since 1955, there has been little improvement in life expectance. Deaths from parasitic and infectious diseases were so few by the mid-1950s that further improvements in this area had little effect on the overall death rate.[127] The infant mortality rate has been reduced from 42 per thousand in 1956, to 35 in 1967.[128] This gain, however, has been offset for among adult blacks, as among whites, there has been an increase since the mid-1950s in death rate from heart diseases, cancer, diabetes, emphysema and cirrhosis and, among the older population, from pneumonia.[129]

---

121 Philip P. Jacobs, *The Control of Tuberculosis in the United States* (New York: National Tuberculosis Association, 1940), p. 205; Gunnar Myrdal, *An American Dilemma,* I (New York: McGraw-Hill, 1964), Chap. xvi.

122 Herman P. Miller, *Rich Man, Poor Man* (New York: Thomas Y. Crowell, 1964), p. 42; U. S., Bureau of the Census, *Historical Statistics . . . ,* Series E-113.

123 Sam Shapiro, Edward R. Schlesinger, and Robert E. L. Nesbitt, *Infant and Perinatal Mortality in the United States,* U. S., National Center for Health Statistics, Vital and Health Statistics, Series 3, Number 4 (October, 1965), p. 65.

124 U. S., Bureau of the Census, *Vital Statistics of the United States: 1937,* Part 1, Table 14.

125 U. S., National Office of Vital Statistics, *Vital Statistics of the United States: 1955,* Vol. II, Table 53.

126 U. S., National Center for Health Statistics, *Vital Statistics of the United States: 1960,* Vol. II, Table 1-B.

127 Moriyama, *op. cit.,* p. 38.

128 U. S., National Center for Health Statistics, "Annual Summary for the United States: 1967," *Monthly Vital Statistics Report,* Vol. 16, No. 13 (July 26, 1968), Table 6.

129 A. Joan Klebba, *Mortality Trends in the United States: 1954–1963,* U. S., National Center for Health Statistics, Vital and Health Statistics, Series 20, No. 2 (June, 1966), pp. 14–50.

Summary

Between the end of the Reconstruction era and the beginning of World War II, the black population became more widely dispersed throughout the United States. Within the northern and western states, the black population grew much more rapidly than in the southern states. A movement to the cities also occurred. By 1940, the largest concentrations of blacks were in the North, in New York City and in Chicago.

During this period, the growth rate of the Negro population changed from a figure in excess of 2 percent per year to a rate of less than 1 percent per year. The reason for this change was a decrease in fertility rates. Family size was reduced, for a larger and larger proportion of black women came to bear either no children or a small number.

The mortality trend is much more difficult, if not impossible, to describe. Apparently, there was some decline in the death rate and some extension of the life span prior to the Depression decade, although these improvements may have been slight. The major reduction in mortality occurred between the late 1930s and the mid-1950s.

Chapter 4

RECENT CHANGES IN NEGRO FERTILITY

The previous chapter described some of the major demographic changes among the black population. In recent years, the rates which have fluctuated most rapidly have been the fertility rates, and the future growth of the black population will be most influenced by fertility trends. In this chapter, these trends and changes in family size are described in greater detail.

Fertility Rate Trends

Two types of fertility rates are frequently used by demographers to study changes in childbearing and population growth. Period fertility rates are most frequently employed. Such rates measure the fertility level of a specified period, usually a one-year span. They are computed by relating the births which occur in a year to the group of women eligible to bear the children. The general fertility rate, for instance, relates births to women aged 15 to 44. Figure 4–1 shows the general fertility rate for non-whites for the years 1920 to 1967.[1] This rate fell steadily between 1920 and the mid-thirties, sinking to a minimum in 1936 when there were only 95 births per 1,000 non-white women of childbearing age. After the 1930s, the general fertility rate rose; slowly during World War II and then more rapidly following demobilization. A peak was reached in 1959 when 163 children were born per 1,000 women. Since 1959, this rate has fallen and the drop appears to be as precipitous as that which occurred during the 1920s; yet, the general fertility rate for 1967, 123, was well above the minimum reached during the Depression.

---

[1] General fertility rates shown in Figure 4–1 for years prior to 1934 refer to the Birth Registration Area.

The general fertility rate indicates year to year fluctuations in fertility, but it leaves many questions unanswered. Were fertility rates low during the Depression because young women delayed starting their families or because older women stopped after they had one or two children? Was the post-World War II baby boom due to more young girls starting families, or was it the older women who added "many fifth and sixth" children? How great have been the changes in family size or in the incidence of childlessness? What accounts for the recent downturn in fertility rates? Are women who are now young, bearing fewer children and starting their families more slowly than their older sisters? A comparison of cohort fertility rates answers these questions.

Cohort fertility rates, suggested by Whelpton in the 1940s, are the second type of rates frequently used by demographers.[2] Cohort fertility rates differ from period rates for they analyze the fertility histories of women born in a given year rather than describe year to year changes in childbearing. These rates are calculated by tracing the fertility patterns of women born in different years.

Cohort fertility rates aid the precise study of childbearing patterns, for they enable us to ascertain how rapidly each group of women began childbearing, and how rapidly these women enlarged their families. An important use of cohort fertility information is to determine the effects which major events had upon the childbearing of different groups of women. For instance, women who reached childbearing ages during the Depression years can be compared to women who attained the same ages during the prosperous period which followed World War II to determine what effects these events had upon family formation.

An examination of cohort fertility trends indicates that black women born in different periods of this century structured their families in very different ways. Women who reached childbearing ages just prior to the Depression delayed starting their families and then bore a small number of children. They completed their childbearing with an average of 2.6 offspring—a reproduction rate only slightly above replacement levels. Much higher fertility characterized women who started bearing children after World War II. These women, born during the 1930s, had many children while they were quite young and then added

---

[2] Pascal K. Whelpton, "Cohort Analysis of Fertility," *American Sociological Review*, XIV (December, 1949), 735–749; *Cohort Fertility* (Princeton: Princeton University Press, 1954).

many more children as they grew older. They will complete their families with an average of at least four children.

The Computation of Cohort Fertility Rates

Many computations and methodological considerations were involved in the derivation of cohort fertility rates. These will be very briefly outlined at this point. Chapter 10 describes them in greater detail.

Six major steps were used to construct cohort fertility rates. First, we ascertained the number of Negroes born in the United States each year between 1935 and 1966. We began with the registered number of Negro births occurring each year and made a correction for unregistered births. Estimates of under-registration were obtained from the 1940 and 1950 tests of birth registration completeness.[3]

Then we determined the census undercount of native Negro females at ages under 15 in 1950. This was done by taking annual female births for the years 1935 to 1949 and surviving these births to the date of the Census of 1950. Survival rates from national life tables were used. This procedure resulted in estimates of how many native Negro females under 15 should have been counted in 1950 if the census had enumerated everyone. The actual number of females counted by the census was then compared to the expected number and the discrepancy was assumed to be net census undercount. This technique produced estimates of the net census undercount of Negro females ages 0 to 14 in 1950.

The third step was to estimate the census undercount of Negro females ages 15 to 44 in 1950. The undercount rates calculated for Negro females under 15 in 1950 were used, and an assumption was made about the similarity of undercounts in the censuses of 1940 and 1950. An iterative technique was then employed to estimate the extent of census undercount at ages 15 to 44 in 1950.[4] From these computations, we were able to determine the "correct size" of the Negro female population at ages under 45 in 1950. This population was needed for the next calculation.

The fourth step determined how many Negroes were born each year from 1920 to 1934, and how many Negro females reached age 14—the start of the childbearing period—each year

---

[3] U. S., National Office of Vital Statistics, *Vital Statistics of the United States: 1950*, I. 108–127.

[4] This technique is described in: Coale, *loc. cit.*

from 1920 to 1966. A revival technique was used to estimate the births which occurred before 1935. This technique can be illustrated by considering the women age 19 in 1950. These women are survivors of a cohort of women who reached age 9 in 1940 and who were born during 1930. If we know the level of mortality rates for this span, we can begin with the number of women alive in 1950 and ascertain how many were born in 1930. This is the method which was used to estimate the number of females born annually from 1920 to 1934. Once the number of female births was known, the sex ratio at birth was used to calculate the total number of births which occurred each year.

A similar revival procedure was employed to determine how many females became 14 years old each year before 1950. Negro women age 44 in 1950, for example, were survivors of a group of Negro women who were 14 years old in 1920.

To estimate how many women became 14 years old each year after 1950, a survival technique was used. This is the opposite of the revival technique. For instance, women who were age 5 years in 1950, for example, were survived to age 14 years to determine how many women reached childbearing age in 1959. Mortality rates from recent life tables were used in these computations.

The fifth step was to divide annual births for the years 1920 to 1966 by age of mother and order of child. We had to determine how many births occurred to women of each age and how many of the births were first, second, third or higher order births. Distributions of registered births by age of mother and order of child served as a guide for this step.

The final step related births to the women eligible to bear the children. We might consider the women who became 14 years old in a given year. Between their fourteenth and fifteenth birthdays, a few of these women will bear a first child and a very small number will die. Between their fifteenth and sixteenth birthdays, some of the women who did not have a first child at age fourteen will bear a first child and a few of the women who had a first child at age 14 will bear a second child. Between their sixteenth and seventeenth birthdays, some women will have first children while others will bear second or third children. Using the distributions of children by age of mother calculated in step five, as well as mortality rates, the childbearing pattern for each cohort of Negro women was traced.

The results of these computations were cohort fertility rates. The first cohort for which the necessary information was avail-

able was the cohort born in 1906—women who began their childbearing in 1920. It was not possible to calculate rates for earlier
cohorts because there is very little reliable information about the
number of Negro births which occurred prior to 1920. For recent
cohorts, we have incomplete fertility histories. Women born in
1940, for instance, started childbearing in 1954. The cohort fertility information ends with data about births which occurred in
1966. Thus, for women born in 1940, we are able to describe only
that portion of their childbearing which occurred before they
reached age 26.

Cohort Fertility Trends

Our analysis of fertility trends begins by looking at changes in
the number of children that cohorts of Negro women have borne
when they attained specific ages. These are called cumulative fertility rates because they indicate the total fertility of a group of
women before they reached a given age.

Table 4–1 shows cumulative fertility rates for cohorts of
Negro women. The first panel in this table indicates the fertility
of women prior to the time they reached age 18. The second panel
shows childbearing prior to the time women became 21, while
other panels show cumulative fertility before ages 24, 27, 30, 35,
40 and 45.

It is cumbersome to present fertility rates for individual cohorts of Negro women. For this reason, the fertility rates of sin-
gle-year cohorts have been averaged. For instance, the first line
of the first panel shows the average fertility of women born 1945
to 1948. By age 18, an age these women attained during the years
1963 to 1966, there was an average of 313 children born per 1,000
women. The second line of this same panel indicates the average
fertility of Negro women born 1940 to 1944. By the time these
women reached age 18, they had borne an average of 336 children
per 1,000 women.

The term parity refers to the number of children a woman
has borne. A zero parity woman has never become a mother while
a first parity woman has borne one child. Table 4–1 also provides
information about the parity distribution of women when they
attained specific ages. The first line in the first panel indicates
that among women born 1945 to 1948, 764 per 1,000 reached age
18 without bearing a child. If 764 became 18 without having a
child, then 236 per 1,000 must have borne at least one child before

Figure 4–1
Births per 1,000 Non-white Women 15 to 44, 1920–1967

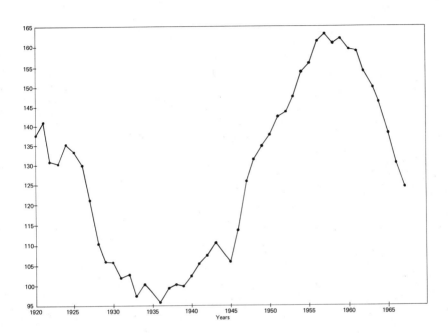

Sources:
> U. S., National Center for Health Statistics, *Vital Statistics of the United States: 1966*, Vol. I, Tables 1–2 and 1–20; *Monthly Vital Statistics Report*, Vol. 17, No. 9, Table 1. Data for each year have been corrected for under-registration of births.

their eighteenth birthday. This number is shown in the appropriate column of Table 4–1. Some of the women, born 1945 to 1948, had more than one child by age 18. Table 4–1 indicates that 64 per 1,000 had two or more children and 11 per 1,000 had three or more children by this age. It is important to remember that these are cumulative parity rates. They indicate what proportion of the women have had one or more, two or more, or three or more children. They are presented in this fashion so that the fertility of different cohorts may be easily compared.

TABLE 4–1
Cumulative Fertility Rates for Selected Ages for Cohorts of Negro Women

Cohorts Born	Years Reaching Ages	Child per 1,000 Women	Zero Parity	1	2	3	4	5	6	7
			Before Age 18							
1945–48	1963–66	313	764	236	64	11	1			
40–44	58–62	336	747	253	70	12	1			
35–39	53–57	341	740	260	69	11	1			
30–34	48–52	321	756	244	66	10	1			
25–29	43–47	263	793	207	47	8	–			
20–24	38–42	247	789	211	31	3	–			
15–19	33–37	205	822	178	24	2	–			
10–14	28–32	202	824	176	23	2	–			
06–09	24–27	193	831	169	21	2	–			
			Before Age 21							
1940–45	1961–66	1045	442	558	301	129	43	10	2	1
35–39	56–60	1096	422	578	323	138	44	11	2	1
30–34	51–55	1020	457	543	303	125	36	9	2	1
25–29	46–50	861	507	493	237	86	36	6	1	1
20–24	41–45	761	518	482	192	65	18	5	1	–
15–19	36–40	678	564	436	171	54	13	3	1	–
10–14	31–35	661	569	431	162	50	12	3	1	–
06–09	27–30	689	552	448	144	54	14	3	1	–
			Before Age 24							
1940–42	1964–66	1834	264	736	514	307	163	73	27	8
35–39	59–63	1921	253	747	537	335	179	81	29	9
30–34	54–58	1803	289	711	510	312	163	71	25	8
25–29	49–53	1543	334	666	440	249	119	46	16	5
20–24	44–48	1271	375	625	340	173	82	33	11	4
15–19	39–43	1154	439	561	309	167	75	28	10	3
10–14	34–38	1108	447	553	293	155	70	25	8	2
06–09	30–33	1179	419	581	312	167	77	28	10	3
			Before Age 27							
1935–39	1962–66	2599	176	824	646	464	305	183	103	45
30–34	57–61	2514	205	795	633	450	295	173	93	42
25–29	52–56	2175	249	751	530	380	239	135	66	28
20–24	47–51	1761	289	711	444	270	163	93	46	20
15–19	42–46	1572	370	630	393	248	149	83	40	17
10–14	37–41	1475	395	605	361	230	141	76	36	14
06–09	33–36	1578	363	637	385	251	156	84	38	16

Table 4–1 (Cont'd)

Cohorts Born	Years Reaching Ages	Child per 1,000 Women	Zero Parity	1	2	3	4	5	6	7
			Before Age 30							
1935–36	1965–66	3187	124	876	729	554	397	270	172	99
30–34	60–64	3078	163	827	702	534	383	264	168	98
25–29	55–59	2732	203	797	625	468	330	220	137	77
20–24	50–54	2209	238	762	517	345	235	154	96	53
15–19	45–49	1909	326	674	447	301	201	132	81	45
10–14	40–44	1807	352	648	409	281	192	124	76	41
06–09	36–39	1804	349	651	412	288	202	131	78	41
			Before Age 35							
1930–31	1965–66	3622	157	843	735	590	450	337	244	168
25–29	60–64	3403	165	835	696	546	415	305	219	132
20–24	55–59	2810	196	804	584	424	315	231	166	114
15–19	50–54	2406	283	717	504	363	260	188	135	85
10–14	45–49	2181	329	671	445	322	238	169	122	85
06–09	41–44	2264	312	688	452	333	251	183	132	91
			Before Age 40							
1925–26	1965–66	3604	158	842	692	546	422	324	244	178
20–24	60–64	3170	181	819	604	457	352	269	203	151
15–19	55–59	2569	264	734	531	395	294	222	168	128
10–14	50–54	2487	310	690	465	348	265	197	151	114
06–09	46–49	2562	295	705	472	355	276	211	159	120
			Before Age 45							
1920–21	1965–66	3135	193	807	588	435	336	263	202	152
15–19	60–64	2850	261	739	536	401	302	231	177	137
10–14	55–59	2587	305	695	474	375	272	205	158	122
06–09	51–54	2657	277	723	477	361	283	215	140	103

Source:
    See text for methods of computation.

There are many data contained in Table 4–1. To summarize trends in cumulative fertility, Figure 4–2 shows a bar graph of the fertility of groups of cohorts.

Trends in Cumulative Fertility

Table 4–1 and Figure 4–2 show a number of important changes in Negro fertility. There have been changes in the total number of children borne by different cohorts of Negro women. Data described in the previous chapter indicate that women who were born during the middle of the last century completed their childbearing with an average of at least six children. The cohort

Figure 4–2
Numbers of Children Ever Born, by Age, to Cohorts of Negro Women

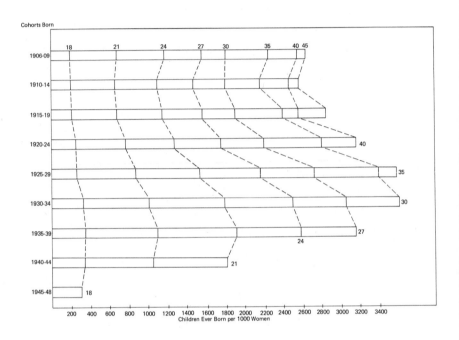

Source:
    Table 4–1.

fertility rates of Table 4–1 show that women born 1906 to 1909 completed their childbearing with an average of only 2.6 children. This comparison indicates there was a long-run downward trend in completed family size among Negroes.

The minimum fertility level was attained by the cohorts born 1910 to 1914. These women reached marriage and childbearing age during the Depression years. Many of them must have postponed marriage and childbearing, for Table 4–1 indicates that when young, they had fewer children than either the cohorts who came before them or the cohorts following them. At the more mature ages, these Depression affected cohorts did not compensate for their low fertility at young ages. Even when these women were in their late twenties and thirties, their fertility rates were not exceptionally high.

The trend toward smaller completed families came to an end with the women born 1910 to 1914, and later cohorts will complete their childbearing with much larger families. In particular, women who started childbearing after 1945 will have large families. These women have borne exceptionally many children at young ages. Thirty percent of the women born 1930 to 1934 had two or more children before age 21; 16 percent had at least four children by age 24, and almost 10 percent had six children before they reached age 27.

These women have been so prolific at young ages that their completed fertility will exceed the completed fertility of earlier cohorts by wide margins. Women attaining age 27, during the late 1950s and early 1960s, can be compared to women who attained age 45 during the same years. Table 4–1 shows that the cumulative birth rates of these two groups of women are similar—about 2600 children per 1,000 women. Thus, the younger women, who have been old enough to bear children for only about twelve years, have been as fertile in this short time as the older women were during their entire childbearing period. Even if the future fertility rates of these younger women are low, they will have large completed families since they will be exposed to the possibility of childbearing for many more years.

It is not certain which cohorts of Negro women will have the largest completed families, but it is likely to be the cohorts born during the early years of the Depression. When the cohorts born around 1930 reached age 35, they had an average of 3.6 children. It is impossible to know how rapidly these women will bear children between age 35 and the end of their childbearing span. However, if they bear children at a low rate, that is, if they have children at these older ages only as frequently as did the low fertility cohorts born 1910 to 1914, they will complete their families with an average of four children. In an historical context, this is a high fertility rate, for the last group of black women to average four or more children in their lifetime were the women born 1865 to 1874.[5]

---

[5] U. S., Bureau of the Census, *Sixteenth Census of the United States: 1940*, Population, Differential Fertility: 1940 and 1910, Women by Number of Children Ever Born, Table 12.

Women born during the latter years of the Depression got off to an even faster start on their childbearing than the women born during the early 1930s. For instance, by age 24 there was an average of 1921 births per 1000 women born 1935 to 1939, compared to 1803 births per 1000 women among the cohorts born 1930 to 1934. It is possible that the women born 1935 to 1939 will have the largest families. However, these women may reduce their fertility at older ages and finish with an average of fewer than four children.

There is some evidence that the trend toward high fertility at young ages and rapid family formation has slackened, for the most recent cohorts to begin their childbearing seem to be initiating a pattern of lower fertility. For example, the cohort born in 1948 had an average of 311 children per 1000 women by age 18, compared to a figure of 351 children per 1000 women, by age 18, among the cohort born one decade earlier. However, this drop in fertility may chiefly reflect a shortage of eligible marriage partners. Women typically marry men who are a few years older than themselves.[6] The sharp change in the numbers of annual births between 1945 and 1947 produced a disparity between the number of prospective brides and grooms. For every 100 female Negroes born in 1948, for example, there were only 77 male Negroes born in 1945.[7] It is impossible to know what will be the full impact of this "marriage squeeze" but it seems likely that the shortage of males will lead to lower marriage and fertility rates among the women born in the late 1940s.

The Timing of Childbearing

One of the most striking post-World War II changes in childbearing has been the increase in the fertility rates of young black women. A pattern has developed in which many Negro girls bear a child very shortly after they attain puberty. Among the women born since 1930, about 2 percent have had a baby before they became 15 years old, about 7 percent prior to their sixteenth birthday and about 15 percent by age 17.

Changes in the timing of childbearing may be analyzed by using the cohort fertility data. It is possible to determine the

---

6 U. S., Bureau of the Census, *Census of Population: 1960*, PC (2)–4E, Table 8.

7 U. S., National Center for Health Statistics, *Vital Statistics of the United States: 1965*, I. Table 1–1.

Figure 4–3
Birth Rates by Single Years of Age for Cohorts of Negro Women

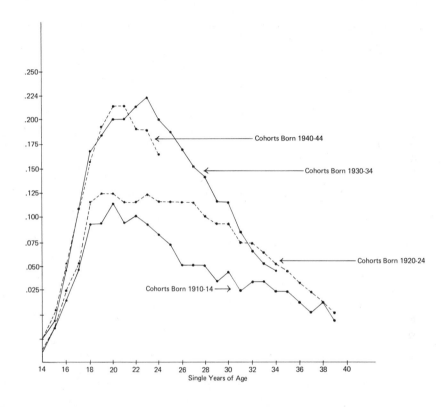

Source:
See Table 4–1.

birth rate for women in each cohort for single years of age. Such birth rates are shown in Table 4–2. The first line of this table, for instance, indicates the birth rate at age 14 for different groups of cohorts and the second line shows birth rates for age 15. Figure 4–3 indicates graphically birth rates for four groups of cohorts.

TABLE 4–2
Birth Rates by Single Years of Age for Cohorts of Negro Women

Ages	1945–49	1940–44	1935–39	1930–34	1925–29	1920–24	1915–19	1910–14	1906–09
14	.02	.02	.02	.02	.02	.01	.01	.01	.01
15	.05	.05	.05	.04	.04	.03	.03	.03	.03
16	.09	.10	.10	.09	.08	.07	.06	.06	.06
17	.15	.15	.16	.15	.12	.10	.10	.09	.09
18	.20*	.20	.22	.21	.18	.16	.14	.14	.14
19	.23*	.24	.25	.23	.20	.17	.15	.14	.16
20		.26	.27	.25	.20	.17	.17	.16	.18
21		.26	.28	.25	.20	.16	.15	.14	.15
22		.24*	.27	.26	.23	.16	.16	.15	.16
23		.24*	.27	.27	.23	.17	.16	.14	.16
24		.21*	.25	.25	.22	.16	.15	.13	.14
25			.22	.23	.21	.16	.13	.12	.13
26			.19	.22	.20	.16	.13	.10	.11
27			.17*	.20	.19	.16	.11	.10	.10
28			.16*	.19	.19	.15	.12	.10	.11
29			.14*	.16	.17	.14	.11	.08	.08
30				.16	.16	.14	.11	.09	.10
31				.13	.13	.12	.09	.07	.06
32				.11*	.13	.12	.09	.08	.08
33				.10*	.11	.11	.10	.08	.07
34				.09*	.10	.10	.08	.07	.07
35					.09	.09	.08	.07	.06
36					.07	.08	.07	.06	.07
37					.06*	.07	.06	.05	.05
38					.05*	.06	.06	.06	.06
39					.05*	.05	.05	.04	.05

* The asterisks indicate that not all cohorts in a group reached the specific age by 1966, the last year for which data were available.
Source:
    Data from Table 4–1.

Table 4–2 and Figure 4–3 show very clearly the changes which have taken place in the timing of childbearing. Among the older cohorts—women born before 1920—the birth rate rose rapidly and reached a peak at about age 20. At this age of maximum fertility, the birth rate was about 16 births per 100 women annually. These women, who began their childbearing during the Depression, did not have high fertility rates at older ages; the age specific fertility rates dropped off quite rapidly after the peak age of childbearing.

Negro women who began childbearing during the 1940s have very different fertility patterns. Among these women, the birth rate at young ages rose very rapidly and peak rates of child-bearing were attained between ages 20 and 22. At these ages, the birth rate was greater than 25 births per 100 women. Since these cohorts got off to such a vigorous start in childbearing, they might be expected to compensate by curtailing their fertility at older ages. However, the evidence in Table 4–2 and Figure 4–3 suggests that, rather than reducing their fertility, they continued to bear children frequently as they grew older. The completed fertility of these women will be high, because they got off to a rapid start in forming their families and they continued to have children frequently as they reached older childbearing ages.

There is evidence that the black women who were in their twenties during the 1960s were bearing fewer children at these ages than the women who were these same ages one decade before. The time period when these age specific fertility rates were at a peak may have passed.

Trends in Family Size

Increases in the birth rate have produced changes in the age at which black women begin their childbearing and increases in the size of their families. Among the older cohorts, about one woman in six bore a child before age 18, upwards of 60 percent reached age 21, and 45 percent reached age 24 before becoming a mother. This is no longer true, for early childbearing character-izes the women who started their families after World War II. About one out of four of these women had a child prior to their eighteenth birthday, and the proportion childless at age 21 fell from 60 percent to about 45 percent.

There has been an increase not only in the rate at which women are having their first child but also a change in how rap-idly second, third, and higher order births are added. One conve-nient way to summarize these trends is to analyze parity progres-sion ratios. These ratios indicate what proportion of the women at one parity level went on to bear an additional child by a speci-fied age.[8] Table 4–3 shows parity progression ratios for cohorts of Negro women. The top panel of this table indicates parity

---

[8] Wilson H. Grabill, Clyde V. Kiser and Pascal K. Whelpton, *The Fer-tility of American Women* (New York: John Wiley & Sons, 1958), pp. 165–173 and 350–355; Clyde V. Kiser, Wilson H. Grabill and Arthur A. Campbell, *Trends and Variations in Fertility in the United States* (Cambridge: Har-vard University Press, 1968), pp. 201–203 and 294–295.

progression by age 21. The first line shows that among cohorts born 1940 to 1945, 56 percent of the women had a first child before they reached age 21. By this same age; 54 percent of the women with a first child went on to have a second; 43 percent of those with two children had a third, and 33 percent of those who had three also bore a fourth.

A study of the parity progression ratios in Table 4–3 reveals there have been a number of important changes. First, there has been a substantial rise in the parity progression ratio from level zero to level one. This indicates there has been a decrease in the proportion of black women who remain childless.

Second, there has been a major jump in the parity progression ratio from one to two. In the past, many of the women who had one child stopped at that level, but this has changed. We can

TABLE 4–3
Parity Progression Ratios for Cohorts of Negro Women*

Years Cohorts Born	Years Reaching Specified Ages	Parity Progression Ratios						
		0–1	1–2	2–3	3–4	4–5	5–6	6–7
		Parity Progression before Age 21						
1940–45	1961–66	56	54	43	33	25	20	23
35–39	56–60	57	55	42	32	24	20	26
30–34	51–55	54	55	41	29	23	20	37
25–29	46–50	48	51	42	33	28	23	41
20–24	41–45	48	39	35	26	24	23	44
15–19	36–40	43	39	31	24	22	28	34
10–14	31–35	43	37	30	24	23	29	33
06–09	27–30	45	38	32	25	25	33	30
		Parity Progression before Age 24						
1940–42	1964–66	68	64	59	53	44	37	32
35–39	59–63	74	72	62	53	45	36	30
30–34	54–58	71	71	61	52	43	34	31
25–29	49–53	66	66	56	47	39	33	31
20–24	44–48	62	54	51	47	40	35	33
15–19	39–43	56	55	53	45	37	35	33
10–14	34–38	53	53	52	44	35	33	30
06–09	30–33	58	53	54	46	37	33	26
		Parity Progression before Age 27						
1935–39	1962–66	82	79	71	65	59	53	45
30–34	57–61	79	79	71	65	60	52	45
25–29	52–56	75	74	67	62	56	49	42
20–24	47–51	71	62	60	60	56	49	43
15–19	42–46	62	62	63	60	55	48	42
10–14	37–41	60	60	64	61	54	47	39
06–09	33–36	63	60	65	62	53	46	40

Table 4–3 (Cont'd)

Years Cohorts Born	Years Reaching Specified Ages	Parity Progression Ratios						
		0–1	1–2	2–3	3–4	4–5	5–6	6–7
		Parity Progression before Age 30						
1935–36	1965–66	88	83	76	72	68	63	57
30–34	60–64	83	83	76	71	68	63	58
25–29	55–59	80	79	73	70	66	61	56
20–24	50–54	76	67	66	67	65	62	56
15–19	45–49	67	66	67	66	65	61	55
10–14	40–44	63	63	68	68	64	61	53
06–09	36–39	66	63	70	70	64	60	53
		Parity Progression before Age 35						
1930–31	1965–66	84	87	80	76	75	72	69
25–29	60–64	83	84	79	76	74	71	69
20–24	55–59	81	74	73	75	73	72	69
15–19	50–54	73	70	71	72	72	71	69
10–14	45–49	68	66	72	73	71	71	69
06–09	41–44	68	65	73	75	72	71	69
		Parity Progression before Age 40						
1925–26	1965–66	84	81	79	77	76	74	73
20–24	60–64	80	74	75	76	76	75	73
15–19	55–59	73	72	74	74	75	77	75
10–14	50–54	68	68	74	76	74	76	75
06–09	46–49	69	67	75	77	75	76	75
		Parity Progression before Age 45						
1920–21	1965–66	80	73	73	77	78	76	75
15–19	60–64	73	72	74	75	76	76	77
10–14	55–59	69	68	74	76	74	77	76
06–09	51–54	70	67	75	78	76	77	77

* These ratios show the percent of women at one parity level who had an additional child by the specified age.
Source:
See text for methods of computation.

speculate that among the cohorts born after 1930, 90 percent or more of the Negro women who bear one child will also bear a second. The proportion of children who are only children is waning.

Third, there have been modest but consistent increases over time in the proportion of second, third and fourth parity women who add another child. This has had the consequence of increasing Negro family size.

Finally, there have been small changes in the parity progression ratios at the higher parity levels, that is five to six and six to seven.

Changes in these parity progression ratios have produced increases in the average number of children Negro women bear. Among the lowest fertility cohorts—those women born 1910 to 1914—only one-quarter had as many as four children in their entire lifetime. In contrast to these women, among the high fertility cohorts born during the 1930s, approximately one-quarter had four children by age 27. It appears that more than 45 percent of the women born during the 1930s will bear at least four children.

It may not be surprising that an increasing proportion of women are having three or four children since surveys of fertility desires indicate that many women want this number of children. More surprising is the rise in the proportion of black women who are having six, seven or more children. Whelpton observed long term changes in family size among whites and noted that even during the post-World War II baby boom the proportion of white women with large families decreased. He concluded that "sixth and higher order births will not be important numerically during the next few decades."[9] This is not the case among Negroes. Despite the urbanization of blacks and changes in educational attainment, more, rather than less, women are going on to have six or seven children. The most recent cohort to reach age 35 was born in 1931. Eighteen percent of these women had seven or more children by this age. It is possible that one-quarter of the women born during the 1930s will bear seven children. The parity progression ratios give an indication of how these high fertility levels come about. Generally, women with five or six children are not adding appreciably to this increase. Parity progression ratios at these higher levels have remained constant for a long time. Rather, the increase has been in the proportion of women who go on to have four or five children.

A Comparison with Nineteenth Century Women

Negro women are now starting their childbearing earlier and having children more rapidly than Negro women born during the period between the Civil War and the turn of this century. This is an unexpected finding since the majority of black women alive at the turn of this century lived in the rural South. Information about the fertility of women born in the last century comes from the Census of 1910. This information is not exactly compar-

---

[9] Grabill, Kiser and Whelpton, *op. cit.*, p. 363.

TABLE 4–4
Distributions of Negro Women by Numbers of Children Ever Born

Years Cohorts Born	Year Attaining Specified Age	Children Ever Born Per 1000 Women	Women by Number of Children					
			Total	None	One	Two	Three	Four or More
By Ages 20 to 24								
1940–44	1964	1316	100%	39%	24%	18%	11%	9%
35–39	59	1380	100	37	24	19	12	9
30–34	54	1260	100	41	23	18	11	8
25–29	49	1068	100	44	25	17	18	5
20–24	44	920	100	47	28	14	6	4
15–19	39	827	100	53	26	12	6	3
10–14	34	789	100	54	26	12	5	3
1885–89	1909	1036	100	50	18	14	9	9
By Ages 25 to 29								
1935–39	1964	2593	100	18	17	19	16	30
30–34	59	2495	100	21	16	18	16	29
25–29	54	2152	100	26	19	18	14	24
20–24	49	1732	100	30	27	18	10	16
15–19	44	1547	100	38	23	14	10	15
10–14	39	1444	100	42	24	13	9	14
1880–84	1909	2132	100	34	15	13	11	27
By Ages 30 to 34								
1930–34	1964	3359	100	15	12	16	15	42
25–29	59	3022	100	19	15	16	14	37
20–24	54	2445	100	22	23	17	11	27
15–19	49	2101	100	31	22	14	10	22
10–14	44	1909	100	36	23	12	8	21
1875–79	1909	3087	100	26	14	11	9	39

Sources:

Table 4–1; U. S., Bureau of the Census, *Sixteenth Census of the United States: 1940, Population*, Differential Fertility: 1940 and 1910, Women by Number of Children Ever Born, Tables 6 and 12.

able to the cohort fertility information for women born 1906 and later, so we must be cautious in drawing conclusions about the childbearing of women born during the last century.

Table 4–4 shows distributions of Negro women by numbers of children ever born. In this table, cohorts have been grouped in a fashion different from that used in previous tables to facilitate comparisons with data from the Census of 1910. As an illustration, the women born 1940 to 1944 might be considered. During 1964, these women reached ages 20 to 24; that is, women born in

1940 became 24, women born in 1941 became 23 and so forth. Table 4–4 shows the fertility of cohorts grouped in this manner. This table indicates that Negro women born 1910 to 1914 got a more conservative start on their childbearing than did the nineteenth century women, and that childlessness was more common among these women than among women born in the last century.

More impressive are comparisons of women born during the 1930s to women born 1875 to 1889. The proportion who had children while they were young was higher among women born during the Depression than among women born during the post-Civil War era. For example, only 50 percent of the women born 1885 to 1889 had a child by the time they attained ages 20 to 24, but 63 percent of the women born 1935 to 1939 had become mothers by these same ages. In addition, proportionally more of the recent cohorts of Negro women added higher order children at young ages. We can conclude that the Negro women who began childbearing after World War II did indeed get a more vigorous start on family formation than any other group of black women since Reconstruction.

Trends in Childlessness

One of the greatest changes in family patterns among blacks has been in the proportion of women who never bear a child. This is of particular interest for fertility analysis, since many studies indicate that very few married women desire no children. Childlessness, then, may represent the outcome of fecundity problems rather than the effect of birth control.

It is difficult to be certain about trends over time in childlessness. The cohort fertility figures provide information about Negro women born since 1906 and do indicate that very many of the women in the low fertility cohorts born 1910 to 1914 had no children. However, the cohort fertility data do not supply information about women born before 1906. To study long term trends, census tabulations showing women by number of children ever born were analyzed. These statistics are not ideal for the study of childlessness, since all single women were assumed to have no children. Also, if we wish to make inferences about the fertility of women born in a given period, we must rely upon the fertility data given by women who survived to a later census date. For instance, estimates of childlessness among women born 1835

TABLE 4-5

Estimated Proportions of Women Childless by Color

Date of Birth of Cohorts	Source of Data	Age at Time of Observation	Negro		White	
			Ever Married Women	Total Women	Ever Married Women	Total Women
1835–44	Census of 1910	65–74	6%	10%	8%	15%
1845–54	" " "	55–64	7	11	8	15
1855–59	" " "	50–54	8	13	9	17
1860–64	" " "	45–49	9	13	10	19
1865–74	Census of 1940	65–74	11	16	13	23
1875–84	" " "	55–64	16	21	15	24
1885–94	" " "	45–54	20	25	15	23
1895–99	Census of 1960	60–64*	26	29	19	24
1900–04	" " "	55–59*	27	32	20	26
1905–09	" " "	50–54	29	33	20	27
1910–14	" " "	45–49	28	32	17	25
1915–19	" " "	40–44	25	30	13	18
1920–24	Survey, 1965	40–44*	18	25	10	15
1925–29	" "	35–39*	13	19	8	12
1930–34	" "	30–34*	9	20	7	12

* Data for these cohorts refer to non-whites.

Source:

U. S., Bureau of the Census, *Sixteenth Census of the United States: 1940*, Population, Differential Fertility: 1940 and 1910, Women by Number of Children Ever Born, Tables 1–6; *Census of Population: 1960*, PC (2)–3A, Tables 4, 5 and 8; *Current Population Reports*, "Marriage, Fertility, and Childspacing: June, 1965," Series P-20, No. 186 (August 6, 1969), Table 1.

to 1844 come from answers to fertility questions posed in 1910 to women who were then 65–74.

Table 4–5 contains information about childlessness among cohorts of Negro women and white women. The sources of information and the ages of the respondents at the time the data were collected are indicated. Figures are shown for ever-married women and for the total women in each cohort.

Few of the black women born around the middle of the last century remained childless, perhaps no more than 10 percent of each cohort. This gradually changed and among Negro women born toward the end of the century, about one-fifth to one-quarter of the women never bore children. Childlessness was even more common among the women born in the first decades of this century, for approximately one-third of these women remained childless. This was a peak proportion for childlessness and later cohorts will exhibit very different patterns. We do not know about the completed childbearing of women who are presently under 45 years old, but we can infer from Table 4–1 and Table 4–5 that fewer than 10 percent of the women born during the Depression will remain childless.

Among whites, the pattern of change over time in childlessness is similar to that among Negroes. Few of the white women born during the middle of the nineteenth century remained childless but among the white women born early in this century there were many who did not become mothers. Later cohorts have changed this pattern, and the childless proportion will be lower among white women born in the 1920s and 1930s than among white women born during the nineteenth century.

Among women born before the end of Reconstruction, childlessness was more common among whites, but among women born since that time, childlessness has been more common among blacks. This appears to be a persistent trend, for among the most recent cohorts to reach age thirty, the blacks have had the higher rates of childlessness.

Comparison of the Fertility of Whites and Negroes

Pascal Whelpton computed cohort fertility rates for native white women in the United States.[10] A comparison of the childbearing patterns of Negro women and white women reveals many similarities. Among both whites and Negroes, women who were born in 1910 to 1914—women who started their families during the Depression—had distinctively low fertility. White women in these cohorts completed their childbearing with an average of 2.3 children while Negro women bore an average of 2.6 children. Although these average numbers of children are similar, the distributions of women by number of children ever borne are dissimilar. Among Negroes, childlessness was much more common than among whites. As indicated in Table 4–5, about one-third of the Negro women born in the period 1910 to 1914 never had a child, while among whites, the proportion who were childless was about 20 percent. Childlessness, then, was a much more important component of the low Negro fertility rates than it was of the white fertility rates. Yet very large families were also more common among Negroes than among whites. More than 12 percent of the

---

[10] Whelpton, *Cohort Fertility;* Grabill, Kiser and Whelpton, *op. cit.,* Chap. ix.

black women in these low fertility cohorts bore at least seven children, but among whites no more than 4 percent had such a large number of offspring.[11]

White women who began their childbearing during and after World War II were similar to Negro women in that they adopted a pattern of high fertility. They had many children while they were young and will complete their families with a much larger number of offspring than the white women whose fertility was affected by the Depression.

There are, however, important differences between white and Negro women who recently started bearing children. First, although white women had many children at young ages, their fertility rates at these ages were still low when compared to those of Negro women. We noted, for instance, that about one out of four Negro women born during the 1930s had a child before she reached age 18. We can infer that no more than 10 percent of the white women who were born during the same period had a baby by age 18.[12] Thus, Negro women began childbearing earlier than did white women; in particular, blacks had many more children while they were teenagers.

Second, Negro women in the post-World War II era added children to their families at a more rapid rate than did white women. We might consider women born in 1934. About six percent of the white women had four or more children prior to age 24, whereas among Negroes, 17 percent had at least four children by this age.[13]

Third, in spite of a general rise in fertility, high order births have become increasingly rare among whites. There has been a continual reduction in the proportion of fourth parity white women who added a fifth child and in the proportion of fifth parity white women who added a sixth child. Thus, among whites, the long term trend toward fewer and fewer large families has continued but among Negroes this has not occurred.

Because of these differences, there will be racial differences in completed family size. White women born during the early Depression years will likely complete their families with an aver-

---

[11] Grabill, Kiser and Whelpton, *op. cit.*, p. 343.

[12] The data from which this inference is drawn refer to the total female population, not only to whites. Pascal K. Whelpton and Arthur A. Campbell, *Fertility Tables for Birth Cohorts of American Women, Part 1, Annual and Cumulative Birth Rates, by Age, by Order of Birth for All Women in Cohorts of 1876 to 1943*, U. S., National Office of Vital Statistics-Special Reports, Selected Studies, LI, No. 1 (January 29, 1960), Table 4.

[13] *Ibid.*

age of 3.2 children, while Negro women born during the same years will have an average of four or more children.

Fertility rates for specific age groups of Negro and white women are shown in Figure 4–4.[14] The rates of both racial groups have followed identical general trends. After 1940, fertility rates increased. Full mobilization toward the end of World War II temporarily depressed fertility, but the postwar baby boom more than compensated for the low rates of 1944 and 1945. In the late 1950s, the fertility rates reached a maximum and since then they have decreased. Among both races, the fall began at the same time and the declines are of about the same magnitude among both whites and Negroes. Despite this recent decrease, the age specific fertility rates among both races were higher in the mid-1960s than in 1940.

During the World War II years, Negro fertility rates at the young ages—under 25—were higher than those for whites, but at ages over 25, whites had the higher rates. This trend changed during the postwar period; among women over 25, Negro fertility rates increased more rapidly than white. As a result, the fertility rates of blacks came to exceed those of whites at all ages. In recent years, the fertility of older Negro women has decreased a bit more rapidly than the fertility of older white women. At present, there is a substantial racial difference in fertility at young ages but, at ages over 25, Negro fertility rates exceed those of whites by only a small margin.

The one fertility rate which has moved in an unusual manner is that of black women 15 to 19. This rate increased after World War II, reached a peak in the late 1950s, declined from 1960 to 1963, but has risen since then. The decrease in the early 1960s may be the result of the "marriage squeeze." The women who became 15, 16 or 17 years old in the early 1960s were born just after World War II and were most affected by the shortage of eligible males. Women who attained these ages after 1965 were less affected by the "marriage squeeze," and their high fertility indicates that these young Negro women have not participated in the general decline in Negro fertility which has been occurring since the late 1950s.

---

[14] The fertility rates for blacks include corrections for the under-registration of births and the census undercount of women. The rates for whites include a correction for the under-registration of births. A correction was not made for the census undercount of white women since the undercount rates at these ages have been estimated at no more than 1 or 2 percent. The U. S., Bureau of the Census, "Estimates of the Population of the United States and Components of Change, by Age, Color, and Sex 1950 to 1960," Table C-2.

Figure 4-4
Age Specific Fertility Rates of Negroes and Whites: 1940–1967

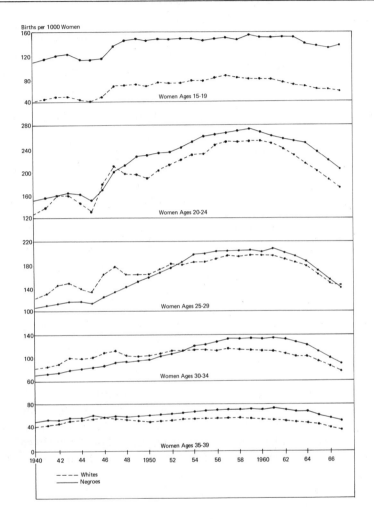

Source:
    See Figure 4–1.

Summary

Completed family size among Negroes declined over a long span. Women born 1910 to 1914 averaged less than three children. This change resulted from a rise in childlessness and a decrease in large families. During the 1940s, fertility rates began to climb, and during the 1950s, they increased very rapidly. The trend toward smaller families stopped and the women born during the Depression years will probably complete their childbearing with an average of at least four children. This increase was brought about by a drop in childlessness and an increase in the proportion of women who had five, six or more children.

Since the late 1950s fertility rates have decreased. Many of the women who got off to a rapid start on childbearing during the 1940s, or early 1950s, are reducing their fertility rates at older ages. While this has the effect of lowering the overall fertility rates for specific years, these cohorts of women will still have large families because of the many children they bore while they were young.

There is no way to know the completed family size of women who began bearing children during the late 1950s and the 1960s, for they are still very young. At these young ages, they have borne children quite rapidly. If their fertility rates at older ages are low—and the present trend seems to be toward lower fertility—they may complete their childbearing with moderate sized families. On the other hand, they are young enough to bear many additional children.

The previous chapter indicated that Negro mortality rates decreased sharply between the late 1930s and the mid-1950s. Changes in fertility combined with changes in mortality to produce fluctuations in the growth rate. During the Depression decade, the black population grew less than one percent each year. The growth rate increased, and during the span 1955 to 1960, the annual growth rate was 2.5 percent. Since 1960, population growth has slowed because mortality rates have remained constant while fertility rates have decreased. The growth rate decreased to an average rate of 1.7 percent for the period 1967 to 1969.[15]

---

[15] U. S., Bureau of the Census, "Estimates of the Population of the United States and Components of Change: 1940 to 1969," *Current Population Reports*, Series P-25, No. 418, (March 14, 1969), Table 2.

Chapter 5

DIFFERENTIALS IN NEGRO FERTILITY

Previous chapters discussed fertility trends for the total black population. They described the high fertility rates of the nineteenth century, the decline in fertility which occurred between the Civil War and the Depression, and the post-Depression rise in fertility. Differentials in fertility have not yet been described. We might ask whether Negro women in the South bear more or fewer children than Negro women who live in the North or whether women with extensive educations have smaller families than women who have finished only a few years of schooling. If there are regional or socio-economic differences in fertility, we must measure how great they are and whether they have changed over time.

This chapter investigates fertility differentials. The first section describes fertility differences for women living in different places. The second section assesses what effect the urbanization of Negroes has had for fertility. The third section studies fertility differentials by place of birth in an effort to measure the consequences of rural background for fertility. The final section relates fertility to such socio-economic variables as education, income, or occupation of husband, and describes changes over time in these relationships.

Sources of Data

Ratios of Children to Women

One measure frequently used to describe differentials in fertility is the ratio of Negro children at ages under 5, to Negro women ages 15 to 44. We have noted that this is a sensitive measure of childbearing and can be computed for any areal unit, such

101

as a city, a state, or a region for which a tabulation of Negroes by age and sex has been published. Since 1890, the decennial censuses have published such tabulations for many different areas. This record makes the ratio of children to women a particularly useful measure for analyzing historical trends in regional or rural-urban fertility differences.

However, in studying these ratios it is necessary to keep in mind two sources of possible error. First, not all the children under 5 years of age are living with their mothers. If urban women send many of their young children to live with sisters or relatives on farms, the ratios of children to women for cities will underestimate fertility, while those for rural areas will overestimate fertility. It is impossible to take this factor completely into account, for the census does not indicate the location of a child's mother. However, we can be certain there has been little change over time in the proportion of black children who live with their mothers. In 1910, 87 percent of the Negro children under five lived with their mothers, and in 1960, 85 percent of the children had this status. In the North, the proportion of children with their mothers fluctuated between 89 percent in 1910, and 87 percent in 1960; and in the South, from 87 percent to 84 percent.[1] These figures imply that fluctuations in the proportion of children who lived with their mothers had only a limited impact upon the estimated fertility rates.

Second, changes in infant mortality rates may affect the ratios of children to women. Suppose that women in two different areas bore offspring at the same rate, but that there were large differences in infant mortality. Then the ratios of children to women would differ and the difference would reflect infant mortality instead of real differences in fertility. It is difficult to correct for this source of bias since we do not know the level of infant mortality among Negroes prior to the 1930s.

Women by Number of Children Ever Born

A second source of data for studying fertility differentials is tabulations of women by number of children ever born. Six national censuses have asked women what number of children they have borne, but the answers have been tabulated only for the

---

[1] U. S. Bureau of the Census, *Negro Population of the United States: 1790–1915*, p. 182; *Sixteenth Census of the United States: 1940*, Population, Differential Fertility; 1940 and 1910, Women by Number of Children Under 5 Years Old, Table 6 and 69; *Census of Population: 1960*, PC(2)–1C, Table 1; PC(2)–3C, Table 27.

censuses of 1910, 1940, 1950 and 1960.[2] This is a very useful measure, for women can be grouped by their educational attainment or by the occupation of their husband and then the average number of children born to women in each category can be determined. In this way, the relationship of socio-economic status to fertility can be assessed. Similarly, women can be categorized by place of birth or by husband's income to study whether these variables influence fertility.

Some difficulties with this measure should be noted. The question about children ever born was asked only of women who reported they had been married. If a women reported herself single, the census enumerator was instructed not to ask the fertility question. Wilson Grabill has argued that the ommission of fertility information for single women introduced relatively little bias. He believed that many unmarried women who had young children in their homes reported themselves married and then reported on their fertility.[3]

Not all married women who were asked about their childbearing answered this question, introducing another possible source of error. In 1910, 11 percent of the married Negro women failed to answer this question;[4] in 1940, 15 percent did not answer;[5] and in 1960, 10 percent did not report on their childbearing.[6] Grabill examined schedules from the Census of 1940 and inferred that women who did not answer typically had borne fewer children than the women who did answer.[7] In 1950 and in 1960, allocation procedures were developed which assigned a specified

---

[2] Information about the number of children born to women who lived in the East North Central states in 1900 has been tabulated. See: Clyde V. Kiser, "Fertility of Social Classes in Various Types of Communities of the East North Central States in 1900," *Journal of the American Statistical Association*, XXVII, No. 180 (December, 1932), 371–382; Clyde V. Kiser, "Trends in the Fertility of Social Classes from 1900 to 1910," *Human Biology*, V, No. 2 (May, 1933), 256–273.

[3] U. S. Bureau of the Census, *Sixteenth Census of the United States: 1940*, Population, Differential Fertility: 1940 and 1910, Women by Number of Children Ever Born, p. 2; *Census of Population: 1950*, P-E, No. 5C, p. 6; *Census of Population: 1960*, PC(2)–3A, p. x.

[4] U. S. Bureau of the Census, *Sixteenth Census of the United States: 1940*, Population, Differential Fertility: 1940 and 1910, Women by Number of Children Ever Born, Table 1.

[5] *Ibid.*

[6] U. S. Bureau of the Census, *Census of Population: 1960*, PC(2)–3A, Table A-1. It is impossible to determine non-reporting rates specific for color in 1950.

[7] U. S. Bureau of the Census, *Sixteenth Census of the United States: 1940*, Population, Differential Fertility: 1940 and 1910, Women by Number of Children Ever Born, pp. 408–410.

number of children to each non-reporting woman. In 1950, the allocation was made on the basis of the composition of the household in which the woman lived.[8] In 1960, characteristics of the woman's household as well as characteristics of other women who lived in the same area were used in making allocations.[9] The rates of children ever born, calculated from 1910 and 1940 census data, probably overestimate the fertility of married women by a small margin since they include no compensation for the low fertility of those married women who did not report on their childbearing.

Data concerning numbers of children ever borne are available only for women who survived to be enumerated. If women who died prior to the census had very different fertility rates from those who survived, then the estimates of fertility from this source are biased. Investigations of this topic have not ascertained whether a woman's chances of dying are systematically related to the number of children she has borne.[10] The tabulations in this chapter refer to women under 45 years of age. Since female death rates at these ages are quite low, selective mortality should not seriously affect the estimates of fertility.

Fertility Differences by Place of Current Residence

Region of Residence

There are persistent and substantial regional differences in Negro childbearing. Women who live in the South have been more fertile than women outside the South at each date for which information is available. This trend is indicated by the ratios of children to women shown in Table 5–1.

This table demonstrates that the national trends in fertility have operated within all regions of the country. The period 1880 to 1940 was one of declining fertility both for women who lived in the South and for women outside the South. We can be certain, then, that the long term decline in Negro fertility was not simply

---

[8] U. S. Bureau of the Census, *Census of Population: 1950*, P-E, No. 5C, p. 181.

[9] U. S. Bureau of the Census, *Census of Population: 1960*, PC (2)–3A, p. xvii.

[10] Grabill, Kiser and Whelpton, *op. cit.*, p. 403; Bettie C. Freeman, "Fertility and Longevity in Married Women Dying after the End of the Reproduction Period," *Human Biology* (September, 1935), 392–418; Harold F. Dorn and Arthur J. McDowell, "The Relationship of Fertility to Longevity," *American Sociological Review*, IV (April, 1939), 234–246.

TABLE 5–1
Ratios of Children Ages 0 to 4 to Women 15 to 44
for Negroes by Region of Residence: 1880–1967

Areas	1880	1890	1900	1910	1920	1930	1940	1950	1960	1967
Total United States	759*	619*	582	519	429	393	368	513	694	660
North and West	505*	400*	288	279	262	293	256	402	634	606
Northeast	–	–	293	274	268	299	245	372	554	–
North Central	–	–	339	290	258	291	269	422	694	–
West	–	–	269	231	236	239	234	442	683	–
South	793*	648*	619	551	463	423	404	573	740	685

* Ratios marked by asterisks refer to the non-white population.

Sources:

> Walter Willcox, Negroes in the United States, U. S. Bureau of the Census, Bulletin 8 (June 1, 1904), p. 67.
> U. S. Census Office, Twelfth Census of the United States: 1900, Population, Part II, pp. 120–121.
> U. S. Bureau of the Census, Negro Population: 1790–1915, pp. 166 and 194.
> U. S. Bureau of the Census, Fourteenth Census of the United States: 1920, Population, II, pp. 156 and 170–187.
> U. S. Bureau of the Census, Fifteenth Census of the United States: 1930, Population, II, pp. 577 and 602–611.
> U. S. Bureau of the Census, Sixteenth Census of the United States: 1940, Population, Characteristics of the Nonwhite Population by Race, Table 3.
> U. S. Bureau of the Census, Census of Population: 1960, PC(2)–1C, Table 1.
> U. S. Bureau of the Census, Census of Population: 1950, P-E, No. 3B, Table 2.
> U. S. Bureau of the Census, "Negro Population: March, 1967," Current Population Reports, Series P-20, No. 175 (October 23, 1968), Tables 1 and 3.

a consequence of Negroes moving away from the South, for fertility levels within the South declined during this period. There were regional differences in the rates of decline. In the North, fertility fell rapidly between 1880 and 1900, but by this year fertility had been reduced to a relatively low level and fell very little thereafter. Within the South, the pattern was different for, throughout the entire period from 1880 to 1940, fertility declined quite rapidly.

In all sections of the country, fertility increased between the end of the Depression and 1960. The increases were greatest in the North where fertility levels had been low. As a result of this change, regional differences in fertility were greatly reduced.

It is difficult to know about changes in regional fertility levels since 1960. However, some tabulations of Negroes by age and region have been published and from these data ratios of children to women were estimated. These figures are shown in Table 5–1 and they suggest that within both regions of the country Negro fertility has declined.

TABLE 5–2
Ratios of Children 0 to 4 To Women 15 to 44
for Negroes by Rural or Urban Residence. 1910–1960

Place of Residence	1910	1920	1930	1940	1950	1960
Total United States	519	429	393	368	513	694
Total Urban	275	247	268	246	424	652
Urban, North & West	242	240	279	246	379	631
Urban, South	290	251	261	246	449	677
Total Rural	645	555	521	519	710	838
Rural non-farm	–	433	426	399	638	826
Rural farm	–	604	567	584	773	866

Sources:

U. S. Bureau of the Census, Negro Population: 1790–1915, pp. 166 and 182.

U. S. Bureau of the Census, Fourteenth Census of the United States: 1920, Population, II, pp. 156, 371, 376, and 377.

U. S. Bureau of the Census, Fifteenth Census of the United States: 1930, Population, II, pp. 517, 587–590, 704–712 and 756.

U. S. Bureau of the Census, Census of Population: 1950, P-E, No. 3B, Table 2.

U. S. Bureau of the Census, Census of Population: 1960, PC(2)–1C, Table 1.

Rural-Urban Fertility Differences

Rural-urban differences in childbearing have been observed since the time John Graunt authored the first demographic volume; in this country, rural-urban differences were evident as early as the eighteenth century.[11] Among Negroes, this differential can be studied from 1910 to the present. Each of the decennial censuses since that date has published the age distribution of blacks in urban, rural non-farm, and rural farm areas. Urban residents are those who resided in cities or towns of 2500 or greater,[12] rural non-farm residents are people who lived in rural areas but not on productive farms, while rural farm residents lived on farms on which there was a specified amount of agricultural activity or production. Table 5–2 shows ratios of children to women for urban and rural areas.

This table reveals that there has always been a large rural-urban difference in Negro fertility. Rural fertility levels have been, and still are, very much above those of urban areas. The

---

[11] Grabill, Kiser and Whelpton, op. cit., p. 12.

[12] In 1950, the definition of urban was changed to include those individuals who lived in densely populated but small suburbs or in unincorporated areas which were contiguous to large metropolitan areas. U. S. Bureau of the Census, Census of Population: 1950, P-C1, p. viii.

high rates of childbearing in rural areas sustained Negro population growth because, prior to the end of World War II, the fertility of urban blacks was much below the level needed for replacement of the population. In 1910, for instance, a ratio of children to women of 448 would have been required just to maintain a stationary population.[13] The actual fertility ratio among blacks in cities was 275, indicating the low fertility of urban Negro women. Warren Thompson analyzed these fertility ratios from the Census of 1920 and observed that the only blacks replacing themselves were those on southern farms. He concluded, "For a Negro to leave the rural South means that he has taken a long step toward becoming sterile."[14]

The timing of fertility decline was different in rural and urban areas. In cities, the fertility level was low in 1910, but changed very little from 1910 to 1940. In rural areas, the trend was quite different. From 1910 to the end of the Depression, the fertility level in rural areas declined. The factors producing lower fertility rates apparently had their effects in cities prior to 1910, but in the rural areas they continued to operate until 1940.

There was no rural-urban difference in the timing of the post-Depression rise in childbearing. In rural areas and in cities of both the South and North, fertility increased very rapidly from 1940 to 1960. As a consequence of this quick change, rural-urban fertility differences were reduced, and, in 1960, the fertility levels of the two areas were more similar than at any earlier date. Before World War II, the rural ratio of children to women was about twice as large as that for urban areas, but in 1960 it was only one and one-third times that of urban areas.

The figures in Table 5–2 suggest that fertility trends in southern cities were similar to those in northern cities. At most dates, women in the southern cities had the higher fertility ratios but the differences were quite small. Apparently, the effect of urban living upon fertility was much the same whether the city was located in the North or South.

The very high fertility levels of 1960 deserve further comment. Many sociologists and demographers have argued that ur-

---

[13] This ratio is an estimate derived from a life table for Negroes, in 1910, who lived in ten northern states and the District of Columbia. U. S. Bureau of the Census, *United States Life Tables 1910* (Washington: Government Printing Office, 1916), pp. 28–29.

[14] Warren S. Thompson, *Ratio of Children to Women: 1920;* U. S. Bureau of the Census, Census Monograph XI (1931), p. 149.

ban living and high fertility rates are incompatible, and the theory of demographic transition claims that as a population becomes urbanized its fertility will fall. The fertility rates of the black women who lived in cities during the 1950s lend no support to these arguments. The urban fertility ratio of 652 in 1960 was very much higher than the urban fertility ratio at any previous date. In fact, the urban fertility ratio in 1960 was higher than the rural fertility ratio in 1910.

During the post-Depression period, the fertility rates of rural women were much higher than those of urban women. In 1960, the Growth of American Families Study interviewed a selected sample of non-white women and asked about childbearing and the use of contraception.[15] It was discovered that two-thirds of the non-white women on farms had never attempted to control their fertility. Consequently, they bore large numbers of children. Census statistics indicating the numbers of children born to Negro women testify to the extremely high fertility of the rural Negro population. Shown below are average numbers of children born to rural farm women in 1910 and 1960.[16]

| | Children Ever Born | |
Age of Women	1910	1960
15–19	892	1225
20–24	1994	2960
25–29	3346	3584
30–34	4566	5461
35–39	5829	5994

For each age group, fertility was higher in 1960 than fifty years earlier. A comparison of 1960 and 1910 fertility rates for rural non-farm women revealed very much the same pattern. Thus, in the 1960s there remained in rural areas a group of Negro

---

15 Whelpton, Campbell, and Patterson, *op. cit.*, p. 356.

16 U. S. Bureau of the Census, *Sixteenth Census of the United States: 1940*, Population, Differential Fertility: 1940 and 1910, Fertility for States and Large Cities, Table 4; *U. S., Censuses of Population and Housing: 1960*, 1/1,000, 1/10,000, Two National Samples of the Population of the United States, Description and Technical Documentation. Certain data used in this monograph were derived from a computer tape file furnished under a joint project sponsored by the U.S. Bureau of the Census and the Population Council and containing selected 1960 Census information from a 0.1 percent sample of the population of the United States. Neither the Census Bureau nor the Population Council assumes any responsibility for the validity of any of the figures or the interpretations of the figures published herein based on this material. In subsequent parts of this monograph, this source of data is referred to as Records of 1 in 1,000 sample of 1960 Censuses.

women who had very high fertility rates, rates which were probably quite similar to those of the national population in the early nineteenth century. These women will complete their families with an average of more than seven children. While rural residents have become a smaller and smaller component of the total Negro population, they are by no means few in number. In 1960, there were over five million Negroes—27 percent of the total black population—living in rural areas.[17] The distinctively high fertility of this group guarantees that a sizable proportion of the future Negro population will have a rural background.

Unintentional Fertility and Sterility

Recent studies of the fertility desires of American women indicate that relatively few married women desire either to bear no children or to have very many children.[18] While most of these studies have explored the attitudes of white women, there have been some studies of Negroes or non-whites. These studies reveal that non-white women have fertility desires similar to those of white women; if anything, non-whites may wish to have slightly smaller families.[19] Apparently, few Negro women intend to reach menopause with either no children or many children.

We cannot know how family size preferences have changed over time, and it is possible that some time in the past, many women wanted to have large families. We can, however, examine trends to determine what changes have occurred in the proportion of women who either bore no children or many children. We can make the assumption that few married women deliberately reached menopause in either of these categories. If a high proportion bore no children, it may reflect high rates of sterility, and if many women had five or more children, we probably have a good indication that effective birth control techniques were not used. Changes over time in the proportion of women with no children or with many children, probably reflect changes in health conditions and changes in the use of family planning.

---

[17] U. S. Bureau of the Census, *Census of Population: 1960*, PC(2)–1C, Table 1.

[18] Freedman, Whelpton and Campbell, *op. cit.*, pp. 220–226; Whelpton, Campbell and Patterson, *op. cit.*, pp. 32–44.

[19] Ronald Freedman, David Goldberg and Larry Bumpass, "Current Fertility Expectations of Married Couples in the United States: 1963," *Population Index* XXXI (January, 1965), 3–19; Whelpton, Campbell, and Patterson, *op. cit.*, pp. 336–351.

TABLE 5–3
Proportion of Ever-Married Negro Women Childless or with Five or More Children, by Urban or Rural Residence: 1910 to 1960

	1910*	1940*	1950*	1960
Proportion Childless				
Total United States	21%	32%	32%	19%
Total Urban	31	37	35	20
Urban, North and West	38	37	37	21
Urban, South	28	38	34	19
Total Rural	16	23	23	15
Rural non-farm	18	28	26	16
Rural farm	15	21	21	15
Proportion with Five or More Children				
Total United States	25%	13%	12%	18%
Total Urban	14	8	8	14
Urban, North and West	11	7	6	12
Urban, South	16	9	9	17
Total Rural	31	21	22	33
Rural non-farm	26	16	17	29
Rural farm	35	24	26	42

* Data for these years refer to non-white women. Rates in this table have been standardized for age using the age distribution of Negro women ages 15 to 44 in 1960 as a standard.

Sources:

U. S. Bureau of the Census, *Sixteenth Census of the United States: 1940*, Population, Differential Fertility: 1940 and 1910, Fertility for States and Large Cities, Tables 1, 2, 15 and 16.

U. S. Bureau of the Census, *Census of Population: 1950*, P-E, No. 5C, Table 32.

U. S. Bureau of the Census, *Censuses of Population and Housing: 1960*, 1/1,000, 1/10,000, Two National Samples of the Population of the United States, Description and Technical Documentation. Certain data used in this monograph were derived from a computer tape file furnished under a joint project sponsored by the U.S. Bureau of the Census and the Population Council and containing selected 1960 Census information from an 0.1 percent sample of the population of the United States. Neither the Census Bureau nor the Population Council assumes any responsibility for the validity of any of the figures or the interpretations of the figures published herein based on this material. In subsequent parts of this monograph, this source of data is referred to as Records of 1 in 1,000 sample of 1960 Censuses.

Table 5–3 contains information pertinent to this topic. It shows the proportion of ever-married women, specific for place of residence, who had no children and the proportion who had five or more children. The data refer to Negro women 15 to 44 and have been standardized for age to eliminate effects of changes in the age structure.

At each date, childlessness was more common among urban women than among rural women. In 1910, it was particularly common among women in the cities, for almost one-third of them reported they had never borne a child. In northern cities, childlessness was considerably more common than in southern cities. Childlessness increased from 1910 to 1940 among women in all areas, but the increases were greater among rural women than among urban women thus reducing the rural-urban difference. After 1940, the trend toward greater childlessness was reversed and rural-urban differences declined still further. In 1910, the proportion of childless Negro women was much higher in cities than in rural areas. Fifty years later, this had changed and cities no longer had such a large proportion of childless women.

Early in this century, the proportion of Negro women ages 15 to 44 who had at least five children was quite high. Approximately one-quarter of such women had large families. Between that time and 1940, fertility rates declined, and it became less common for women to bear as many children. This trend, however, did not persist into the post-World War II era. Fertility rates increased and the proportion of women with five children went up. This rise was not restricted to farm women, for among Negro women in cities, as well as those in rural areas, the proportion with at least five offspring was as high or higher in 1960 as in 1910.

A Comparison with White Women

Trends in the fertility of whites can be compared to those of Negroes by studying ratios of children to women. Among whites as among Negroes, there have always been rural-urban fertility differences, and the fertility ratios for rural areas have always been greater than those for cities.[20] The period before 1940 was one in which the fertility of whites in both urban and rural areas declined. Between 1940 and 1960, rates of childbearing went up in both areas, but the gains in cities were greater than the gains in rural areas and this led to a reduction of the rural-urban fertility differential among whites. Recent studies of family planning suggest that rural white women will have families which are only slightly larger than those of urban women.[21] It appears that the same general trend involving decreasing fer-

---

[20] Okun, op. cit., Chapter i, Part C.
[21] Whelpton, Campbell, and Patterson, op. cit., pp. 116–117; Freedman, Whelpton, and Campbell, op. cit., pp. 314–318.

tility rates before 1940, increasing rates from 1940 to 1960, and reductions in rural-urban differences, characterize both the white and Negro populations.

Nationally, the fertility rates of Negroes have always been as high or higher than those of whites. This is not true of the fertility rates within specific areas. During the period prior to 1940, ratios of children to women in urban areas were lower for Negroes than for whites. A comparison of census data suggest that, for a long span, blacks in cities had lower fertility rates than whites. This must be a cautious interpretation, for racial differences in infant mortality affected the ratios of children to women. Since 1940, the picture has changed. Negro fertility rates in cities increased rapidly and Negro women bore children much more frequently than white women in cities during the period following World War II.

In rural areas, the fertility ratios of blacks have always exceeded those of whites. Racial differences in rural fertility were large early in this century; they diminished during the 1920s and 1930s and then once again widened, for the post-1940 increase in rural fertility was greater among Negroes than among whites.

The Effect of Urbanization on Negro Fertility Rates

The period 1910 to 1940 was one of declining fertility among Negroes. Two important components of this drop can be identified: the change in fertility rates within both urban and rural areas, and the shifting distribution of population. In 1910, only one out of four Negroes lived in a city or town, while in 1940 almost one-half of the Negro population lived in urban areas. Table 3–2 indicates the urban proportion of the Negro population from 1890 to 1960. As the urban proportion increased, we would expect fertility rates for the total population to fall merely because urban women bear fewer children than rural women.

It is possible to isolate the effects of both changing fertility rates and shifts in the rural-urban distribution of Negroes. The methodology known as components of difference between two rates is useful for such an analysis. Results of this investigation are shown in Table 5–4. Negro women were divided into three place of residence categories: those who lived in the North and West, those who lived in the urban South, and those who lived

TABLE 5–4
Components of Change in Ratios of Children to
Women: Negroes, 1910 to 1940 and 1940 to 1960

Ratios of Children 0–4 to Women 15–44

Areas	1910	1940	1960
Total United States	519	368	694
North and West	279	256	634
Urban South	290	246	527
Rural South	652	527	847

Components of Change in Ratio of Children to Women

	From 1910 to 1940	From 1940 to 1960
Total Change	—151	+326
Change attributable to:		
Fertility rates in North and West	—3	+93
Fertility rates in urban South	—11	+141
Fertility rates in rural South	—80	+182
Shifting distribution of population	—78	—95
Interaction of factors	+21	+5

Sources:
    U. S. Bureau of the Census, *Negro Population of the United States: 1790–1915*, p. 82.
    U. S. Bureau of the Census, *Sixteenth Census of the United States: 1940, Population, Characteristics of the Non-white Population by Race*, Table 3.
    U. S. Bureau of the Census, *Census of Population: 1960*, PC(2)–1C, Table 1.

in the rural South. Almost all Negroes in the North and West lived in cities. Ratios of children to women for each of these areas are shown in Table 5–4.

We might first consider the 1910 to 1940 change in the fertility ratio for the entire population. We might ask what the ratio of children to women would have been in 1940 if there had been no shift in the areal distribution of population and had no fertility ratio changed, except the fertility ratio in the North and West. If this had been the case, the national fertility ratio in 1940 would have been 516. In 1910, the ratio of children to women was 519. If the only change between 1910 and 1940 had been the change in the fertility rates of women in the North and West, the fertility ratio would have dropped only three points from 519 to 516. In this fashion, we have singled out the effect of this one component of change. In a similar manner, we isolated the changes attributable both to fluctuations in fertility rates and shifts in the areal distribution of the population.

Between 1910 and 1940, Negro fertility did not decline because the Negro women who lived in cities reduced their child-bearing. Changes in urban fertility rates were quite inconsequential. From 1910 to 1940, fertility did not decline singularly as a result of the urbanization of blacks. The decrease in child-bearing by rural southern Negroes played a role every bit as important as urbanization in bringing down the national fertility rate. Had there been no shift to urban residence, there still would have been a large decrease in Negro fertility. This means that the long term decline in Negro fertility must have been the result of the reduced childbearing of those Negro women who remained on the farms of the South.

The components of difference technique was also used to study the post-Depression rise in fertility and the results are shown in Table 5–4. The 1940 to 1960 increase in national fertility was a consequence of higher birth rates in each area of the country. Increases in urban fertility were an important component of the overall rise. The shifting distribution of Negroes did dampen the increase somewhat, for there was a migration away from the area with the highest fertility, the rural South. If this migration had not occurred, the 1960 ratio of children to women would have been even higher than it was.

Fertility Differences by Region of Birth

Demographers have observed that women who are reared in rural areas have different fertility patterns than those raised in cities. David Goldberg determined that women who migrated from farms to cities had substantially higher fertility rates than women who grew up in cities. Furthermore, among farm-born women who moved into cities, there were socio-economic differentials in fertility, while this was not the case among women from urban backgrounds.[22] O. Dudley Duncan recently studied a national sample of women and found that either coming from a non-farm background or having a high school education was sufficient to lead to controlled fertility.[23]

---

[22] David Goldberg, "Another Look at the Indianapolis Fertility Data," *Milbank Memorial Fund Quarterly* XXXVIII, No. 1 (January, 1960), 23–36; "The Fertility of Two Generation Urbanites," *Population Studies* XII, No. 3 (March, 1959), 214–222.

[23] Otis Dudley Duncan, "Farm Background and Differential Fertility," *Demography* II (1965), 240–249.

United States censuses have not asked women if they were born on farms or if they were reared in rural areas. They have asked questions about region of birth. Tabulations showing the fertility of women born in different regions may be used to make inferences about the effect rural background has on fertility. Until the mid-1950s, more than half of the Negroes in the South lived in rural areas, and fertility rates in rural areas were higher than those in urban areas. Women who were 15 to 44 in 1960 were born prior to 1945. We can be certain that in 1960 the majority of southern-born women at childbearing ages were born in rural areas. Earlier in this century, a much greater proportion of southern Negroes lived in rural areas. This implies that most of the southern-born women at childbearing ages in 1910 or 1940 were born in rural areas. The data in Table 3–2 show that, the majority of blacks who lived outside the South resided in urban places. Therefore, most northern-born Negroes were born and, presumably, raised in cities.

The top panel of Table 5–5 indicates the average number of children born to Negro women 15 to 44 by region of birth and region of current residence; the middle panel indicates the proportion of married women who were childless, and, the bottom panel shows the percentage of married women who had borne five or more children. The figures in this table have been standardized for age.

Table 5–5 contains some interesting findings. First, we observe that an identical fertility trend characterizes both southern and northern-born women. Fertility rates were lower in 1940 than in 1910 and childlessness was more common in 1940 than in 1910 among women born in both regions. Since 1940, fertility rates have gone up among women born in both regions.

Second, southern-born women are definitely more fertile than northern-born women. At each date, southern-born women had the higher average number of children and the higher proportion with five or more children. Apparently, being born and raised in a city did lead to lower fertility among Negroes.

Third, migrants apparently bear children at a different rate than non-migrants. Black women who were born in the South but moved North, bore fewer children than southern born women who remained in the South. In 1910 and 1940, these women who migrated to the North had even lower fertility rates than northern born women who remained in their region of birth. This indicates that first generation Negro migrants to northern cities

TABLE 5-5

Fertility Information for Negro Women, 15 to 44, by Region of Birth and Region of Present Residence, 1910, 1940 and 1960*

	1910	1940	1960
	Children Ever Born per 1000 Married Women		
Total	3017	1963	2526
Born in South	3100	1995	2676
Living in South	3214	2137	2913
Living outside South	1779	1482	2240
Born outside South	1962	1606	2056
Living in South	2392	1834	2513
Living outside South	1914	1589	1987
	Percent of Married Women Childless		
Total	21%	32%	19%
Born in South	21	32	19
Living in South	19	30	18
Living outside South	37	39	20
Born outside South	33	34	22
Living in South	36	39	9
Living outside South	34	33	23
	Percent with Five or More Children		
Total	25%	13%	18%
Born in South	26	15	19
Living in South	27	15	23
Living outside South	14	8	13
Born outside South	13	8	10
Living in South	18	14	14
Living outside South	13	8	10

* Rates in this table have been standardized for age. The age distribution of Negro women 15 to 44 in 1960 was chosen as the standard.

Sources:
  U. S. Bureau of the Census, *Sixteenth Census of the United States: 1940,* Population Differential Fertility: 1940 and 1910, Women by Numbers of Children Ever Born, Tables 6, 9, 12, 35, 38, 41 and 44; Records of 1 in 1,000 sample of 1960 Censuses.

have not had excessively large families. In fact, they typically bore fewer offspring than northern born women.

Northern-born women who moved to the South were very fertile, much more fertile than northern born women who remained in the North.

There is something anomalous about the fertility of women who migrated away from their region of birth. At each date, southern-born women who lived in the North bore fewer children than did northern born women who lived in the South. Selective migration may be a partial explanation. On the one hand, southern born women who have no children or few children or those who marry at late ages may find it easiest to move into the North. On the other hand, northern born women who get an early start on their childbearing may find it difficult to care for their children in northern cities. They may decide to migrate to the South and move in with relatives, perhaps in rural areas. Unfortunately, the censuses do not provide sufficient data to test these speculations.

Fertility Differences by Occupation of Husband

For many decades, the United States censuses have inquired about socio-economic status by asking about occupation or the ownership of property.[24] However, fertility was not related to socio-economic indicators until compilations were made from the Census of 1910, a census which provided tabulations of a woman's fertility by her husband's occupation. Similar information is available from the Censuses of 1940, 1950, and 1960 making it possible to study changes over time in the relationship of this socio-economic variable to fertility.

This information is available only for those Negro women who were married once and lived with their husbands at the time the census was taken. This is a selected group of Negro women. The figures below indicate that somewhat over one-half of the Negro married women ages 15 to 44 were in this married-once-spouse-present category.

Percentage of Married Negro Women Ages 15 to 44
Who Were Married-Once Spouse-Present[25]

1910	64%
1940	54%
1950	59%
1960	60%

Table 5–6 contains fertility information for Negro women grouped by their husband's occupation. The methods used to

24 A question about occupation was first asked in the Census of 1840; a question about value of property owned was first asked in the Census of 1850. Wright, *op. cit.*, p. 84–130.

25 U. S. Bureau of the Census, *Sixteenth Census of the United States: 1940*, Population, Differential Fertility: 1940 and 1910, Women by Number of Children Ever Born, Tables 18 and 20; *Census of Population: 1950*, P-E, No. 5C, Table 17; Records of 1 in 1,000 sample of 1960 Censuses.

TABLE 5–6
Fertility of Married-Once Spouse-Present Negro
Women 15 to 44 by Occupation of Husband, 1910–1960[a]

	1910	1940	1950	1960
	Children Ever Born Per 1000 Married Women			
Total	3274	2147	2115	2730
White collar[b]	2155	1308	1517	1915
Craftsmen	2542	1798	1876	2699
Operative	2615	1755	1982	2673
Service worker	1783	1378	1516	2294
Non-farm laborer	2670	1879	2042	2993
Farmer, farm laborer	3912	3005	3200	4098
	Percent of Married Women Childless			
Total	22%	33%	31%	19%
White collar[b]	33	46	34	25
Craftsmen	28	36	32	17
Operative	26	40	31	18
Service worker	40	46	37	19
Non-farm laborer	27	37	30	17
Farmer, farm laborer	16	22	20	15

[a] Rates in this table have been standardized for age using the age distribution of Negro women 15 to 44 in 1960 as a standard. Figures for 1950 refer to non-whites. Methods of defining occupation and labor force status of husband vary from census to census. See sources for details.

[b] White collar includes professional, managerial, clerical and sales occupations.

Sources:

U. S. Bureau of the Census, *Sixteenth Census of the United States: 1940*, Population, Differential Fertility: 1940 and 1910, Fertility by Duration of Marriage, Tables 12 and 14.

U. S. Bureau of the Census, *Census of Population: 1950*, P-E, No. 5C, Table 29; Records of 1 in 1,000 sample of 1960 Censuses.

define labor force participation and to define occupational categories changed between 1910 and 1960. The sources which are listed in the table provide specific details.

This table indicates very clearly that there are socio-economic differentials in Negro fertility and that these have existed for as long as data have been available. The fertility rates of Negro women do vary in a systematic fashion according to husband's occupation. Women who were married to white collar workers or service workers had low fertility rates, the wives of blue collar workers had higher fertility rates, and the wives of farmers and farm laborers had the highest fertility. This has been true from 1910 to the present.

It seems reasonable that wives of white collar workers should have low fertility, for these women are likely to be well educated, to marry later in life and to live in cities. Presumably, these factors lead to smaller families. It is more mysterious why low fertility and a high incidence of childlessness should characterize wives of service workers. An examination of this occupational category reveals that, until recently, many of the Negro men who worked at service occupations were employed as janitors, sextons, porters or domestic servants.[26] Some of these men may have been required to live at their places of work. Perhaps because of this requirement, service employers selected Negro couples who had either no children or very few children.[27]

At each date, wives of craftsmen, operatives and non-farm laborers had fertility rates which were quite similar. There is no evidence to suggest that there were childbearing differentials within the blue collar group. Wives of the most highly skilled and highly paid blue collar workers—wives of craftsmen—had fertility rates which were similar to those of women married to manual workers.

Between 1910 and 1940, fertility rates declined and childlessness increased among women in each occupation-of-husband category. Occupational differentials in fertility changed very little during this time period. Since 1940, fertility rates have gone up among women in each group. The increases, however, have been greatest among wives of blue collar workers and least among wives of white collar workers. This has led to greater occupational differentials in fertility. Even if the wives of farmers are excluded, it is obvious that occupational differences in childbearing were greater in 1960 than in 1940 or 1910. On the other hand, differentials in childlessness have decreased, and, among each category of women, childlessness was lower in 1960 than fifty years earlier. In 1960, the only women with an unusually high incidence of childlessness were the Negro women married to white collar workers.[28]

Among whites, there have been occupational differences in fertility from 1910 to the present. However, recent investigations have found that occupational differences in white fertility are rapidly diminishing. Wives of farmers expect and bear a larger

---

[26] U. S. Bureau of the Census, *Sixteenth Census of the United States: 1940*, Population, Occupational Characteristics, Table 1; *Census of Population: 1950*, P-E, No. 1B, Table 7; *Census of Population: 1960*, PC(2)–7A, Table 7.

[27] Grabill, Kiser, and Whelpton, *op. cit.*, p. 149.

[28] *Ibid.*, p. 135; U. S. Bureau of the Census, *Census of Population: 1960*, PC(2)–3A, Table 31.

number of children, but there are only small differences in the childbearing patterns of white wives who are married to non-farm workers and these differences are apparently being eliminated.[29]

Educational Attainment Differentials

It has often been asserted that educational attainment is inversely related to fertility. In the last century, Herbert Spencer claimed that educated women bore fewer children than less educated women,[30] and studies conducted during the 1930s[31] and early 1940s[32] demonstrated that this, indeed, was the case. Data for the national population concerning the relationship of educational attainment to childbearing first became available with the Census of 1940 and succeeding censuses have provided additional information. Table 5–7 shows fertility data for Negro women grouped by their educational attainment. The top panel indicates the average number of children born per 1,000 women, the middle panel shows the proportion of women who were childless, and the bottom panel shows the proportion of women who had five or more children.

Educational attainment is inversely related to fertility among blacks. At each date, the women with the highest fertility were those who had no more than an elementary school education. The proportion childless was lowest and the proportion with five or more children was greatest among those Negro women who completed few years of school.

Negro women who graduated from high school or who attended college bore relatively few children and a large proportion of these women remained childless for their entire lives. College educated women bore far fewer children than similarly educated white women.[33] For instance, among Negro women ages 40 to 44, in 1960, who had a high school education, there was an

---

29 Freedman, Whelpton, and Campbell, *op. cit.*, pp. 305–309; Grabill, Kiser, and Whelpton, *op. cit.*, p. 181; Whelpton, Campbell and Patterson, *op. cit.*, p. 113.

30 Herbert Spencer, *The Principles of Biology*, II (New York: Appleton and Co., 1968), p. 485.

31 Clyde V. Kiser, *Group Differences in Urban Fertility* (Baltimore: Williams and Watkins, 1942), p. 91.

32 Pascal K. Whelpton and Clyde V. Kiser (eds.), *Social and Psychological Factors Affecting Fertility*, I (New York: Milbank Memorial Fund 1946), p. 31.

33 Clyde V. Kiser and Myrna E. Frank, "Factors Associated with the Low Fertility of Nonwhite Women of College Attainment," *Milbank Memorial Fund Quarterly* XLV (October, 1967), 427–450.

average of 2100 children per 1000 women, and about 23 percent were childless.[34] Among the similar group of white women, only 14 percent were childless and there were 2300 children per 1000 women.[35] For a group of women to bear enough children to replace themselves in the next generation, they must have an average of about 2.4 children in their lifetimes.[36] A study of the data used to compute Table 5–7 reveals that, as of 1960, no group of Negro women who graduated from high school had borne enough children to replace themselves.

Between 1940 and 1960, the fertility of women at each educational level increased and childlessness became less common. During this span, educational differentials in fertility gradually widened because the fertility of women with few years of school completed increased more rapidly than the fertility of women with many years of education. A look at trends in childlessness and the proportion of women with five children indicates more about these widening fertility differentials. The change in childlessness would have reduced fertility differences, other things being equal, because it decreased among women in all groups. On the other hand, there was a sharp rise in the proportion of women with a grammar school education who had at least five children but only a modest rise in this proportion among the college educated. We can infer that the fertility differential increased because a larger proportion of the women with little education added fifth, sixth, and higher order children. Although there was a rise in fertility among the highly educated women, there was little change in the proportion who had five or more children.

It would be interesting to trace educational differences in fertility to see if they developed recently or if they are of long-standing duration. The Census of 1910 provided some relevant information, for fertility rates were tabulated for literate and illiterate women. Persons were designated as literate if they answered, "Yes," to a question asking if they could read English

---

[34] Records of 1 in 1,000 sample of 1960 Censuses.

[35] U. S. Bureau of the Census, *Census of Population: 1960*, PC (2)–3A, Table 25.

[36] At 1940 mortality levels, Negro women would have had to average 2.5 children in order to replace themselves. At 1950 and 1960 mortality levels, the figure was 2.3 children. U. S. Bureau of the Census, *Sixteenth Census of the United States: 1940*, United States Life and Actuarial Tables: 1939–41, Table 9; U. S., National Office of Vital Statistics, *United States Life Tables: 1949–51*, Vital Statistics Special Reports, Vol. XLI, No. 1 (November 23, 1954), Table 9; U. S., National Center for Health Statistics, *Life Tables: 1959–61*, I, No. 1 (December, 1964), Table 9.

TABLE 5–7
Fertility Information for Negro Women 15 to 44
by Educational Attainment: 1940 to 1960*

Educational Attainment	1940	1950	1960
	Children Ever Born per 1000 Ever Married Women		
Total	1963	1902	2526
College 4+	810	955	1352
College 1–3	1137	1148	1738
High school 4	1291	1316	1920
High school 1–3	1647	1807	2602
Elementary	2103	2170	3048
	Percent of Ever Married Women Childless		
Total	32%	32%	20%
College 4+	56	48	29
College 1–3	47	42	25
High school 4	43	39	26
High school 1–3	35	31	17
Elementary	30	29	16
	Percent of Ever Married Women with Five or more Children		
Total	13%	12%	18%
College 4+	2	2	3
College 1–3	5	4	5
High school 4	6	5	11
High school 1–3	9	10	18
Elementary	15	12	25

* The figures in this table have been standardized for age using the age distribution of Negro females 15 to 44 in 1960 as the standard. Figures showing fertility by educational attainment for 1950 pertain to non-whites.

Sources:

U. S. Bureau of the Census, *Sixteenth Census of the United States: 1940*, Population, Differential Fertility: 1940 and 1910, Women by Number of Children Ever Born, Table 50.

U. S. Bureau of the Census, *Census of Population: 1950*, PE-5C, Table 22.

U. S. Bureau of the Census, *Census of Population: 1960*, PC(2)–3A, Table 8; Records of 1 in 1,000 sample of 1960 Censuses.

or any other language. In 1910, 70 percent of the Negro population age 10 years and over reported they were literate.[37] Shown below is fertility information for women ages 15 to 44 in 1910.[38]

---

[37] U. S. Bureau of the Census, *Thirteenth Census of the United States: 1910*, I. p. 1191. These rates have been standardized for age.

[38] U. S. Bureau of the Census, *Sixteenth Census of the United States: 1940*, Population, Differential Fertility: 1940 and 1910, Women by Number of Children Ever Born, Table 53.

	Children Ever Born per 1,000 Women	Proportion Childless	Proportion with Five or more Children
Literate	2,829	23%	23%
Illiterate	3,273	17	30

These figures indicate that educational differences in black fertility are of long standing duration, for early in this century literate women had substantially lower fertility rates than illiterate women. This was not simply the result of literate women living in cities; in both urban and rural areas illiterate black women bore many more children than literate women.[39]

Among white women, educational attainment is also inversely related to childbearing but there are racial differences in the relationship of these variables. Data from the Census of 1960 indicate that, at lower educational attainment levels, the fertility of Negro women has exceeded that of white women. At the higher educational attainment levels, that is among women with some college education, it is the Negro women who bear fewer children.[40]

The 1955 Growth of American Families Study found that the crucial educational distinction among white women was whether or not the woman had some high school education. The only women who had unusually large numbers of children or who were particularly unsuccessful at planning their families were women who had not gone beyond grammar school.[41] Among white women, those women with a college education were about as fertile as women who had a complete high school education. Among Negro women, the pattern is different, for each increment in educational attainment is associated with a substantial decrease in fertility.

Recent studies of national trends in white fertility suggest that educational differences are declining.[42] Apparently, almost all white women are going to bear two to four children regardless of their educational attainment. Among Negroes, educational differentials are apparently not diminishing; rather, they grew larger between 1940 and 1960.

---

[39] *Ibid.*, Table 118.
[40] U. S. Bureau of the Census, *Census of Population: 1960*, PC(2)–3A, Table 25.
[41] Freedman, Whelpton, and Campbell, *op. cit.*, pp. 290–291.
[42] Freedman, Whelpton, and Campbell, *op. cit.*, p. 393; Grabill, Whelpton and Kiser, *op. cit.*, pp. 225–227.

TABLE 5–8
Fertility of Married-Once Spouse-Present Negro Women
15 to 44 in 1960 by Characteristics of Husband*

	Children Ever Born per 1000 Women	Percent Childless	Percent with Five or More Children
Educational Attainment of Husband			
College 4+	1694	24%	10%
College 1–3	2327	12	11
High school 4	1952	26	9
High school 1–3	2462	21	17
Eiementary school	3152	16	27
Income of Husband in 1959			
$5,000 or more	2215	19%	12%
$4,000 to 4,999	2648	15	19
$3,000 to 3,999	2520	23	16
$2,000 to 2,999	2884	18	24
$1,000 to 1,999	2941	20	25
Less than $1,000	3324	20	29

* These data refer to Negro women 15 to 44 in 1960 who were married-once, spouse-present. They have been standardized for age.

Source:
Records of 1 in 1,000 sample of 1960 Censuses.

Fertility Differences by Husband's Education or Husband's Income

Two frequently used indicators of socio-economic status are a man's income and his educational attainment. Tabulations showing wife's fertility by these variables are available from the Census of 1960. Table 5–8 contains these fertility data. It indicates the average number of children ever born, the proportion of women childless and the proportion of women with five or more children. These data pertain to women who were married once and who were living with their husbands at the time of the Census of 1960.

The husband's educational attainment is related to childbearing, for women who are married to men who have only an elementary school education bore almost twice as many children as women married to men who had a complete college education.

Similarly, husband's income in 1959 was related to fertility, for wives of men who earned less than one thousand dollars had borne many more children than wives of men who earned five thousand dollars or more. The proportion of women who went on to have large families, that is, five or more children, was also inversely related to the husband's socio-economic characteristics. Childlessness, on the other hand, was not linked to socio-economic variables in any systematic manner. It appears that by 1960, the proportion of black wives who were childless was pretty much the same regardless of the husband's income or his education.

Summary

In this chapter, differentials in the fertility of blacks have been analyzed and the evidence leads to a number of conclusions. It is clear that differentials in Negro fertility are very similar to those observed among white women in the United States. Black women in rural areas have higher fertility rates than black women in urban areas. Negro women who are married to men with white collar jobs bore fewer children than women married to men with less prestigious jobs, and women who are well educated have had fewer offspring than women who attended school for only a short time. In addition, we can infer that Negro women from an urban background typically completed their families with a smaller number of children than women from a rural background. Thus, black women resemble other groups of women in that socio-economic variables and rural or urban status affects their fertility.

We can be certain that the same general trends in fertility occurred among all groups of black women, although there were differences in the timing of fertility changes. From the late nineteenth century until the Depression, fertility rates declined. This was true among women in rural areas as well as among women who lived in cities; among women with the characteristics of higher social status, and among those who had little education or who were married to unskilled workers. It was true among both women from rural and urban backgrounds. Not only did fertility rates fall prior to 1940, but also the proportion of married women who were childless increased among all groups of black women. It is impossible to isolate any major groups of Negro women who did not participate in the pre-1940 fall in fertility or the post-1940 increase.

It is more difficult to draw unqualified conclusions about whether differentials in Negro fertility have diminished or grown wider. Generally, as fertility rates declined before 1940, socio-economic and rural-urban differentials decreased just a bit. Since then, the differentials appear to have grown wider, for the fertility rates of urban women and women of higher socio-economic status increased less than did the fertility rates of rural women or women of lower socio-economic status. A comparison of changes in the proportion of women who have five or more children suggests that there may be emerging differences in the control of fertility. The proportion of women with large numbers of children increased most rapidly among rural women and among women of lower status. This recent widening of fertility differentials then, may indicate that since the end of the Depression, some groups within the black population have adopted effective control of fertility while others have not.

Finally, data presented in this chapter indicate that the fertility rates of black women generally exceeded those of similar groups of white women. To be sure, this is not true of all groups. For instance, until after World War II, black women in cities bore children at a lower rate than white women in cities. Also, college educated Negro women have had lower fertility rates than college educated white women. These, however, are the exceptions. Among rural women and among women who have little education, Negro fertility rates have been much higher than those of comparable white women at all dates for which data are available.

Chapter 6

TRENDS IN MARITAL STATUS AND THEIR EFFECT UPON FERTILITY

Previous chapters discussed national trends in Negro fertility and described differentials in childbearing. However, important questions remain unanswered. We have said little about marriage and family among blacks. We need to analyze marital status trends, for changes in fertility levels could possibly be the result of changes in marital status. Since World War II, the proportion of blacks with the characteristics of higher social and economic status has increased. For instance, in 1940, only 5 percent of the employed Negro males worked at white collar jobs but, in 1967, 23 percent worked at such jobs.[1] Just prior to World War II, 6 percent of the Negro males age 25 and over had a complete high school education but, by 1968, 29 percent of the same age group had graduated from high school.[2] These changes in social and economic status may have made it easier for black men to marry, and, once married, easier for them to remain married. Such a change in marital status may have increased the number of Negro women at risk of bearing a child and this may have contributed to the changing fertility rates.

Many differentials in black fertility were described, but there

---

[1] The figure for 1940 refers to employed Negro males 14 and over, while the figure for 1967 refers to employed non-white males 16 and over. U. S. Bureau of the Census, *Sixteenth Census of the United States: 1940*, Population, Characteristics of the Non-white Population by Race, Table 8; "Recent Trends in Social and Economic Conditions of Negroes in the United States," *Current Population Reports*, Series P–23, No. 26 (July, 1968), p. 16.

[2] U. S. Bureau of the Census, *Sixteenth Census of the United States: 1940*, Population, Characteristics of the Non-white Population by Race, Table 6; "Educational Attainment: March, 1968" *Current Population Reports*, Series P–20, No. 182 (April 28, 1969), Table 1.

was one which was omitted, namely marital status differentials. We did not determine whether women who remained married to their first husband bore more children than did women whose marriage was interrupted by divorce or desertion.

This chapter discusses changes in marital status of blacks and the effect these changes have had upon fertility rates.

Perspective on the Family System of Blacks

The Views of Frazier

The most extensive description of the development of the Negro family system in the United States and trends in marital status was written by E. Franklin Frazier.[3] In Frazier's view, economic factors, rather than cultural values, were a primary determinant of the family system of Negroes. He believed there were three major economic and social periods for the black family in this country. First was the era of slavery extending from the time blacks entered the colonies until the Civil War. The second period lasted from the Emancipation to World War I. The final period, characterized by the urbanization of blacks, began during World War I and continues to the present.

Frazier observed that before coming into the colonies, Africans were stripped of their social heritage. Slaves from different tribes and language groups were mixed in the caravans in Africa and during Middle Passage. If they wished to communicate they had to use the language of their captors. Once they reached the Americas, their masters attempted to inculcate some European religious practices and cultural values. Many of the slaves brought into the United States were descendents of West Indian blacks. The time spent in the West Indies supposedly removed African customs and made blacks more docile and obedient to their masters.[4]

Besides the cultural vacuum, other factors worked against the development of a stable family system. In the early days of slavery, the black population contained many more males than females. Frazier argued that this unbalanced sex ratio encouraged casual sexual contacts.[5] In addition, numerous slave owners

---

[3] E. Franklin Frazier, *The Negro Family in the United States*, rev. ed. (Chicago: University of Chicago Press, 1966).

[4] *Ibid.*, Chap. i.

[5] *Ibid.*, p. 24.

looked upon their black women as accessible sexual partners, and many black females were used as concubines regardless of the ties these women had to their own children or husband.[6] Even more important, Frazier believed, was the absence of legal marriage. A male slave could not guarantee support for his own wife and children since he was employed only so long as his master wished. The slave could not own property or secure an income to support a family. He could not prevent his wife from leaving him for another man nor could he keep his children with him.[7]

Within this cultural milieu, Frazier believed that a maternal family system developed. The most important bonds, and in some cases the only bonds, were the ties of affection which linked a mother to her small children. The husband's involvement varied. In some cases, the husband played an important role and remained with his wife permanently; in other cases, the father's involvement ceased with impregnation.

Prior to Emancipation, about 10 percent of the black population was free.[8] About one-half of the free Negroes lived in the South, the other half in the North.[9] Although little is known about these free Negroes, Frazier believed that their family system was very different from that of slaves.[10] He presented a number of examples of free men in New Orleans, Philadelphia and Charleston who learned trades, established businesses, and maintained stable families and households. In Frazier's view, a stable family system gradually emerged among these free blacks even before the Civil War.

To many blacks, Emancipation meant the freedom to move about; as we noted in Chapter 3, many slaves left their plantations and flocked to the Union lines or to southern cities upon hearing of their freedom. Frazier believed that promiscuous sex and casual mating became the pattern after the Civil War, for blacks moved frequently and changed their mates just about as

---

[6] In 1860, 13 percent of the Negro population or 600,000 people were enumerated as mulattoes. This suggests that interracial mating was not uncommon. However, as noted in Chapter 2, the term mulatto was not rigorously defined. U. S. Bureau of the Census, *Negro Population in the United States: 1790–1915*, pp. 207–208.

[7] E. Franklin Frazier, "The Changing Status of the Negro Family," *Social Forces* IX, No. 3 (March, 1931), 386.

[8] U. S. Bureau of the Census, *Negro Population in the United States: 1790–1915*, p. 55.

[9] *Ibid.*, p. 55.

[10] E. Franklin Frazier, *The Free Negro Family* (Nashville: Fisk University Press, 1932), Chap. iii.

often. Families may have been even more disrupted in this period than before, because the ties which bound a slave to his plantation and which restricted the movement of slaves were no longer binding.[11]

For most of the black population, there was a continuation of the matriarchal family system after the Civil War. Often, these were inter-generational families in which a woman cared both for her own children and for her daughter's children. Illegitimacy was common and carried no stigma. Indeed, additional children might be welcome because many blacks were sharecroppers or lived on one-horse farms where children could chop and pick cotton at an early age.

Some blacks discovered economic opportunities during and after Reconstruction. In rural areas, sometimes with the aid of the Freedman's Bureau, it became possible for Negroes to own their own farms. In the growing cities of the South, some black men found steady jobs in the service trades, with manufacturing firms or on railroads, and a few became teachers or ministers. Frazier argued that these aspiring middle class Negroes adopted the norms and values of white society.[12] Many saved money and purchased their own homes, and by 1890, one-quarter of the rural black families and one-sixth of those who lived in cities owned their own homes.[13] These Negroes attempted to educate their children within their stable patriarchal families:

> Generally, these families have attempted to maintain standards of conduct and to perpetuate traditions of family life that were alien to the majority of the Negro population. Where they have been few in numbers, they have often shut themselves up within the narrow circle of their own families in order not to be overwhelmed by the flood of immorality and vice surrounding them. In some places, they have been numerous enough to create a society of their own in which they could freely pursue their way of life and insure a congenial environment to their children. Often intensely conscious of their peculiar position with reference to the great mass of the Negro population, they have placed an exaggerated valuation upon moral conduct and cultivated a puritanical restraint in opposition to the free and uncontrolled behavior of the larger Negro world.[14]

---

[11] Frazier, *The Negro Family in the United States*, Part 2.
[12] *Ibid.*, Chap. xii.
[13] *Ibid.*, p. 247.
[14] *Ibid.*, p. 246.

The boll weevil entered the United States in 1893 and gradually spread eastward from Texas, devastating crops in state after state and reducing the number of people who could be supported by cotton. Particularly hard hit were sharecroppers and tenant farmers who lacked the financial resources to either control weevils or shift into other crops. During World War I, manufacturing output increased, but immigration from Europe ceased. Therefore, northern firms recruited labor in the South. The combination of economic stagnation in rural areas and job opportunities in the North produced an out-migration of Negroes from the South.

Frazier believed this stream of urban migrants included two very different groups of Negroes. One group was composed of unattached men and women who moved about in search of jobs and excitement. These people did not come from a background of stable families and were not interested in binding marital ties. Frazier presented the picture of a "Black Ulysses" wandering from city to city, from job to job and from woman to woman.[15]

Another component of the migration stream was men with stable families who moved into cities and either brought their families with them or intended to do so. However, once in the city, they found it impossible to maintain their families. First, there was the problem of housing. The accomodations available to blacks were in the most dilapidated sections of town. Even in these areas, housing was so scarce and expensive that one family frequently had to take in another family or roomers in order to pay the rent. Second, there was the problem of income. Jobs were plentiful during World War I but manufacturing output and employment declined during the 1920s. During the Depression, the shortage of jobs became even more critical. Black men found themselves out of work, without marketable skills and unable to support their children. Faced with these difficulties, many men left their families and joined the growing number of "Black Ulysses." Family dissolution and high rates of illegitimacy were, in Frazier's view, inevitable consequences of the urbanization of Negroes.[16]

Frazier wrote during the 1930s. Looking ahead, he foresaw two conflicting trends. On one hand, diminishing opportunities

---

[15] E. Franklin Frazier, "The Impact of Urban Civilization upon Negro Family Life," *American Sociological Review* II (October, 1937), 611.

[16] Frazier, *The Negro Family in the United States*, Chaps. xv and xvi.

in southern agriculture would force more and more blacks to move into cities. Once in cities, these people would find themselves impoverished, ignorant and segregated. They would be unable to earn enough money or find sufficient housing to maintain a family. Since the majority of blacks were in this category, Frazier foresaw a trend toward increasing familial instability.

On the other hand, a more differentiated social structure was going to emerge among blacks in cities. More Negroes would obtain an education and qualify for high paying jobs. The expanding black population would provide a market for goods and services produced or sold by other blacks. These expanded economic opportunities insured the growth of a black middle class— a class which would, in Frazier's opinion, rapidly adopt the stable family norms of white society.[17]

The Moynihan Report

In 1965, the Department of Labor published a report entitled "The Negro Family: The Case for National Action."[18] Daniel Patrick Moynihan wrote this report which elicited much response from civil rights leaders and prompted vigorous discussion by the press of the state of the Negro family and the appropriate role for government action in this field.[19]

Moynihan argued that numerous changes favorable to the Negro occurred during the 1950s and early 1960s. Typical of these changes were the Supreme Court decision of 1954 outlawing segregated schools, the initiation of various federal programs for job retraining, the civil rights bills enacted by Congress, the investigations of discriminatory practices carried out by federal agencies and the continuing years of prosperity. As a result of these developments, Moynihan argued, the economic status of many Negroes improved and a large proportion of young blacks was advancing to opportunities denied to all blacks just a few years earlier.[20]

---

17 *Ibid.*, Chapter xx. Frazier's impressions of socio-economic differences in the types of urban Negro families are also discussed in E. Franklin Frazier, *Negro Youth at the Crossways* (New York: Schocken Books, 1967), Chap. ii.

18 U. S., Department of Labor, *The Negro Family: The Case for National Action* (Washington: Department of Labor, Office of Policy Planning and Research, 1965).

19 Lee Rainwater and William L. Yancey (eds.), *The Moynihan Report and the Politics of Controversy* (Cambridge: The M. I. T. Press, 1967).

20 U. S., Department of Labor, *op. cit.*, p. 4.

However, at the same time that one segment of the Negro population was making great socio-economic advances, Moynihan believed that there was another segment of the black population which was not sharing the prosperity. Their earning power and opportunities were not increasing and they were falling behind, not only the white population, but also behind middle class blacks.[21]

A breakdown in Negro family life, symptomatic of the problems of the impoverished blacks, exacerbated the troubles of the next generation. Moynihan argued that Frazier's prediction had indeed come true. Negro family life was becoming less stable. Moynihan reached this conclusion after observing that: the percentage of non-white births which were illegitimate had gone up since 1948;[22] the percentage of married Negro women who were separated[23] or divorced[24] increased since the mid-1950s; the proportion of Negro families headed by a woman went up since the early 1950s;[25] and the number of Negro children assisted by Aid-to-Dependent Children programs increased steadily.[26]

The breakdown of Negro families insured, in Moynihan's view, that many black children would grow up facing insurmountable handicaps. Negro children who lived apart from both of their parents were likely to achieve at a low level when they were enrolled in school,[27] and to drop out of school at an early age.[28] They were more likely to engage in delinquent activities[29] than children who lived with both parents.

The major reason for the continuing increase in the disruption of Negro families, Moynihan believed, was the lack of economic opportunities for Negro men. Despite general prosperity, there was a persistently high level of unemployment among Negroes. During the early years of the 1960s, between one-tenth and one-eighth of the Negro males were out of work.[30] As a result of this economic insecurity many Negro men were unable to support their wives and children.

---

21 *Ibid.*, p. 5.
22 *Ibid.*, p. 59.
23 *Ibid.*, p. 58.
24 *Ibid.*, p. 77.
25 *Ibid.*, p. 62.
26 *Ibid.*, p. 63.
27 *Ibid.*, p. 36.
28 *Ibid.*, p. 37.
29 *Ibid.*, pp. 39–40.
30 *Ibid.*, p. 67.

Trends in Marital Status

Few studies have analyzed the extensive data collected by the decennial censuses to determine what changes over time have occurred in the marital or family status of Negroes or what implications changes in marital status have for fertility. This chapter analyzes these data.

National Trends

Since 1890, the decennial censuses have asked adults whether they were currently single, married, widowed or divorced. More recently, the Census Bureau has asked this question annually of a sample of the population. Table 6–1 shows the marital status distribution of Negroes ages 15 and over for the period 1890 to 1968. The age composition of any population affects its marital status distribution. For example, a population of teenagers includes many single persons while a population composed of the elderly includes many widows and widowers. To eliminate the confounding effect of fluctuations in the age structure, the fig-

TABLE 6–1
Marital Status of Negroes 15 and Over: 1890–1967.*

	Negro Females				
Date	Total	Single	Married	Widowed	Divorced
1890	100%	20%	57%	22%	1%
1900	100	21	56	22	1
1910	100	19	58	22	1
1920	100	19	59	21	1
1930	100	19	57	22	2
1940*	100	20	58	20	2
1950*	100	18	62	17	3
1957*	100	21	60	16	3
1958*	100	21	60	16	3
1959*	100	20	61	16	3
1960*	100	20	62	14	4
1961*	100	20	61	15	4
1962*	100	22	60	14	4
1963*	1C0	22	60	14	4
1964	100	20	63	13	4
1965	100	21	62	13	4
1966	100	21	61	14	4
1967*	100	21	61	14	4
1968	100	21	59	15	5

Table 6–1 (Cont'd)

			Negro Males		
Date	Total	Single	Married	Widowed	Divorced
1890	100%	29%	65%	6%	–
1900	100	30	62	8	–
1910	100	29	62	8	1%
1920	100	28	63	8	1
1930	100	28	63	8	1
1940*	100	31	61	7	1
1950*	100	27	65	6	2
1957*	100	31	63	4	2
1958*	100	31	62	5	2
1959*	100	31	61	5	3
1960*	100	28	64	5	3
1961*	100	30	63	5	2
1962*	100	31	61	5	3
1963*	100	31	62	4	3
1964	100	30	64	4	2
1965	100	29	64	4	3
1966	100	30	62	4	4
1967*	100	29	63	5	3
1968	100	28	64	5	3

* These data have been standardized for age. The age distribution of the Negro population ages 15 and over in 1960 was used as the standard. Data for dates marked with an asterisk refer to non-whites.

Sources:

U. S., Census Office, *Eleventh Census of the United States: 1890*, Part III, p. 18.

U. S. Bureau of the Census, *Twelfth Census of the United States: 1900*, Vol. II, Table XLIX.

U. S. Bureau of the Census, *Thirteenth Census of the United States: 1910*, Vol. 1 Marital Condition, Table 14.

U. S. Bureau of the Census, *Fourteenth Census of the United States: 1920*, Vol. II Marital Condition, Table 2.

U. S. Bureau of the Census, *Fifteenth Census of the United States: 1930*, Vol. II, Marital Condition, Table 5, *Census of Population: 1960*, PC(1)–1D. Table 177.

U. S. Bureau of the Census, *Current Population Reports*, Series P–20, Nos. 81, 87, 96, 114, 122, 135, 142, 155, 168, 170, and 187.

ures in Table 6–1 have been standardized for age. The standard age distribution was that of blacks age 15 and over in 1960.[31]

Between 1890 and 1968, there was a geographic redistribution of blacks and a change in their economic and social position. Despite this shift away from rural farm residence, there has been little change in the marital status of blacks. In 1968, as in 1890, about one-fifth of the Negro females and three-tenths of the Negro males reported themselves single; that is, never mar-

---

[31] U. S. Bureau of the Census, *Census of Population: 1960*, PC(2)–1C, Table 1.

ried. Persons who had ever married should have reported themselves as married, widowed, or divorced.

Although there has been some fluctuation during the last eighty years in the proportion of single Negroes, it is difficult to detect any major long run shifts in the timing of marriage. As examination of the data used to construct Table 6–1 reveals, there have been some periods in which the marriage pattern changed so appreciably that the marital status distributions of all adult Negroes were altered. After the turn of the century, very slight decennial decreases in the proportion that was single were recorded. During the Depression decade, however, the marriage rate was atypically low; and the Census of 1940 found that an unusually large proportion of adults were single. In contrast, during the prosperous 1940s, age at marriage fell and the Census of 1950 recorded that only a small proportion was single.

While there has been little change in the single proportion, there has been a shift over time in the current marital status reported by blacks who report themselves as having married at some time in the past. The proportion who are widowed has fallen rather steadily. Around the turn of the century, more than one-fifth of the adult Negro women reported they were widows; by the 1960s, only one-seventh were widows. Among males, the proportion reporting themselves as widowers fell from about 8 to 4 percent during the same period.

At this point, we need to observe that there are large differences between the marital status distributions of Negro males and females. At each date, the proportion *single* was much higher among males than among females, but the proportion *widowed* was higher among women. There are many causes for this discrepancy. There are differences in the age composition of the male and female populations and sex differentials in undercount; that is, censuses enumerate females more completely than males.[32] Also, remarriage rates are much higher among males than among females.[33] Many men who become widowers may remarry and this would have the effect of reducing the proportion of males who report they are widowers. Divorced or widowed women, on the other hand, may find it difficult to remarry since the number

---

[32] Coale, *loc. cit.*, p. 29; U. S. Bureau of the Census, "Estimates of the Population of the United States and Components of Change, by Age, Color, and Sex: 1950 to 1960," Table C–2.

[33] U. S. Bureau of the Census, *Census of Population: 1960*, PC(2)–4E, Table 2.

of older women far exceeds the number of men in similar age brackets. Studies of census accuracy indicate that marital status is not very reliably reported.[34] Vital statistics tabulations show that, in recent years, about one-quarter of the Negro births occur to unmarried women. Many of these women who have children may be reported by census takers as widowed or divorced, and this would reduce the proportion of women who are single but would have no affect upon the proportion of men in this marital status category. It is impossible to correct for these sources of error but they should be borne in mind when analyzing changes in marital status.

To return to a discussion of changes in reported current marital status, we note that the decrease in the relative numbers of widowers and widows has occurred almost entirely since 1930. The timing of the decrease in widowhood is similar to the timing of improvements in the mortality experience of blacks as indicated by vital statistics data. Negro mortality rates did not fall significantly until public health programs were initiated in the 1930s, but thereafter, they fell rapidly.[35] One very clear result of this change was a reduction in the frequency with which death terminated marriages. Increases in the rate at which widowed persons remarry have helped to reduce the proportion of adults who are widowed.

Divorce has become more common as a reported current marital status although, at present, no more than 4 percent of the adult Negroes report themselves divorced and not remarried at the time of the census. The rise in divorce has occurred since 1940. Among Negro women, increases in divorce have been more than offset by decreases in widowhood, but among men, the rise in divorce has matched the decrease in widowers.

The outcome of these opposite trends in the relative frequency of widowhood and divorce has been a modest increase in the proportion currently married among black females; from 57 percent in 1890 to about 60 percent in the mid-1960s. Among males, there has been neither an increase or decrease in the proportion who report they are married, which has consistently been about five-eighths of the adult population.

---

[34] U. S. Bureau of the Census, "Accuracy of Data on Population Characteristics as Measured by CPS-Census Match," *Evaluation and Research Program of the U. S. Censuses of Population and Housing: 1960*, Series ER 60, No. 5 (1964), Table 27.

[35] Moriyama, *op. cit.*

Trends in the marital status of different age groups were examined to see if there were different patterns of change. Among the young—people 15 years old to 24 years old—there have been substantial fluctuations in the proportion *single* and in the proportion *married*, reflecting the changing marriage rates of the different decades. Among people ages 25 to 44, the proportion who report they are currently married has increased, chiefly due to a sharp decrease in the proportion widowed. There has been little change in the marital status of Negroes ages 45 and over. The proportion widowed has fallen only slightly because the drop in the death rate at older ages has been smaller than the drop in the death rate at younger ages. There is little evidence of an increase in divorce among Negro men or women in this older age group.

Among whites, the long term trends in marital status have been similar to those among Negroes. The proportion that never married, that is, single, among both white men and women has fallen since 1900. The decrease has been greater among the men. Part of this change may be attributed to lower mortality rates, but there is another important cause. Early this century, foreign born immigrants comprised about 15 percent of the nation's white population.[36] This migration stream included large numbers of unmarried males, many of whom apparently remained unmarried for many years after they entered the United States.[37] The decrease in European migration to the United States has played some role in reducing the proportion of adult whites who are single.[38]

There have been persistent racial differences in reported marital status. The proportion who report they are single has always been slightly greater among Negroes than among whites, while the proportion currently married has been slightly greater among whites. Widowhood has been much more frequently reported by blacks but there has been little racial difference in the proportion divorced.

Changes in Age at Marriage

It is not easy to determine changes over time in the age at which people marry for this nation has never had, and still does

---

[36] C. Taeuber and I. B. Taeuber, *op. cit.*, p. 77.

[37] U. S., Census Office, *Twelfth Census of the United States: 1900*, Part II, pp. 254–255.

[38] U. S. Bureau of the Census, *Thirteenth Census of the United States: 1910*, Vol. I, p. 522; *Census of Population: 1960*, PC(1)–1D, Table 177.

Figure 6–1
Marital Status Distribution of Non-white Males and
Females by Age, 1960

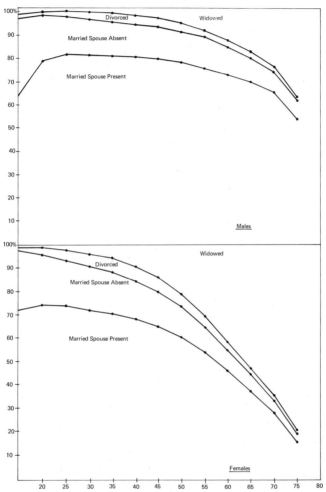

Source:
    U. S., Bureau of the Census, *Census of Population:* 1960 PC(1)–10
Table 176.

not have, a national system for registering marriages.[39] Four
censuses have included a question asking women when they married, but the format of this question was changed each time which

[39] In 1963, the Marriage Registration Area provided data for non-
whites in thirty-three states. U. S., National Center for Health Statistics,
Vital Statistics of the United States: 1963, Vol. III, Table 1–10.

TABLE 6–2
Proportion of Negroes Married by Specified Ages: 1890–1965.

	Males		Females	
Dates	15–19	20–24	15–19	20–24
1890	.9%	34.2%	15.0%	62.0%
1900	1.8	35.3	16.6	60.2
1910	2.3	39.9	18.2	65.1
1920	4.0	44.8	21.2	68.4
1930	3.9	45.1	22.0	66.9
1940	3.1	39.6	19.0	62.8
1950	4.4	45.3	21.1	68.8
1960	3.9	43.3	16.4	65.1
1965	1.4	43.9	11.3	65.8
1968	2.0	40.1	10.7	57.8

Source:
    Table 6–1.

hinders comparability.[40] Information about age at marriage must be inferred from census tabulations which show the proportions of various age groups who had married by the time of the census.

Table 6–2 shows the percentages of blacks who had married by the time they reached ages 15 to 19 and 20 to 24 for the period 1890 to 1965. Changes in these percentages reflect trends in the age at marriage. For instance, if youthful marriage becomes popular, the percentage of 15 to 19 year-olds who had married would go up. A rise in average age at marriage would be reflected by a decline in the proportion who had married by these young ages.

Table 6–2 reveals there have been changes in the ages at which blacks marry, although the changes appear quite small. Between 1890 and 1930, there was a trend toward earlier mar-

---

[40] In 1910, *married-spouse-present* women were asked how many years they had been married. In 1940, ever-married women were asked their age at first marriage. In 1950, men and women were asked the number of years they had spent in their current marital status. In 1960, men and women were asked in what year they had first married. Tabulations concerning age at marriage from the censuses of 1910, 1940 and 1950, have been published only for women who had married once and who lived with their husband at the time of the census. Leon E. Truesdell, *The Development of Punch Card Tabulation in the Bureau of the Census, 1890–1940* (Washington: Government Printing Office, 1965) ; U. S. Bureau of the Census, *Sixteenth Census of the United States: 1940*, Population, Differential Fertility: 1940 and 1910, Fertility by Duration of Marriage, p. 3; *Census of Population: 1950*, P-E, No. 2E, p. 4; *Census of Population: 1960*, PC(2)–4D, p. x.

riage, and the median age at which black men and women married declined during this span. The economic difficulties of the Depression encouraged blacks to delay marriage and the trend toward earlier marriage was reversed during the 1930s. Early marriage occurred frequently after World War II, and the Census of 1950 discovered that an unprecedentedly large proportion of the young population was married. This particularly affected the cohorts of black women born 1930 to 1934, cohorts which have distinguished themselves by their high fertility. The 1950s and 1960s witnessed a rise in the age at marriage. Table 6–2 indicates that a very small proportion of young Negroes in 1965 or in 1968 had married. This low percentage of married may indicate a new trend toward later marriage. However, these age groups were affected by the marriage squeeze and the low percentage of women who were married may only reflect a shortage of grooms. On the other hand, males were not affected by the marriage squeeze and the low proportion of this group which had married suggests a trend toward a rising age at marriage among blacks.

Among whites, trends in the age at marriage have moved in the same direction as among Negroes. Between 1890 and 1930, there was an increase in youthful marriages. The Depression had less effect upon age at marriage among whites than among Negroes, but in the following decade, the increase in early marriage was apparently greater among whites. Since 1960, there has been a trend toward older age at marriage among both whites and Negroes.

There has been very little fluctuation in the proportion of blacks who marry at some point in their lives. Table 6–3 shows estimates, derived from census data, of the proportion of birth cohorts of Negroes who ever married. About 95 percent of both the black males and females report that they married at some time. The only distinctive proportion ever-married belongs to the people who were born 1900 to 1909. These birth cohorts reached marriagable ages just before and during the Depression. The Depression, seemingly, had a lasting effect upon these Negroes, because an unusually large proportion remained single.

The pattern among whites is somewhat different than that among Negroes. There has been a consistent increase in the proportion of birth cohorts of whites who marry at some point in their life.[41]

---

[41] U. S. Bureau of the Census, *Census of Population: 1960*, PC(1)–1D, Table 177.

TABLE 6–3
Estimates of the Proportions of Cohorts of Negroes Who Are Ever-Married

Year Cohorts Born	Females	Males
1865–69	93.2%	95.9%
1870–74	92.9	95.8
1875–79	94.9	96.1
1880–84	94.4	96.1
1885–89	93.6	95.6
1890–94	93.0	95.6
1895–99	92.2	95.3
1900–04	89.6	93.1
1905–09	91.1	93.8
1910–14	91.5	94.1

Source:

  U. S. Bureau of the Census, Census of Population: 1960, PC(1)–10, Table 177; Negro Population in the United States: 1790–1915, p. 243.

Rural-Urban Trends

Frazier contended that some changes in the Negro family system resulted from urbanization. Information about the marital status of blacks, specific for rural or urban residence, is available for the period 1910 to the present. Table 6–4 contains this information. Again, the data have been standardized for age. The Bureau of the Census designated as urban all those people who lived in cities or towns of 2500 or more. The remainder of the population has been classed as rural.[42]

At one point in time, there were substantial rural-urban differentials in marital status. In 1910 and 1920, the proportion of blacks who reported they were single was very much greater in cities than in rural areas. In 1910, one-third of the men in cities, but only one-quarter of the men in rural areas, were single. Among those who had ever-married, there were also rural-urban differences, the proportion widowed or divorced being higher in cities than in rural areas.

---

[42] Beginning in 1950, the Bureau of the Census included as urban those individuals who lived in places of less than 2500 and in unincorporated areas if these areas were within or contiguous to the fringes of a large city of 50,000 or more. U. S. Bureau of the Census, *Census of Population: 1950*, P–C1, p. x.

TABLE 6–4
Marital Status of Negroes in Rural and Urban Areas: 1910–1960*

	Males						Females					
	1910	1920	1930	1940	1950	1960	1910	1920	1930	1940	1950	1960
Urban												
Total	100	100	100	100	100	100	100	100	100	100	100	100
Single	33	32	30	33	27	28	22	20	20	22	18	20
Married	57	58	59	59	65	64	51	53	52	53	60	61
Widowed	9	9	9	7	6	5	26	25	26	23	19	15
Divorced	1	1	2	1	2	3	1	2	2	2	3	4
Rural												
Total	100	100	100	100	100	100	100	100	100	100	100	100
Single	26	26	26	29	27	30	18	18	18	18	18	20
Married	65	66	65	64	67	64	64	63	61	64	67	65
Widowed	8	7	8	6	5	4	17	18	19	17	14	13
Divorced	1	1	1	1	1	2	1	1	2	1	1	2

* Standardized for age.

Sources:

U. S. Bureau of the Census, *Thirteenth Census of the United States: 1910,* Population, I, 586.

U. S. Bureau of the Census, *Fourteenth Census of the United States: 1920,* Population, II, 576.

U. S. Bureau of the Census, *Fifteenth Census of the United States: 1930,* Population, II, 848.

U. S. Bureau of the Census, *Sixteenth Census of the United States: 1940,* Population, IV, Part I, Table 6.

U. S. Bureau of the Census, *Census of Population: 1950* PC-1, Table 104.

U. S. Bureau of the Census, *Census of Population: 1960,* PC(1)–10, Table 176.

Rural-urban differences in marital status have decreased and have been nearly eliminated. The proportion single has gradually declined in cities and increased in rural areas. Widowhood has decreased as a reported marital status more rapidly in cities. As a result of these trends, cities no longer contain a distinctly small proportion of blacks who report they are currently married.

Trends in Desertion

The marital status data in Table 6–1 do not pertain to desertion; for some women, desertion may precede widowhood or divorce. On the other hand, if a woman's husband left her many years before the census date, she should report herself as married unless she has obtained a divorce or knows that her husband is dead. To minimize this difficulty, the Census Bureau introduced the categories "married-spouse-present" and "married-spouse-absent." If a woman reported that she was currently married, the enumeration schedule for her household was scanned to see if her husband was living with her. Similarly, if a man reported that he was currently married, the enumeration form was checked to ascertain the presence or absence of his wife. Thus, information about the presence of a spouse was obtained, not by asking a question, but rather by observing household composition. While the married-spouse-absent category includes women who have been deserted, other women are also in this group.

> This group includes married women whose families have been broken by separation (often preceding divorce), immigrants whose husbands were left abroad, wives of persons enumerated as inmates of institutions and other married women whose usual place of residence was not the same as that of their husbands, including wives of soldiers, sailors, men in labor camps, etc.[43]

Figure 6–1 shows the marital status distribution in 1960 of non-white males and females who had ever been married. At each age, the proportion living with a spouse was greater among males than among females. Upwards of three-quarters of the males and three-fifths of the ever-married women lived with their spouse when the Census of 1960 was taken. Among both sexes, the proportion *married-spouse-present* was at a peak for persons 20 to 29 and then declined at older ages.

The reasons for marital disruption changed with age. At the youngest ages, the absence of a spouse was the most common reason for disrupted marriages. Military service explains only a small portion of the separations reported by young women. For instance, in 1964, only 12 percent of the non-white women ages 14 to 24 who were married but did not live with their husbands, reported that their husbands were in military service.[44] At the older ages, the absence of a spouse became less common as the cause of marital disruption, and the death of the spouse was more frequently reported.

Trends over time in the current marital status of the ever-married population are shown in Table 6–5. These data have been

---

[43] U. S. Bureau of the Census, *Sixteenth Census of the United States: 1940*, Population, Differential Fertility: 1940 and 1910, Women by Number of Children Ever Born, p. 3.

[44] U. S. Bureau of the Census, "Marital Status and Family Status: March, 1964 and 1963," *Current Population Reports*, Series P-20, No. 135 (April 28, 1965), Table 4.

standardized for age to eliminate any effects that changes in the age composition might have. The data are shown for all years for which information is available.

The frequency with which desertion is discussed sometimes suggests that many married blacks live apart from their spouses. Such is not the case. At each date, about four-fifths of the married men and three-fifths of the married women lived with their mates.

Between 1910 and 1940, the proportion of ever-married women who lived apart from their husbands increased. Table 6–5 shows that only 5 percent of the women were *married-spouse-absent* in 1910, but this rose to 11 percent in 1940. During this span, there was very little change in the proportion of ever-married women who reported they were either widowed or divorced. As a result, the rise in the proportion *married-spouse-absent* had the net effect of reducing the proportion of married Negro women who lived with their husbands from 67 percent in 1910 to 62 percent in 1940.

Between 1940 and the present, the proportion of black women who were *married-spouse-absent* continued to increase; by 1968, 17 percent of the ever-married women were in this cate-

TABLE 6–5
Distribution of Ever-Married Negroes by
Current Marital Status: 1910–1967*

	Negro Females				
Date	Total	Married-Spouse-Present	Married-Spouse-Absent	Widowed	Divorced
1910	100%	67%	5%	27%	1%
1940	100	62	11	25	2
1950*	100	62	14	21	3
1957*	100	63	13	20	4
1958*	100	61	15	21	3
1959*	100	59	18	20	3
1960*	100	62	15	18	5
1961*	100	61	15	19	5
1962*	100	61	16	18	5
1963*	100	60	16	18	6
1964*	100	61	17	17	5
1965	100	60	18	17	5
1966	100	60	17	17	6
1967*	100	61	17	17	5
1968	100	58	16	19	6

Table 6–5 (Cont'd)

Date	Total	Married-Spouse-Present	Married-Spouse-Absent	Widowed	Divorced
		Negro Males			
1910		(Not Available)			
1940	100%	78%	11%	9%	2%
1950*	100	76	13	8	3
1957*	100	79	10	6	4
1958*	100	77	12	7	4
1959*	100	75	13	8	4
1960*	100	76	14	6	4
1961*	100	79	11	7	3
1962*	100	77	12	7	4
1963*	100	76	13	6	5
1964*	100	80	11	5	4
1965	100	77	13	6	4
1966	100	77	11	6	6
1967*	100	78	12	6	4
1968	100	76	13	7	4

* These data have been standardized for age. The age distribution of the Negro population ages 15 and over in 1960 was used as the standard. Data for dates marked with an asterisk refer to non-whites.

Sources:

U. S. Bureau of the Census, *Sixteenth Census of the United States: 1940*, IV, Part 1, Table 8; Differential Fertility: 1940 and 1910, Women by Number of Children Ever Born, Tables 12 and 16.

U. S. Bureau of the Census, *Census of Population: 1950*, PC–I, Table 104.

U. S. Bureau of the Census, *Census of Population: 1960*, PC(1)–1D, Table 176.

U. S. Bureau of the Census, *Current Population Reports*, Series P–20, Nos. 81, 87, 96, 114, 122, 135, 142, 155, 168, 170 and 187.

gory. There has also been a rise in the proportion who report they were divorced. Despite these changes, there has not been a fall in the proportion of women who lived with their husbands because of the rapid decline in widowhood. We conclude that in the last twenty-five or thirty years there has been little change in the proportion of married Negro women who lived with their husbands.

Examination of trends for specific age groups of women reveals much the same pattern. In particular, among women in the child rearing ages, decreases in widowhood have offset the recent increases in the proportion of women who were married but lived apart from their husbands.

Figures showing the presence of wives for Negro husbands are available only for the post-Depression period. During this span, there has been no change in the proportion of married men who lived with their wives. Increases in divorce have been offset by decreases in widowhood.

Moynihan and Frazier were correct in describing increases in desertion, but this observation needs elaboration and qualification. Improvements in health conditions and living standards have engendered greater marital stability by reducing the incidence of widowhood and, probably, have increased the ease with which people can remarry if their first marriage is terminated. As a result, there has been very little change in recent years in the proportion of married Negroes who live with their husbands or wives.

It is interesting to note that the proportion of married males reported as *spouse-absent* has not changed since 1940, but the proportion of married women reported as *spouse-absent* has increased. The census data do not indicate the causes of these trends. Since 1940, fertility rates have gone up and illegitimacy has apparently become more common, for the proportion of Negro births reported as illegitimate increased from 17 percent in 1940 to 29 percent in 1967.[45] Perhaps, these higher fertility rates have led to an increase in the number of single women who are reported as *married-spouse-absent* or changing welfare regulations may encourage some married women to indicate they are not living with their husbands. These factors may help to account for the change in the proportion of women who were married but lived apart from their husbands.

The Effects of Urbanization

The consequences of urbanization for marital status are not easy to measure. There have been changes from census to census in the types of tabulations which are provided; and, in addition, census data indicate a person's marital status at one point in time and do not provide either a marital or migration history.

We can infer, however, that city living has an effect, for there have always been rural-urban differences in the proportion of blacks who were married but did not live with a spouse. Information about marital status and desertion in rural and urban areas is contained in Table 6-6 which shows the marital status of

---

[45] U. S., National Center for Health Statistics, *Vital Statistics of the United States: 1967*, I, Table 1–24.

ever-married blacks in four geographic areas: the North and West, the entire South, the urban South, and the rural South. At each date, most blacks in the North and West lived in cities while the southern black population was primarily rural until the mid-1950s.[46] Data are shown for these four areas because few tabulations of marital status by presence of spouse have been published for the entire urban or rural population.

First, we can observe from the data in Table 6–6 that urban living is related to desertion. At each date, the proportion of married Negroes who lived apart from their spouses was higher in the North than in the South and higher in the urban South than in the rural South. Second, changes over time in widowhood and divorce have been the same in each area; the proportion widowed has declined while divorce has become more frequently reported

TABLE 6–6
Distribution of Ever-Married Negroes by Place of Residence and Current Marital Status: 1910–1960*

		Negro Women			
Date	Total	Married-Spouse-Present	Married-Spouse-Absent	Widowed	Divorced
		North and West			
1910	100%	62%	8%	27%	3%
1940	100	58	15	25	2
1950*	100	61	15	19	5
1960*	100	63	16	15	6
		Entire South			
1910	100	68	5	26	1
1940	100	65	10	23	2
1950*	100	65	13	19	3
1960*	100	65	15	16	4
		Urban South			
1910	100	54	8	36	2
1940	100	54	13	32%	
1960*	100	60	17	18	5
		Rural South			
1910	100	74	4	21	1
1940	100	73	7	20%	
1960*	100	72	12	14	2

[46] See Table 3–2.

Table 6–6 (Cont'd)

Date	Total	Married-Spouse-Present	Married-Spouse-Absent	Widowed	Divorced
		Negro Men			
		North and West			
1910	–				
1940	100%	72%	18%	8%	2%
1950*	100	72	16	8	4
1960*	100	75	15	5	5
		Entire South			
1910	–				
1940	100	81	11	7	1
1950*	100	80	12	6	2
1960*	100	79	13	5	3
		Urban South			
1910	–				
1940	–				
1960*	100	77	14	6	3
		Rural South			
1910	–				
1940					
1960*	100	81	12	5	2

* These data have been standardized for age. The age distribution of the Negro popula-tion age 15 and over in 1960 was used as the standard. Data for dates marked with an asterisk refer to non-whites.

Sources:

U. S. Bureau of the Census, *Negro Population in the United States: 1790 to 1915*, (Washington: Government Printing Office, 1918), p. 259.

U. S. Bureau of the Census, *Sixteenth Census of the United States: 1940*, Population, IV, Part 1, Tables 30 and 32; Differential Fertility: 1940 and 1910, Women by Number of Children Ever Born, Tables 71 and 74.

U. S. Bureau of the Census, *Census of Population: 1950*, PC-1, Table 147.

U. S. Bureau of the Census, *Census of Population: 1960*, PC(1)–1D, Table 242.

as a marital status. Third, from 1910 to 1940, the proportion *married-spouse-absent* went up in both regions of the country but, since 1940, the regional trends have been different. In the North, the proportion of married men who were not living with their wives has actually decreased while among women the proportion living apart from their husbands has remained the same. Within the South, the picture is very different, for among both men and women, there has been an increase in the proportion who were married but did not live with their spouse. This indicates there have been regional differences in the timing of changes in the marital status distribution among blacks. In the North and West,

TABLE 6–7

Components of Change in the Proportion of Negro Women Who Were Married-Spouse-Absent, 1910 to 1940 and 1940 to 1960

	1910 to 1940	1940 to 1960
Percentage of Married Women with Spouse Absent—Original Year	6.0%	11.9%
Percentage of Married Women with Spouse Absent—Later Year	11.9	15.9
Total Change	+ 5.9	+ 4.0
Change Attributed to:		
Change in Age Distribution of Women	− 0.3	− 0.8
Change in Areal Distribution	+ 1.3	+ 2.0
Changes in Rates in North and West	+ 0.9	+ 0.1
Change in Rates in Urban South	+ 1.4	+ 1.3
Change in Rates in Rural South	+ 2.2	+ 2.6
Interaction of Factors	+ 0.4	− 1.2

Source:

U. S. Bureau of the Census, *Census of Population: 1960*, PC(1)–1D, Table 242; PC(2)– Differential Fertility: 1940 and 1910, Women by Number of Children Ever Born, Tables 80 and 82.

U. S. Bureau of the Census, *Census of Population: 1960*, PC(1)–1D, Tables 242; PC(2)– 1C, Table 19.

the rise in desertion apparently occurred between 1910 and 1940; since that time, there has been little change in the proportion *married-spouse-absent*. In the South, however, the pattern is different and the proportion of currently married women who did not live with their spouses increased throughout the period from 1910 to 1960.

In the fifty-year period between 1910 and 1960, the proportion of black women who were married but did not live with their husband increased from 6 percent to 16 percent.[47] This resulted from a shift of blacks from rural to urban areas and changes in the proportion of women who were married but lived apart from their spouse in each area of the country as well as from changes in the age distribution of married women. Table 6–7 presents the results of an investigation which attempts to ascertain some of the demographic causes of the increasing proportion of women who were married but spouse-absent. The technique used was the components-of-difference-between-two-rates methodology which was described in Chapter 5.

---

[47] These percentages refer to ever-married black women age 15 to 74.

Results are shown for two time periods; 1910 to 1940 and 1940 to 1960. During the first period, the proportion *married-spouse-present* rose from 6.0 percent to 11.9 percent. Table 6–7 indicates that changes in the age distribution of women did not contribute to this increase. If there had been no movement of blacks away from the South and if the age-specific proportions *married-spouse-absent* in each area had remained constant from 1910 to 1940, the changes in the age distribution would have lowered the overall proportion of married women who lived apart from their husband. This table indicates the shifting areal distribution of blacks between 1910 and 1940 did contribute to a rise in the proportion *married-spouse-absent* for there was movement away from the rural South where the proportion *married-spouse-absent* was lowest. However, even if there had been no shift in the areal distribution, the proportion *married-spouse-absent* would have increased because, among women in the rural and urban South, there were substantial rises in the proportion who were married but did not live with their husband.

Between 1940 and 1960, the proportion *married-spouse-absent* increased from 11.9 percent to 15.9 percent. The movement of blacks away from the South played a part in this rise but increases in the proportion of southern women who were *married-spouse-absent* again played a very important role. Interestingly enough, change in the proportion of women in the North and West who were married but lived apart from their husband had little effect upon the overall rise in the proportion of married women who did not live with their husband.

In conclusion, Table 6–7 indicates that some of the increase in the proportion *married-spouse-absent* can appropriately be attributed to urbanization. A fuller explanation of changes in the marital status of blacks must account for the finding that, since 1940, the proportion of married blacks who live apart from their spouse has gone up within the South but has changed very little outside the South.

Socio-economic Factors and Marital Status

Each of the commentators who have discussed the Negro family have claimed that socio-economic factors are related to marital stability. Supposedly, Negro men who are able to retain good jobs and earn money are in a better position to support their families; their marriages will be more stable than those of men who have limited earning abilities. The relationship of economic factors to marital status is another complex area, for it is not easy to determine the influence of socio-economic variables apart from the effects of age at marriage or rural background.

Educational Differences in Marital Status

We can begin to study the relationship of socio-economic factors to marital status by looking at educational attainment differences in reported marital status. Educational attainment is an important indicator of socio-economic standing and usually does not change during an individual's adult life since most people complete their formal schooling in their teen years or their early twenties. In addition, educational attainment is the one socio-economic indicator which can be related to marital status for three

TABLE 6–8

Marital Status by Educational Attainment
for Negroes 25 to 64: 1940–1960[a]

			Males			
				Distribution of Married Men		
		Single	Married- Sp.-Pres.	Married- Sp.-Abst.	Widowed	Divorced
1940						
College	4	18%	85%	9%	4%	2%
	1–3	17	81	11	5	3
High School	4	17	81	10	6	3
	1–3	15	80	11	7	2
Elementary	5–8	15	80	11	7	2
	0–4	14	82	9	8	1
1950[b]						
College	4	14	84	9	4	3
	1–3	13	81	11	4	4
High School	4	12	81	11	4	4
	1–3	11	79	12	5	4
Elementary	5–8	10	79	13	5	3
	0–4	11	79	13	6	2
1960[b]						
College	4	16	85	9	3	3
	1–3	14	80	12	3	5
High School	4	14	79	13	3	5
	1–3	13	78	14	4	4
Elementary[c]	5–8	13	78	14	4	4
	0–4	15	77	15	5	3

Table 6–8 (Cont'd)

		Single	Married-Sp.-Pres.	Married-Sp.-Abst.	Widowed	Divorced
			Distribution of Married Women			
1940						
College	4	23%	67%	11%	18%	4%
	1–3	16	65	10	20	5
High School	4	13	67	10	19	4
	1–3	9	65	12	19	4
Elementary	5–8	8	66	11	20	3
	0–4	8	65	10	23	2
1950[b]						
College	4	17	70	11	12	7
	1–3	10	70	11	14	5
High School	4	9	69	12	14	5
	1–3	6	66	14	15	5
Elementary	5–8	6	66	14	16	4
	0–4	7	65	14	19	2
1960[b]						
College	4	15	73	11	9	7
	1–3	10	71	12	9	8
High School	4	9	70	14	10	6
	1–3	7	66	17	11	6
Elementary[c]	5–8	8	65	17	14	5
	0–4	11	62	17	18	3

(Table column header spans: *Females* over the distribution; *Distribution of Married Women* spans the Married-Sp.-Pres., Married-Sp.-Abst., Widowed, and Divorced columns.)

[a] These data have been standardized for age.
[b] Data for 1950 and 1960 refer to non-whites.
[c] Elementary 0–4 includes persons who reported no years of schooling.

Sources:

U. S. Bureau of the Census, *Sixteenth Census of the United States: 1940*, Population, Educational Attainment by Economic Characteristics and Marital Status, Table 40.

U. S. Bureau of the Census, *Census of Population: 1950*, P–E, No. 5B, Table 8.

U. S. Bureau of the Census, *Census of Population: 1960*, PC(2)–4E, Table 4.

different census dates, facilitating an analysis of change over time.

Table 6–8 shows tabulations of marital status for Negroes or non-whites who were 25 to 64 years old in 1940, 1950 and 1960. These data have been standardized for age. The first column in each panel of the table shows the proportion of individuals at each educational attainment level who were single. The following four columns show the distribution of the ever-married population by their reported marital status at the time of the census. These last four columns, in each row, sum to 100.

It is clear there are educational attainment differences in marital status. First, we will discuss differences in the proportion that was single. At each date, among both men and women, the proportion *single* was highest among the college educated. In 1940 and 1950, the relationship of education to the proportion that was single was approximately linear. Increases in educational attainment were matched by increases in the proportion *single*. Between 1940 and 1960, the proportion that was single generally decreased and the relationship of education to the proportion that was single changed. In 1940, a singularly high proportion of the college graduates were single, but, by 1960, the proportion that was single was high among both the college educated and elementary school dropouts.

Second, we will discuss the relationship of education to marital status among those blacks who reported they had married. The data in Table 6–8 support the view that socio-economic status is related to marital stability because, at each date, the proportion of married persons who lived with a spouse was greater among the college educated than among those who had only a grammar school education. The reported causes of marital disruption also appear related to educational attainment. Widowhood is most commonly reported by people in the lower educational attainment categories and least reported by the college educated. These figures may reflect educational differences in remarriage rates as well as differences in the likelihood of becoming a widow or widower. Divorce, among women, is much more frequently reported by the college educated than by those with a grade school education. On the other hand, among men there appears to be no relationship between educational attainment and the proportion divorced.

Third, we will summarize changes over time in the relationship of education and marital status. Among blacks at every educational attainment level, widowhood decreased and divorce increased as reported marital statuses. Changes in the proportion *married-spouse-absent* are more difficult to describe. Among individuals at the lower educational levels, there has been a rise in the proportion who were married but did not live with their spouse. However, among persons who had a college education, there has been no change in the proportion *married-spouse-absent*.

What has been the outcome of these changes in divorce, widowhood and proportion *married-spouse-absent?* Among both men and women in the lower educational attainment categories, there has been a slight decrease in the proportion of married persons who lived with a spouse. For instance, the proportion of married men, with 5 to 8 years of schooling who lived with a wife decreased from 80 percent to 78 percent from 1940 to 1960. Among married women at this educational level, the proportion living with a husband fell from 66 to 65 percent. The picture is different at the highest educational attainment levels. Among married women with a college education, the proportion living with a husband has gone up from 67 percent to 73 percent. However, among married men at this education level there has been neither an increase nor a decrease in the proportion who live with their wife.

Occupational and Income Differences in Marital Status

Table 6-9 shows the 1960 distribution of Negro men by their current marital status and their occupation or income. The first column in each panel shows the proportion that remained single and the succeeding columns in each row show the current marital status reported by ever-married men.

This table again indicates there are socio-economic differences in marital status. Income differentials are very clear. One-third of the men who reported no income in 1959 were single compared to only 4 percent single among the men who earned $5,000 or more. Among men who had married, the reasons for their being in disrupted marriages were linked to income. The proportion who were married, but did not live with their wives, was at a maximum among the low income group and at a minimum among the highest income group. Similarly, widowhood and divorce were much more frequently reported by men who had small incomes than by men who earned large sums.

Since these data have been standardized for age, it is impossible to argue that the low income group contains an unduly large number of elderly low income widowers. A more likely explanation for the inverse relationship between causes of marital disruption and income is that men with limited earning power find it difficult or impossible to remarry if their first marriage is terminated. An investigation of this hypothesis revealed that the following percentages of men, whose first marriage was terminated, had remarried by the time of the Census of 1960:[48]

---

48 Records of 1 in 1,000 Sample of 1960 Censuses.

Income of Negro Men, 1959	Proportion Remarried
$5,000 or more	50%
3,000 to 4,999	49
1,000 to 2,999	42
less than 1,000	36
no income	14

Table 6–9 indicates that married men with high earnings are much more likely to be living with their wives than men with low earnings. The figures shown above indicate that this reflects not only socio-economic differences in the termination of marriages, but differences in remarriage rates.

Occupational differences in the marital status of Negro men are similar to educational or income differences. The percentage of married men living with their wives was high among profes-

TABLE 6–9
Marital Status of Negro Men 25 to 64 in 1960 by Income and Occupation

		Distribution of Ever-Married Men*			
	Single	Married-Spouse-Present	Married-Spouse-Absent	Widowed	Divorced
Income in 1959					
$5,000 or more	4%	87%	7%	3%	3%
3,000 to 4,999	7	83	10	3	4
1,000 to 2,999	10	80	15	3	2
less than 1,000	18	73	18	6	3
no income	34	47	37	7	10
Occupation in 1960					
Professionals	12%	88%	7%	2%	3%
Managers	8	87	7	2	4
Clerical Workers	10	87	8	2	3
Sales Workers	12	85	9	3	3
Craftsmen	7	86	8	3	3
Operatives	7	85	9	3	3
Priv. Household Workers	18	55	25	13	7
Service Workers	12	79	13	4	4
Laborers	10	82	11	4	3
Farmers	7	92	4	2	2
Farm Laborers	15	79	13	5	3

* These data have been standardized for age using the age distribution of Negro males 25 to 64 in 1960 as the standard. Marital status by occupation data refer to non-whites.
Source:
    U. S. Bureau of the Census, Census of Population: 1960, PC(2)–4E, Table 5; Records of 1 in 1,000 sample of 1960 Censuses.

sional workers, and the proportion married but not living with their wives was high among service workers and laborers. Two occupations stand out as having unusual marital status distributions. As might be expected, relatively many farmers are married-spouse-present.

The occupational group of private household workers, which accounts for less than one percent of all employed Negro men, is selective of single men and married men who do not live with their wives.

Overview of Findings

This analysis of demographic data has shown, first, that for a long time there has been relatively little change in the marital status of blacks, the age at which blacks marry, or the proportion who marry at some time during their life. Second, the causes for marital disruption have changed. Desertion has apparently increased, for the proportion who are married but do not live with their spouse has gone up. On the other hand, this trend has been offset by a decrease in widowhood. Thus, the increasing proportion who are *married-spouse-absent* has not reduced the proportion of married Negroes who live with a spouse. Third, socio-economic and place of residence variables are linked to marital status and to reasons for marital disruption. The data suggest that, since 1940, desertion has become more common among blacks of lower status and among those within the South, but that the proportion *married-spouse-absent* has remained about the same or even decreased in northern cities and among blacks with the characteristics of higher socio-economic status.

These findings seem consistent with the views of Moynihan and Frazier that Negro marital and family status reflects the social and economic position of Negroes. There is reason to believe that the economic status of blacks improved after the Civil War. We do not know how many Negroes owned property in 1860, but it must have been a very small number since most blacks were enslaved. However, by 1890, home ownership was not rare among Negroes, and from 1890 to 1910 the number of owners increased. Shown below is the proportion of Negro-occupied homes which were owner-occupied.[49]

---

[49] U. S. Bureau of the Census, *Negro Population in the United States: 1790–1910*, pp. 467 and 470.

| | Percentage of Homes Owner-Occupied | |
Year	Farm Homes	Non-farm Homes
1890	21%	17%
1900	25	19
1910	26	22

These changes in home ownership may be indicative of improvements in the social and economic status of blacks, a change which encouraged the development of stable families.

Between 1910 and 1940, marital disruption, particularly desertion, increased among Negroes. The urbanization of blacks was one factor producing this change, but within both rural and urban areas, the proportion of married women who did not live with their husbands went up. The available evidence indicates that the economic position of blacks deteriorated. To be sure, the earnings and occupational levels of many blacks in industrial areas improved during World War I. But, as Myrdal, Spero, and Harris have pointed out, the job picture for blacks did not improve after the War, for Negroes were typically excluded from jobs in new or expanding industries and lost manual jobs because of automation.[50] During the Depression, job opportunities were further constricted and the agricultural programs of the federal government helped to impoverish rural Negroes. Home ownership, which had increased before 1910, remained at approximately the same level between 1910 and 1940.[51] As a result of these economic changes, the position of blacks in 1940 was probably less favorable than in 1910, and this change may help to explain the increases in desertion and marital disruption.

Since the end of the Depression, the incomes of blacks have risen much more rapidly than prices[52] and since 1960, not only have Negro incomes gone up, but the racial difference in income has narrowed.[53] In addition, between 1940 and 1967, there was a

---

[50] Myrdal, op. cit., I, Chapter xiii; Sterling D. Spero and Abram L. Harris, The Black Worker, reprint ed. (New York: Atheneum, 1968), Parts iii, iv, and v.

[51] U. S. Bureau of the Census, Negro Population in the United States: 1790–1910, p 470; Census of Housing: 1960, HC(1)–No. 1, Table H.

[52] U. S. Bureau of the Census, Historical Statistics of the United States: Colonial Times to 1957 (Washington: Government Printing Office, 1961) Series G 147–148 and G 169–190; Historical Statistics of the United States: Continuation to 1962 and Revisions (Washington: Government Printing Office, 1965) Series G 75–149.

[53] U. S. Bureau of the Census, "Income in 1967 of Families in the United States," Current Population Reports, Series P–60, No. 59 (April 4, 1969), Table 3.

substantial occupational upgrading of the Negro labor force.[54] These improvements in living standards have helped to reduce widowhood which used to be a common cause of marital disruption.

We know little about which blacks have benefited most from economic gains in recent years. We can speculate that the economic status of those Negroes in northern cities and those with extensive educations improved most rapidly. Among these Negroes, there has been no increase in the proportion *married-spouse-absent*. In fact, considering both changes in widowhood and desertion, there has been a modest rise in the proportion of blacks in these categories who were married and lived with their spouse. The economic status of Negroes who have little education or those in the rural South may have further deteriorated, rather than improved during this span, and among these Negroes, desertion has apparently increased.

Further studies, using both descriptions of Negro life styles and demographic data, are needed to investigate the hypothesis that, among Negroes who have experienced socio-economic gains, marital stability is increasing while among those who have not experienced such gains, marital instability is continuing to increase.

The Effects of Changes in Marital Status on Fertility

Changes in marital status have been described but their implications for fertility have yet to be measured. Stycos and Back demonstrated that within a society which does not effectively use birth control, the level of fertility will be influenced by marital stability.[55] The higher the proportion of women living with a spouse, the higher the fertility rate. Until recently, few blacks in the United States planned their families effectively.[56] We need to determine if the net effect of changes in age at marriage, proportion of women married, and marital stability has lengthened or shortened the typical period of time during which Negro women are exposed to childbearing.

---

[54] U. S. Bureau of the Census, *Sixteenth Census of the United States: 1940*, Population, Characteristics of the Non-white Population by Race, Table 8; Claire C. Hodge, "The Negro Job Situation: Has It Improved?", *Monthly Labor Review* (January, 1969), 20–28.

[55] J. Mayone Stycos and Kurt W. Back, *The Control of Human Fertility in Jamaica* (Ithaca: Cornell University Press, 1964), p. 151.

[56] The use of birth control by blacks is discussed in Chapter 8.

Before discussing this topic, two caveats must be stressed. First, as we have noted, a substantial proportion of Negro children are conceived and born out of wedlock. During the mid-1960s, approximately one-quarter of all Negro births and about 45 percent of the first births were illegitimate.[57] Second, marital status information comes from the censuses and some unmarried mothers may have been enumerated as married women. Both of these difficulties hamper the analysis of how changes in marital status relate to changes in fertility.

Changes in Exposure to Childbearing

Two kinds of evidence supply answers to questions about change in the proportion of women who are exposed to the risk of childbearing, at least childbearing within marriage. These are contained in Table 6–10. The first column of figures shows the proportion of Negro women ages 14 to 44 who were living with a husband for the years from 1910 to 1967.

Between 1910 and 1940, the proportion of black women living with a husband dropped slightly. After World War II, the age at marriage fell, the marriage rate increased, and the proportion of women who lived with a spouse increased, even exceeding the level of 1910. During the late 1950s, the proportion of all black women who were *married-spouse-present* decreased, reflecting, perhaps, the economic constraints and higher unemployment rates of that period. Since 1960, the proportion living with a spouse has declined. The discussion presented earlier in this chapter suggests this has occurred, not because fewer married women live with their husbands, but because marriage rates among young Negro women are low.

The childbearing span extends for a little more than thirty years, from ages 14 to 44 approximately. We can ask, how many years of this span would a Negro woman spend with a husband if the age-specific marital status rates of a given year were to remain in effect indefinitely?[58] This is analogous to the life table concept, the expectation of life, which indicates how many years

<hr />

[57] U. S., National Center for Health Statistics, *Vital Statistics of the United States: 1966*, Vol. I, Table 1–25; Alice J. Clague and Stephanie J. Ventura, *Trends in Illegitimacy: United States–1940–1965;* U. S., National Center for Health Statistics, Vital and Health Statistics, Series 21, No. 15 (February, 1968).

[58] In computing the expected number of years a woman could live with a husband, no correction was made for mortality of women.

TABLE 6–10

Proportion of Negro Females 14 to 44 Who Lived with a Spouse and Estimates of Expected Years in Married-Spouse-Present Status: 1910 to 1967

Date	Proportion of Negro Women Living with Spouse	Expected Years Married-Spouse- Present**
1910	50.7%	17.1 Years
1940	49.0	15.8
1950*	53.0	16.5
1951*	54.8	17.1
1953*	54.5	17.1
1957*	51.0	16.2
1958*	49.8	15.9
1959*	48.3	15.5
1960	48.6	15.5
1961*	49.8	16.2
1962*	48.4	15.8
1963*	47.1	15.5
1964	48.2	16.1
1965	45.8	15.4
1966	45.0	15.4
1967*	45.1	15.5

* Data for these years refer to non-whites.
** See text for definition.

Sources:
    See Table 6–1.

a person would survive if the age-specific mortality rates of a given year remained constant. The procedure for making this estimate is one type of age standardization and it provides the second type of evidence about exposure to marital childbearing. These expected numbers of years in the *married-spouse-present* state are shown in the second column of Table 6–10. The typical number of years a black woman could expect to spend living with a husband declined between 1910 and 1940, increased after World War II, and has declined since the late 1950s, although the fluctuations have been small.

Between 1910 and 1940, the fertility rates of blacks decreased. Both types of evidence in Table 6–10 suggest that changes in marital status may have played some role in this decline. Immediately after World War II, fertility rates went up corresponding to an increase in the proportion of women who lived with a husband. Throughout the 1950s, fertility rates climbed and, in 1960, they were very much higher than ten or twenty years earlier. However, there were not corresponding changes in marital status, and the proportion of women living with a husband apparently reached a peak in the early 1950s and has declined since then. It is impossible to argue that the post-World War II rise in fertility and the high childbearing rates of the 1950s were a result of a major change in marital status.

Marital Status Differentials in Fertility

How great is the fertility difference between women who have a husband present and women who are widows or who are married but do not live with their husbands? Have there been changes over time in the magnitude of these differences? This section provides answers to these questions by analyzing marital status differentials in childbearing.

To understand fully how marital disruption influences child-bearing, we need the marital and fertility histories of a large sample of women. We would want to know their age at marriage, when each of their marriages was broken and why it was termi-nated. Censuses and surveys do not furnish such information. However, they provide information about the childbearing of women in different marital status categories. These data indicate that marital status does have an important influence upon the number of children a black woman bears but that the magnitude of this influence has gradually waned.

Such a conclusion was reached by examining figures shown in Table 6–11. This table contains fertility information for Negro women ages 15 to 44, by current marital status, for four census dates. These data have been standardized for age to eliminate any confounding effects of changes in the age structure.

Women in unbroken first marriages—those who were mar-ried once and lived with their husband—had the highest fertility at each date. This is undoubtedly a consequence of their being ex-posed to the possibility of becoming pregnant for the longest peri-ods of time. These married-once-spouse-present women had the lowest proportion childless and also the highest proportion with five or more offspring.

Women who report themselves as married, but spouse-ab-sent, bear relatively few children. In fact, at each date, women in this group had the lowest fertility rates, lower even than those of widowed or divorced women. The image of deserted Negro women bearing many children to secure welfare payments is not a valid

TABLE 6–11
Fertility Information for Negro Women 15 to 44
by Current Marital Status: 1910 to 1960[a]

Current Marital Status	1910	1940	1950	1960
Children Ever Born per 1000 Women				
Total	3017	1963	1902	2526
Married-spouse-present[b]	3171	2090	2031	2662
Married once	3274	2147	2115	2730
Married more than once	2926	1897	1816	2528
Married-spouse-absent	2259	1554	1579	2330
Widowed and divorced	2612	1736	1639	2383
Percent of Married Women Childless				
Total	22%	33%	31%	19%
Married-spouse-present	22	32	31	19
Married once	22	33	31	19
Married more than once	15	28	31	18
Married-spouse-absent	25	33	34	21
Widowed and divorced	17	32	34	20
Percent with Five or More Children				
Total	25%	13%	12%	18%
Married-spouse-present	27	15	13	19
Married once	29	16	14	20
Married more than once	22	11	11	16
Married-spouse-absent	16	7	8	14
Widowed and divorced	19	10	8	14

[a] Rates and percentages in this table have been standardized for age. The age distribution of Negro females 15 to 44 in 1960 was used as the standard. Data for 1950 pertains to non-whites.

[b] In 1910, 5 percent of the married-spouse-present women did not report whether they had been married once or more than once. In 1940, 13 percent did not report the frequence of their marriages. The fertility of these women has been included in the married-spouse-present category but not in the married-once or married-more-than-once categories.

Sources:

    U. S. Bureau of the Census, *Sixteenth Census of the United States: 1940*, Population, Differential Fertility: 1940 and 1910, Women by Number of Children Ever Born, Tables 18 and 20.

    U. S. Bureau of the Census, *Census of Population: 1950*, P–E, No. 5C, Table 17.

    U. S. Bureau of the Census, *Census of Population: 1960*, PC(2)–3A, Table 8; Records of 1 in 1,000 Sample of 1960 Censuses.

one, for *married-spouse-absent* women have relatively few children.

Between 1910 and 1960, marital status differentials in fertility diminished. In 1910, *married-once-spouse-present* women—the high fertility group—had borne an average of one more child than married-spouse-absent women—the low fertility group. By 1960, this changed so that the differential was only four-tenths of a child. These figures provide no insights that explain why these differentials have declined. It may be that *married-spouse-absent* women are now exercising some control over their fertility. It is also possible that, among the *married-spouse-absent* group, intervals of husbands' absence are getting shorter, giving rise to higher fertility.

Among all marital status categories, the proportion of women who were childless increased from 1910 to 1940 but declined during the next twenty years. By 1960, marital status differences in childlessness were very small and the proportions childless were generally lower in 1960 than fifty years earlier. At each date, the women who had married but who were not living with their husband had high proportions childless, again indicating the relatively low fertility of this group.

This table shows fertility data for those spouse-present women who had been married once and for those who had been married more than once. Childlessness was more common among those who had only one husband than among those who had more than one husband. Indeed, the married-more-than-once women had the lowest rates of childlessness. These rates may be explained by male sterility. If a certain proportion of all men are sterile, then a woman who has been married more than once has had a greater probability of living with a fecund husband than a woman who has spent her entire married life with one man.

Implications of Changes in Marital Status

The last two sections have described two different but seemingly compensating trends. Fewer women are living with a spouse and the length of the *married-spouse-present* period has gradually decreased. On the other hand, we observed that marital disruption reduces fertility now less than it did in the past. Do these two trends offset each other? To answer this question we need to assess the aggregative effect of marital disruption upon fertility. One method to do this is to study figures shown in Table 6–11. We might consider the number of children born per 1,000 evermarried black women and compare it to the number of children born to those women who were *married-once-spouse-present*. We can assume that this latter fertility rate is the rate which would obtain for the total population if no marriages were disrupted; that is, if all women were *married-once-spouse-present*. This comparison is made below, using, of course, data which have been standardized for age.

Date	Rates of Children Ever Born Per 1,000 Women Ages 15 to 44		Reductions in Fertility Due to Marital Disruption	
	Actual	Assuming No Marriages Were Disrupted	Per 1,000 Women	Percent
1910	3017	3274	−257	− 7.8
1940	1963	2147	−184	− 8.6
1950	1902	2115	−213	−10.1
1960	2526	2720	−204	− 7.5

The effect of marital disruption upon fertility has varied within a narrow range. The trend toward more marital disruption has pretty much been offset by a decline in the influence marital status has upon fertility.

This evidence indicates that it is impossible to argue that increasing marital disruption was either an important component of the drop in fertility which preceded World War II or the recent rise in fertility. It is well to note that these rates refer to *cumulative* fertility for census dates. In a particular year or for a specific cohort, marital disruption may have had a different and more substantial effect upon the fertility rate.

Chapter 7

THE PROCESS OF FAMILY FORMATION

In previous chapters, we showed that various factors were related to marital stability and fertility among blacks. We indicated that women born in the South have more children than women born outside the South; and that educational attainment and age at marriage were inversely related to fertility. Thus far, we have dealt with only two variables at one time. We have not attempted to answer more interesting questions which involve the simultaneous effects of three or four variables. For instance, did northern-born women bear fewer children than southern-born women because they had greater educational attainment; or did being born in the South really have an influence on fertility apart from the influence of educational attainment? Or, did educational attainment have any effect on marital stability and childbearing, independent of the effect of age at marriage? This chapter provides answers to these questions.

Descriptions of marital status and fertility differentials, up to this point, have dealt with women in broad age categories such as 15 to 44 or 25 to 64. Perhaps, there have been changes from cohort to cohort in the effects that education or age at marriage have had on marital stability or fertility. This chapter explores these relationships for different cohorts of women.

In brief, the aim of this section of the monograph is to describe the process of family formation among blacks. This obviously is a very complex process. We can do no more than describe the effects of selected demographic variables.

Sources of Data

The primary source of data utilized in this chapter is the one in one-thousand sample of the population developed from the Censuses of Population and Housing of 1960. This sample includes

166

180,000 individuals. For each of these people, ninety-seven characteristics are shown. These include demographic items such as the respondent's age, sex, race, nationality, place of birth, place of residence, and current marital status; and economic characteristics such as his labor force status, occupation, and income. The characteristics of the respondent's dwelling unit such as its size, value, age and plumbing facilities are also recorded. For married women and for children, characteristics of the head of the household are indicated such as his age, education, and occupation.

We began this analysis by selecting all ever-married black women who were 15 to 59 years of age in 1960. Conceivably, very many of the ninety-seven variables could have been related to marital stability and fertility among these women. However, it is often difficult or impossible to specify the manner in which a variable was linked to marital status or to childbearing. Labor force status is a good example. A number of studies have demonstrated that women in the labor force typically bear fewer children than women who do not work.[1] Recall that the labor force question pertained to activity during the first week of April, 1960, while the fertility question referred to the total number of children a woman has ever borne, some of which may have been borne many years prior to the Census of 1960. Suppose we find that labor force participants have borne fewer offspring than women who are not in the labor force. Should we conclude that women avoided having children in order to work or should we draw just the opposite conclusion and claim that women who had few children elected to take jobs? Unfortunately, census data provide no means for resolving this question.

For this reason, we limited this analysis to important life cycle variables which could be related to the process of family formation in a logical manner. The variables chosen for this analysis were the woman's region of birth, her educational attainment, the age at which she first married, and measures of her marital stability and her fertility. Every one of the black women ages 15 to 59 received a score for each of these variables. These scores were assigned as follows:

REGION OF BIRTH Each woman born outside the South was scored one on this variable while each woman born within the South received a score of zero. This dis-

---

[1] Grabill, Kiser and Whelpton, *op. cit.*, pp. 264–272; Freedman, Whelpton and Campbell, *op. cit.*, pp. 303–305; Kiser, Grabill and Campbell, *op. cit.*, p. 221.

tinguishes between women who were born in the South and women born in other regions.

EDUCATIONAL ATTAINMENT Each woman was given a score on this variable equal to the total number of years of school she had completed.

AGE AT MARRIAGE This variable equals the woman's reported age at *first* marriage.

MARITAL STABILITY Each woman who had married only once and who was living with her husband at the time of the Census of 1960 was scored one on this variable. All other ever-married women—that is, women who had married more than once and who were living with a second husband and women who were widowed or divorced—were scored zero on this variable. This variable distinguishes women who were in unbroken marriages from all other ever-married women.

FERTILITY This variable equals the total number of children the woman reported she had borne by the time of the 1960 Census. The women were told to exclude stepchildren, adopted children and stillbirths.

The reasons for selecting these variables are clear. In the previous chapters, we have shown that each of them is related to childbearing. We note that the region-of-birth variable comes closest to measuring whether or not a woman came from a rural background. Almost all the women scored one on this variable; that is, women born outside the South were born, and presumably raised, in cities. On the other hand, greater than two-thirds of the southern-born women of childbearing age in 1960 were born in rural areas and, hence, they had some rural background.

Having chosen variables to study, the next step is to specify how these variables influenced family formation. Figure 7–1 is a schematic diagram which orders the variables in what is believed to be a chronological or causal sequence. Other demographic studies have found that there were regional differences in educational attainment.[2] Northern born women typically attended school for more years than did southern born women. Thus, educational attainment is thought of as a function of the region of birth. For most women, marriage either occurs after the completion of

---

[2] John K. Folger and Charles B. Nam, *Education of the American Population*, A 1960 Census Monograph (Washington: Government Printing Office, 1967), pp. 153–155; Beverly Duncan, "Trends in Output and Distribution of Schooling," in *Indicators of Social Change*, Eleanor Bernert Sheldon and Wilbert E. Moore, (eds.) (New York: Russell Sage Foundation, 1968), pp. 622–626.

schooling or means the end of formal education. Consequently, age at marriage is viewed as depending upon educational attainment and region of birth. Marital stability may have been influenced by schooling, age at marriage, and region of birth; for that reason, it is placed to the right of these variables. Finally, at the far right in Figure 7–1 is fertility because the number of children a woman bore was (to some degree), a result of these other variables. The arrows in Figure 7–1 indicate the hypothesized directions of effects.

There are arrows leading from outside the model to each of the dependent variables in Figure 7–1. This is to indicate that many factors which are not incorporated in this model affected these variables. Educational attainment, for instance, was obviously influenced by more than just region of birth. Intelligence and parental support, to name just two of a large number of factors, affected education. Contraceptive use and fecundity impairments influenced childbearing, but are not explicitly taken into account by this model. Their effects are subsumed by the arrow leading to fertility from outside the model.

The advantage of a model such as Figure 7–1 is that it summarizes the effects that the variables had on family size. In addition, since data are available for each of the variables, the magnitudes of the effects of the variables can be measured and compared. This allows us to discuss, in an orderly and rigorous manner, what consequences these variables had for family formation. If, in the future, more data become available, new variables can be incorporated into this model, or the model can be rejected and, if the data warrant, supplanted with a better one.

Family Formation among Negro Women Ages 15 to 44

This analysis was begun by considering black women who were ages 15 to 44 in 1960. The one-in-one-thousand sample included 2706 Negro women in this age range who had been married at least once.[3] Listed below are the means and standard deviations of the five variables for this age group of women.

---

[3] The sample included 2,748 black women 15 to 44, but 42 of them were listed as having married before age 13. These women were excluded from analysis, for their reported age at marriage was apparently incorrect. The Bureau of the Census used an editing procedure designed to insure that no respondents reported ages at first marriage of less than 14. U.S., Bureau of the Census, *Census of Population: 1960*, PC (2)–4D, p. xix; Records of 1 in 1,000 sample of 1960 censuses.

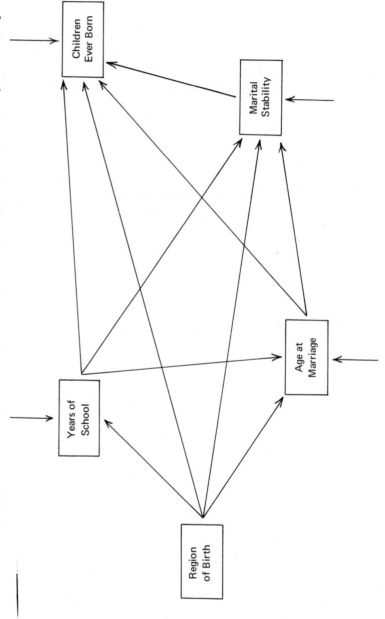

Figure 7–1

Schematic Diagram Showing Ordering of Variables Used in Analysis of Marital Stability and Fertility

Variable	Mean	Standard Deviation
Region of Birth	.19	.39
Educational Attainment	9.5 years	3.1
Age at First Marriage	20.1 years	4.5
Marital Stability	.60	.49
Children Ever Born	2.85	2.67

The mean for the region of birth variable is .19. Women born outside the South received a score of one on this variable, while southern-born women were scored zero. The mean indicates that about one-fifth of the black women ages 15 to 44 were born outside the South, while the remainder, four-fifths were born in the South. On the average, the women completed nine and one-half years of schooling and married at an average age of 20.1 years. The marital status variable has a mean of .60. This indicates that three-fifths of the women were in unbroken first marriages, while the other two-fifths had married but experienced some marital interruption. These women had borne an average of 2.8 children.

A first step in measuring the effects of the variables in this model involves a zero order regression analysis. Table 7–1 contains correlation and regression coefficients which indicate how these five variables were interrelated. The first column of numbers in this table shows correlation coefficients. The first coefficient, for instance, was calculated from the equation which regressed educational attainment upon region of birth. Its value, .193, is positive, indicating that women born outside the South completed more years of school than women born within the South. The square of this correlation coefficient indicates what proportion of the variance in educational attainment can be attributed to the independent variable, region of birth. We might ask how much greater was the educational attainment of northern-born women. The answer is given by the regression coefficient calculated from the same equation. Regression coefficients are shown in the second column of Table 7–1. Among Negro women, 15 to 44, those born outside the South completed an average of one and one-half (1.537) more years of school than women born in the South. The final column of Table 7–1 shows standard errors of the regression coefficients. Since these calculations were made from sample data, there is a question of the appropriate level of significance. As an arbitrary rule, we assume that any regression coefficient which is greater than twice as large as its standard error is significantly different from zero.

TABLE 7–1
Zero Order Correlation and Regression Coefficients:
Negro Women 15 to 44 in 1960

Dependent Variable	Independent Variable	Correlation Coefficient	Regression Coefficient	Standard Error of Regression Coefficient
Education	Region of Birth	.193	1.537	.150
Age at Marriage	Education	.111	.161	.028
	Region of Birth	.047	.548	.222
Marital Stability	Age at Marriage	.109	.012	.002
	Education	.087	.014	.003
	Region of Birth	.004	.004	.024
Fertility	Marital Stability	.068	.371	.104
	Age at Marriage	−.205	−.122	.011
	Education	−.219	−.189	.016
	Region of Birth	−.113	−.775	.131

Source:
U. S., Bureau of the Census, Records of 1-in-1,000 sample of 1960 Censuses.

The more years a woman spent in school, the older she was likely to be when she married. This relationship is described by coefficients in the second panel of Table 7–1. The regression coefficient shows that the effect of a one-year increase in education was a delay of marriage for .16 years. The region in which a woman was born did make a difference as to when she married. The regression coefficient which relates age at marriage and region of birth indicates that northern born women married, on the average, about one-half a year later than did southern born women.

In the third panel of Table 7–1, the dependent variable is marital stability. We might expect that women who came from a rural background would have more stable marriages than those from an urban background. The figures in Table 7–1 cast doubt on this notion, for the regression coefficient which links region of birth and marital stability is very close to zero. Southern born black women were no more likely to be *married-once-spouse-present* than were women who were born outside the South. Marital stability, however, was related to educational attainment and to age at first marriage. Both increases in education and delays in marriage had the effect of increasing the likelihood that a woman was living with her first husband at the time of the census.

The final panel of Table 7–1 shows how fertility is related to other variables.[4] Southern born women bore more children than women born outside the South, and the regression coefficient indicates that the average difference was about eight-tenths of a child. Increase in educational attainment and delays in age at marriage both had the consequence of reducing fertility. Each additional year of schooling reduced fertility by about one-fifth child, while each year marriage was delayed lessened fertility by about one-eighth child. The regression coefficient indicates that marital stability was linked to childbearing, for women in unbroken marriages had an average number of offspring which was one-third of a child greater than the average number borne to women whose marriages had been interrupted.

Multiple Regression Models

The independent variables discussed in the previous section are intercorrelated. Both educational attainment and the postponing of marriage led to greater marital stability, but women who completed many years of school were often the same women who married later in life. The zero order regression models do not permit an analysis of the independent effects of education or age at marriage. To make such a study, multiple regression models are used. Table 7–2 contains the results of the multiple regression analysis. These results were obtained by solving the following equations:

> 1) The regression of age at first marriage upon educational attainment and region of birth.
> 2) The regression of marital stability upon age at marriage, educational attainment and region of birth.
> 3) The regression of fertility upon marital stability, age at marriage, educational attainment and region of birth.

The multiple correlation coefficients associated with these equations are listed in Table 7–2. The square of these coefficients indicates what proportion of the variance in the dependent variable is accounted for by the independent variables. Each correla-

---

[4] As we have noted, illegitimacy is quite common among blacks. One might assume that this sample information could be used to study the characteristics of women who bore children out of wedlock. However, single women were not asked about their fertility so it was impossible to determine how many women bore children before they married.

TABLE 7–2
Multiple Correlation Coefficients and Partial
Regression Coefficients: Negro Women 15 to 44 in 1960

Dependent Variable	Independent Variables	Multiple Correlation Coefficient	Partial Regression Coefficients	Standard Error of Partial Regression Coefficients	Partial Regression Coefficients, Standard Form
Age at Marriage		.114			
	Education		.154	.028	.106
	Region of Birth		.312	.225	.027
Marital Stability		.133			
	Age at Marriage		.011	.002	.100
	Education		.013	.003	.079
	Region of Birth		−.021	.024	−.017
Fertility		.311			
	Marital Stability		.578	.100	.106
	Age at Marriage		−.144	.011	−.192
	Education		−.167	.016	−.194
	Region of Birth		−.458	.128	−.067

Source:
U. S., Bureau of the Census, Records of 1-in-1,000 sample of 1960 Censuses.

tion coefficient has a fairly low value indicating that a small proportion of the variance is explained, but these coefficients are of approximately the same magnitude as those reported in other research dealing with similar dependent variables.[5]

Partial regression coefficients are of more interest than the multiple correlation coefficients, for they can be interpreted as measuring the effect of one independent variable upon the dependent variable controlling the effects of other independent variables. Partial regression coefficients, along with their standard errors, are shown in Table 7–2.

Age at first marriage is the first dependent variable to be considered. A woman's educational attainment had an effect upon her age at marriage, independent of where she was born. The partial regression coefficient indicates that the independent effect of a one year increase in schooling was a delay of marriage by .154 years. The partial regression coefficient relating age at

[5] Philip C. Sagi and Charles F. Westoff, "An Exercise in Partitioning Some Components of the Variance of Family Size," in *Emerging Techniques in Population Research*, Proceedings of a Round Table of the Milbank Memorial Fund (New York: Milbank Memorial Fund, 1963), pp. 130–134.

marriage to region of birth, .312, is not twice as large as its standard error, .225. We conclude that educational attainment had the independent effect of delaying marriage, but that region of birth, apart from educational attainment, had no impact upon the timing of marriage.

The number of years of school a woman completed and her age at marriage both had significant independent effects upon the stability of her marriage. The regression coefficients show that either a one year's change in education or a one year's change in age at marriage had approximately the same effect upon marital stability. In Chapter 6, we noted that educational attainment was positively related to marital stability. This relationship did not exist merely because extensively educated black women married at older ages. Rather, educational attainment had the independent effect of increasing marital stability.

The region of birth variable is a peculiar one. Table 7–2 indicates that the region in which a black woman was born had no independent effect upon when she married or the stability of her marriage. However, it had important independent consequences for the number of children she bore. After taking into account differences in education, age at marriage and marital stability, having been born outside the South reduced fertility. This independent effect of being born outside the South was a reduction in fertility of approximately one-half a child.

Educational attainment and age at marriage both had independent consequences for fertility. The partial regression coefficients show that a one year's delay in marriage reduced fertility by about one-tenth child, while the independent effect of a one year's increase in schooling was a reduction in fertility of .17 child. We can be certain that the low fertility of black women who completed many years of education was not simply a result of their marrying at older ages; rather educational attainment had an important independent effect upon black fertility.

Marital stability led to higher fertility. The effect of being in an unbroken marriage, independent of when a woman married, her education or her region of birth, was an increase in fertility of about six-tenths of a child. This demonstrates that marital disruption reduced black fertility and that average family size would have been considerably larger if so many marriages had not been terminated.

The multiple regression information may now be used with the model of family formation to make explicit how these vari-

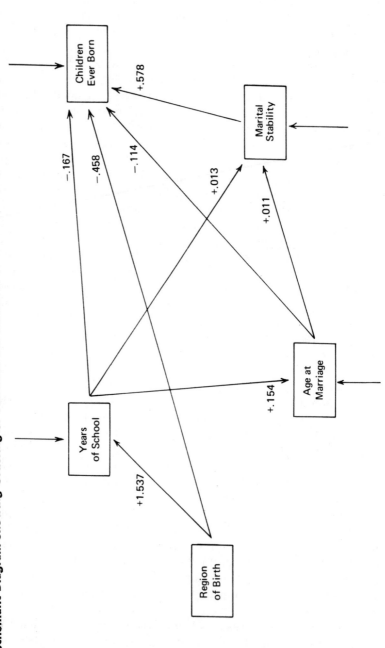

Figure 7–2

Schematic Diagram Showing Ordering of Variables and Measures of Their Influence, Black Women 15 to 44 in 1960

ables affect marital stability and fertility.[6] Figure 7–2 presents these results. In essence, this is a schematic presentation of data contained in Table 7–2. This figure is similar to Figure 7–1 except that two paths of influence are not shown. The multiple regression analysis indicated that region of birth did not have an independent effect upon age at marriage or marital stability so there are no arrows representing these effects in Figure 7–2. The numbers which are attached to the arrows in Figure 7–2 are partial regression coefficients.

This model shows that being born outside the South increased the number of years of school a black woman obtained, and lessened her childbearing. Education had a direct effect, not only upon a woman's fertility but also upon her age at marriage and the likelihood that her marriage would remain intact. A woman's age at marriage affected both her fertility and the stability of her marriage.

Figure 7–2 allows us to ascertain not only the direct effects of the independent variables but their indirect or joint effects. For instance, we might ask if being born outside the South had, in addition to a direct effect on fertility, an indirect effect, because northern-born women attended school longer and educational attainment reduced fertility. It is possible to assess these indirect effects. The regression coefficients show that being born in the North netted a woman 1.54 additional years of education. Each additional year of schooling reduced fertility by .17 child. Consequently the indirect effect of region of birth on fertility through education equals the product of these coefficients, that is .26 children. Indirect effects, then, can be measured by beginning with an independent variable and tracing its paths to the dependent variable. In some cases, there will be more than one intermediate variable.

Listed below are some of the indirect effects of variables upon fertility.

The measures of indirect effects show that education reduced fertility, not only directly, but also because extensively educated women married at older ages. Women who had completed many

---

[6] For further discussion of these models see: Otis Dudley Duncan, "Path Analysis: Sociological Examples," *American Journal of Sociology* LXXXII (July, 1966), 1–16; Kennth C. Land, "Principles of Path Analysis,"; David R. Heise, "Problems in Path Analysis and Causal Inference," Otis Dudley Duncan, "Contingencies in Constructing Causal Models," in *Sociological Methodology, 1969*, Edgar F. Borgatta, (ed.) (San Francisco: Jossey-Bass, 1969), pp. 3–112.

Effects of Independent Variables on Fertility

Age at Marriage	
Direct Effect	—.114 children
Effect through Marital Stability	+.006
Education	
Direct Effect	—.167
Effect through Age at Marriage	—.018
Effect through Marital Stability	+.009
Region of Birth	
Direct Effect	—.458
Effect through Education	—.256
Effect through Education and Age	
at Marriage	—.028

years of school were more likely to be in stable marriages. Since women in stable marriages bore more children, educational attainment had an indirect effect through this variable which increased fertility, but the size of this indirect effect was small.

The most important indirect effects were those involving region of birth. Women born outside the South bore fewer children than women born within the South. First, this region of birth variable had a direct effect which reduced fertility. Second, northern born women completed more years of schooling and this lowered fertility. Third, region of birth had a small negative effect through education and age at marriage. There were additional indirect effects of region of birth but they were of smaller size.

Family Formation among Cohorts of Negro Women

Cohort Differences

We have described the effects of a series of variables for the group of black women ages 15 to 44 in 1960. We have yet to determine whether the relationships among these variables are identical for all cohorts of women. It is possible that the relative influences of the variables have changed over time or differ according to stages of the life cycle. To answer these questions, black women were grouped by age in the following manner.

Year Cohorts Born	Age of Cohorts in 1960
1935–39	20–24
1930–34	25–29
1920–29	30–39
1910–19	40–49
1900–09	50–59

The one in one-thousand sample was scanned and ever-married black women in these age groups were selected. Table 7–3 shows the number of women in each age category, the means, and standard deviations for each of the five variables used in this study.

The data in this table demonstrate very clearly that there have been changes over time in the characteristics of black women. The proportion of women born outside the South has increased, reflecting the shifting distribution of the black population.

Younger cohorts of women have completed more years of school than the older cohorts. Women born 1930 to 1934 completed an average of three and one-half more years of education than did women who were born during the first decade of this century.

There appears to be a decline in the age at which women marry. However, these data in Table 7–3 are really not useful for describing trends in age at marriage; they refer only to women who had married by the time of the census of 1960. Some of the women in the recent cohorts who were not married by 1960, married at later dates, and this affected the average age at marriage among these cohorts.

Cohort fertility trends were discussed in Chapter 4. In brief, we know that women born 1900 to 1920 bore relatively few children. Women born during the 1920s will have considerably higher completed fertility, and the women born during the Depression decade will bear even more children than the women born during the 1920s.

Regression Models

The analysis of the effects of these variables begins with the computation of zero order regression models. This is done in a manner similar to that described previously for women ages 15 to 44. The results of this analysis are contained in Table 7–4.

Correlation coefficients are shown in the top panel of this table. The coefficients in the first row, for example, are those calculated from the equations which regressed education on region of birth. The bottom panel of this table contains regression coefficients. The first row of these coefficients also results from the equations which regress education on region of birth. Regression coefficients which are greater than twice as large as their standard error are marked with an asterisk.

TABLE 7–3

Means and Standard Deviations of Variables Used in Regression Analysis: Cohorts of Negro Women

Years Cohorts Born	Age in 1960	Region of Birth		Educational Attainment		Age at First Marriage		Marital Stability		Children Ever Born		Size of Sample
		Mean	Standard Deviation	Mean	Standard Deviation	Mean	Standard Deviation	Mean	Standard Deviation	Mean	Standard Deviation	
1935–39	20–24	.22	.42	10.0	2.7	18.3	2.3	.67	.47	2.0	1.6	419
1930–34	25–29	.22	.41	10.2	2.9	19.7	3.4	.67	.47	2.8	2.2	475
1920–29	30–39	.20	.40	9.5	3.1	20.8	4.7	.58	.49	3.3	2.9	1134
1910–19	40–49	.12	.33	8.1	3.5	22.1	6.2	.48	.50	3.0	3.1	1014
1900–09	50–59	.13	.33	6.8	3.5	23.0	7.8	.42	.49	2.8	3.1	764

[a] The mean for region of birth equals the proportion of women born outside the South.
[b] The mean for marital stability equals the proportion of women who were in unbroken marriages.

Source: U. S., Bureau of the Census, Records of 1-in-1,000 sample of 1960 Censuses.

TABLE 7–4

Zero Order Correlation and Regression
Coefficients for Cohorts of Negro Women

Age in 1960 Years of Birth Dependent Variable	Independent Variable	20–24 1935–39	25–29 1930–34	30–39 1920–29	40–49 1910–19	50–59 1900–09
	Zero Order Correlation Coefficients					
Education						
	Region of birth	.171	.132	.214	.143	.124
Age at Marriage						
	Education	.248	.285	.145	.115	.074
	Region of Birth	.047	.109	.087	.069	.061
Marital Stability						
	Age at Marriage	.028	.173	.181	.125	.236
	Education	.046	.134	.053	.060	.093
	Region of Birth	.066	−.096	.008	−.010	.002
Fertility						
	Marital Stability	.049	.044	.107	.132	.004
	Age at Marriage	−.377	−.428	−.244	−.271	−.162
	Education	−.280	−.229	−.211	−.210	−.139
	Region of Birth	−.107	−.109	−.140	−.091	−.106
	Regression Coefficients					
Education						
	Region of Birth	1.12*	.93*	1.63*	1.52*	1.30*
Age at Marriage						
	Education	.21*	.33*	.22*	.21*	.17*
	Region of Birth	.26	.90*	1.03*	1.32*	1.44
Marital Stability						
	Age at Marriage	.01	.02*	.02*	.01*	.01*
	Education	.01	.02*	.01	.01	.01*
	Region of Birth	.07	−.11*	.01	−.01	.00
Fertility						
	Marital Stability	.16	.21	.62*	.83*	.02
	Age at Marriage	−.25*	−.28*	−.15*	−.14*	−.06*
	Education	−.16*	−.17*	−.20*	−.19*	−.12*
	Region of Birth	−.41*	−.58*	−1.00*	−.87*	−.99*

* These regression coefficients are at least twice as large as their standard error.

Source:
    U. S., Bureau of the Census, Records of 1-in-1,000 sample of 1960 Censuses.

The data in Table 7–4 show the persistence of region of birth differentials in educational attainment. Northern born women in each group of cohorts completed more years of school than did their southern contemporaries. The regression coefficients indicate that region of birth differences in educational attainment have changed very little over time; women born outside the South averaged slightly over one more year of education than did women born in the South.

Educational attainment was inversely related to age at marriage among each set of cohorts, and northern-born women married later in their lives than did southern-born women.

Marrying at older ages and completing many years of schooling increased marital stability among all cohorts, but region of birth had a significant effect upon marital stability only among women who were 25 to 29 in 1960.

Educational attainment and age at first marriage were inversely related to childbearing among all age groups. Northern-born women consistently bore fewer children than did the southern born women of the same cohort.

We could comment at greater length about the relationships which are described by the zero order regression models. However, it is more interesting to study the independent effects of the predictor variables. To do this, multiple regression models are used. Computations for these multiple regression models were made and the results are contained in Table 7–5. The first panel shows the multiple correlation coefficients and partial regression coefficients for the equations which have age at marriage as the dependent variable. In the second panel, marital stability is the dependent variable, and in the final panel, fertility is the dependent variable.

Among each group of cohorts, except the oldest, education had a significant independent effect upon age at marriage. This is indicated by the regression coefficients in the first panel of Table 7–5. Region of birth, on the other hand, did not have a significant effect upon age at marriage, independent of the effects of educational attainment.

Among women who were 25 years and older in 1960, delays in marriage, independent of education or region of birth, increased the likelihood that a woman would be in an unbroken marriage. Education also seemingly had the independent effect of increasing marital stability, but this requires a cautious interpretation since not all the partial regression coefficients relating education to marital stability are significantly different from zero.

Region of birth had no independent effect upon marital stability among women who were 30 years old or over in 1960. However, region of birth did have an important effect on marital sta-

TABLE 7–5

Multiple Correlation Coefficients and Partial Regression Coefficients, Cohorts of Black Women 20 to 59 in 1960

Dependent Variable	Independent Variable	20–24 1935–39 Mult. R	20–24 1935–39 Reg. Coef.	25–29 1930–34 Mult. R	25–29 1930–34 Reg. Coef.	30–39 1920–29 Mult. R	30–39 1920–29 Reg. Coef.	40–49 1910–19 Mult. R	40–49 1910–19 Reg. Coef.	50–59 1900–09 Mult. R	50–59 1900–09 Reg. Coef.
Age at Marriage		.248		.294		.156		.127		.090	
	Education		.21*		.32*		.20*		.19*		.15
	Region of Birth		.02		.60		.70		1.03		1.24
Marital Stability		.077		.232		.184		.136		.249	
	Age at Marriage		.00		.02*		.02*		.01*		.01*
	Education		.01		.02*		.00		.01		.01*
	Region of Birth		.07		–.14*		–.02		–.04		–.03*
Fertility		.433		.463		.351		.372		.228	
	Marital Stability		.24		.61*		.93*		1.10*		.34
	Age at Marriage		–.22*		–.27*		–.15*		–.14*		–.06*
	Education		–.11*		–.09*		–.16*		–.17*		–.11*
	Region of Birth		–.24		–.19		–.60*		–.43		–.76*

* These partial regression coefficients are at least twice as large as their standard errors.

Source:
   U. S., Bureau of the Census, Records of 1-in-1,000 sample of 1960 Census.

bility among women 25 to 29 in 1960. For women in this age range, being born outside the South significantly increased the probability that a woman's marriage had been disrupted. It is difficult to understand why this variable should have had an important effect only for this age group of women. It may be that this particular relationship is a harbinger of a new trend and that, in the future, northern birth, that is, coming from an urban background, will significantly reduce the probability that a woman is in a stable marriage. On the other hand, it may be an idiosyncrasy of those women born during the Depression and first married during the late 1940s and the early 1950s, years when marriage rates were very high.

Women whose marriages had not been interrupted bore more children than women whose marriages had been interrupted and this was true among all cohorts. The partial regression coefficient for the oldest group of cohorts is not significant, but this is undoubtedly because many of these women became widows after they completed their childbearing. About one-fifth of the women in this age range whose marriages had been interrupted reported they were widows in 1960. Among the other groups of cohorts, the magnitude of the partial regression coefficients measuring the effect of marital stability, increases with age. This suggests that the longer a woman spent in a stable marriage, the more important this stability factor became in determining her fertility.

Age at marriage and educational attainment both independently influenced the fertility of all cohorts. Among the younger women, a one year's delay of marriage had a greater effect upon fertility than a one year increase in education. Among the older cohorts, a one year change in either education or age at marriage had approximately the same consequence for fertility.

Being born outside the South had the independent effect of reducing fertility among all cohorts. The effect of this variable was more pronounced among the older women than among the younger.

Summary of Findings

It is not easy to put together a coherent description of the marital status and fertility trends we have described in this and other chapters. However, there are some themes or ideas which are both common in the literature describing black family patterns and consistent with the findings of the last chapters. First, there is considerable agreement that black women desire to have stable marriages and reasonably sized families. Frazier observed that many blacks intended to have stable marriages and wished to provide secure and happy homes for their children. He argued that assimilation would gradually occur and more blacks would adopt the family norms of white society.[7] More recently, Elliot Liebow studied street-corner Negro men in Washington, D.C., and discovered that their aspirations were similar to those of white men:

> . . . The young, lower-class Negro gets married in his early twenties, at approximately the same time and in part for the same reason as his white or Negro working- or middle-class counterpart. He has no special motive for getting married; sex is there for the taking, with or without marriage, and he can also live with a woman or have children—if he has not done this already —without getting married. He wants to be publicly, legally married, to support a family and be the head of it, because this is what it is to be a man in our society, whether one lives in a room near the Carry-out or in an elegant house in the suburbs.[8]

A number of studies have investigated desired and expected family size among blacks.[9] In general, there seemed to be no desire for very large families; rather, Negroes apparently wanted to have approximately the same sized families as whites.

Second, the characteristics of higher socioeconomic status undoubtedly engender greater marital stability and the control of fertility. Educated men and women have greater earning potential than their compatriots who have learned fewer skills, or attended school for fewer years. In addition, education probably provides information and sophistication which is useful for solving the problems of married life, whether it be securing housing or preventing excess children. By no means is this a new observation, for DuBois made a similar comment after studying Philadelphia blacks in the 1890s. We must note that elevated socio-economic standing is obviously not a necessary and sufficient

---

[7] Frazier, *The Negro Family in the United States*, Chap. xxii.

[8] Elliot Liebow, *Tally's Corner* (Boston: Little, Brown and Co., 1967), p. 210.

[9] Whelpton, Campbell and Patterson, *op. cit.*, Chap. ix; Carl L. Harter, "Male Fertility in New Orleans," *Demography*, X (1968), 61–78; Norman B. Ryder and Charles F. Westoff, "Relationships Among Intended, Expected, Desired, and Ideal Family Size: United States, 1965," *Population Research* (March, 1969), Table 4.

condition for stable marriages and small families, for an immense number of other factors, many of them not susceptible to demographic measurement, influence whether a marriage remains intact or whether a woman bears two or seven children.

We hypothesize that the marital status and fertility of any group of adults depends upon many different factors. It is influenced by their characteristics as adults such as their current income or by their place of residence which may be related to their ability to secure adequate housing. It is also influenced by their background characteristics such as their families of origin and their educational attainment. To explain the marital status and fertility variables discussed in this chapter, we must assess the influence of these different causal variables. We speculate that black women who were born in the South faced a number of difficulties if they were to remain in stable marriages or have just a few children. Being born in the South was indicative of coming from a rural background and this had a direct effect on fertility. We can speculate that small families were more salient to women who had an urban background. In addition, women who grew up in cities may have more role models or peers who had just a few children and who provided information about the use of birth control.

The southern states typically spent less effort and money insuring that their populations received an education than did the northern states. Blacks in the South were at an extreme disadvantage in many states.[10] This meant that southern born black women completed fewer years of school. This lack of schooling had direct effects both on marital status and on fertility, again suggesting that educational attainment facilitated marital stability and the control of fertility. Educational attainment also had indirect effects upon marital stability and fertility since women who attended school for many years postponed their marriage, and this delay led to more stable marriages and smaller families.

This discussion is weakest in accounting for differences in marital stability. We can hypothesize that well-educated women frequently married similarly well-educated men who had greater earning potential, and that characteristics of the husbands, resulting from this marital selectivity, played an important role in determining the stability of marriages. Much more extensive

---

[10] Myrdal, *op. cit.*, I, 337–344; Louis R. Harlan, *Separate and Unequal*, reprint ed. (New York: Atheneum, 1968).

research is needed concerning marital homogeneity and the characteristics of husbands in order to account for the observed patterns of marital stability.

The analysis of data for different cohorts provides some insights into how the variables examined in this chapter influenced family size. Although region of birth, education, age at marriage, and marital stability each affected fertility among all cohorts, the timing of their effects differed. Among young black women, age at marriage had the greatest impact upon fertility. It seems likely that early in marriage, few couples effectively planned their families or limited their fertility. The Princeton Fertility Study found that couples typically did not use contraceptives very proficiently until they had some children or approached their desired family size.[11] Among black women in the early stages of family building, their fertility depended chiefly upon their age at marriage, although among these young women education did have a small significant effect, suggesting that even early in marriage educational attainment led to control of fertility.

As women grew older, other variables, in addition to age at marriage, became important in explaining fertility. For instance, being born outside the South came to have the effect of reducing fertility. It is probable that northern-born women began to use birth control and limited the number of children after they had borne some, but that women from a southern background continued to bear children more frequently. Marital stability came to have a much more pronounced effect, reflecting the results of living with a husband for a longer period of time.

Changes in the socio-economic status of blacks and in their regional distribution should have the consequence of lowering fertility rates in the future. As we have frequently noted elsewhere in this monograph, educational attainment among both black males and females has increased, the occupational and earnings situation has improved during the 1960s and, at the same time, the rural farm population has declined rapidly. We can hypothesize that these changes will lead to greater control of fertility and smaller families. It is more uncertain what effects changes in socio-economic status will have upon marital stability and further research is imperative if this question is to be answered.

---

[11] Westoff, Potter and Sagi, *op. cit.*, Chap. IV.

The Effects of Husband's Characteristics on Fertility

In Chapter 5, we observed that socio-economic characteristics of husbands were related to fertility. Wives of men who held white collar jobs bore fewer children than wives of men who worked as laborers. Similarly, the husband's income and his education appeared related to the wife's fertility. It is possible that the husband's socio-economic characteristics had an important effect upon family size. Men who held white collar jobs or who earned large sums of money may have planned carefully and controlled their family's size in order to be socially mobile. However, it is possible that men who had the characteristics of higher status married older women or married well-educated women. In other words, the husband's characteristics may have had no influence on the couple's fertility apart from the influence of the wife's age at marriage or her educational attainment.

To determine which of these explanations was more plausible, the one-in-one-thousand sample of the 1960 population was scanned and black women, ages 15 to 44 in 1960, who had married only once and lived with their husbands, were selected. It was necessary to eliminate ever-married women who were not living with a husband and also women who had had more than one husband, since there were no data indicating which husband fathered the woman's children or when the children were born. A total of 1,628 women satisfied the criteria for inclusion. The following information was obtained for each of the women:

> Her age at first marriage
> Her educational attainment
> Her husband's educational attainment
> His occupation as of April, 1960
> His total income in 1959
> His age at marriage
> The number of children the wife had borne.

A numerical score was assigned for each of these variables. Age at marriage and education were scored in years. Each husband received an occupational prestige score. These scores were developed by Dudley Duncan and ranged from a high of 75 points, given to men who were professional or technical workers, to a low of 7 points assigned to laborers.[12] Income in 1959 was measured

---

[12] Albert J. Reiss Jr., *Occupations and Social Structure* (New York: Free Press of Glencoe, 1961), p. 155.

in units of one thousand dollars and fertility was measured by number of children. The means and standard deviations of these variables are listed in Table 7–6. It is interesting to observe the educational discrepancy which characterized these couples. The women were better educated: wives averaged 9.7 years of schooling while husbands averaged 8.5 years. This finding was not unique to these couples, for among most age groups of adult blacks, average educational attainment was greater among women than among men.[13]

To determine the effects of husband's characteristics, regression models were used in which fertility was the dependent variable. We tested to determine if the inclusion of a characteristic of the husband accounted for a significant increase in explained variance, over and above the variance accounted for by the wife's age at marriage and her education. The first model, listed in Table 7–6, shows the regression of fertility upon wife's education and her age at marriage. The partial regression coefficients indicate that each year marriage was delayed, fertility was decreased by about one-eighth child, while each year of additional education had the independent effect of reducing fertility by one-fifth child. The multiple correlation coefficient shows that these two variables accounted for 10.7 percent of the variance in fertility.

Model II includes a measure of the husband's occupational status, in 1960, as a third explanatory variable. The partial regression coefficient has a negative sign indicating that, independent of wife's education and age at marriage, the husband's occupational prestige was inversely related to fertility. However, the proportion of variance accounted for is just about the same whether or not the husband's occupation is included as an explanatory variable. The F ratio indicates that the inclusion of this variable does not significantly change the explained variance. This leads to the conclusion that the husband's occupation did not have a substantial effect upon fertility apart from the effects of wife's education and her age at marriage.

A similar analysis, shown in Table 7–6, indicates that the husband's income in 1959 and his age at marriage did not have important independent effects upon fertility. The husband's educational attainment did have an effect upon the couple's fertility. Extensively educated husbands had fewer children than husbands

---

[13] U. S., Bureau of the Census, *Census of Population: 1960*, PC(2)–1C, Table 19.

who had completed only a few years of schooling. Each year of education, on the part of the husband, had the independent effect of reducing the couple's fertility by about one-tenth child.

On the basis of this analysis, we conclude that, although the husband's occupation and income appeared related to the couple's childbearing, this is a spurious relationship. Men with prestigious

TABLE 7–6
Regression of Fertility Upon Characteristics of the Wife and Husband Married-Once-Spouse-Present Black Women, 15 to 44 in 1960 (N = 1628)

Variable	Notation	Mean		Standard Deviation
Children Ever Born	Y	3.00	Children	2.73
Wife's Age at Marriage	X_1	20.75	Years	4.65
Wife's Education	X_2	9.68	Years	3.04
Husband's Occupation	X_3	20.35	Points	14.67
Husband's Income	X_4	3.087	($1,000)	2.10
Husband's Education	X_5	8.51	Years	3.73
Husband's Age at Marriage	X_6	24.95	Years	6.86

Model I. Regression of Fertility Upon Wife's Education and Wife's Age at Marriage
$$Y = 7.56 - .1242 X_1 - .2055 X_2$$
$$R^2 = .1071$$

Model II. Regression of Fertility Upon Wife's Education, Wife's Age at Marriage and Husband's Occupational Prestige Score
$$Y = 7.56 - .1228 X_1 - .1924 X_2 - .0076 X_3$$
$$R^2 = .1085$$

Source	Sum of Squares	D of F	Mean Square	F Ratio
Total	12,121	1627		
Explained by X_1 and X_2	1,298	2		
Additional with X_3	17	1	17	2.56
Unexplained by $X_1 X_2 X_3$	10,806	1624	6.65	

Model III. Regression of Fertility Upon Wife's Education, Wife's Age at Marriage and Husband's Income in 1959
$$Y = 7.58 - .1237 X_1 - .2023 X_2 - .0178 X_4$$
$$R^2 = .1073$$

Source	Sum of Squares	D of F	Mean Square	F Ratio
Total	12,121	1627		
Explained by X_1 and X_2	1,298	2		
Additional with X_4	3	1	3	.45
Unexplained by $X_1 X_2 X_4$	10,820	1624	6.66	

Table 7–6 (Cont'd)

Model IV. Regression of Fertility Upon Wife's Education, Wife's Age at Marriage and Husband's Education

$$Y = 7.72 - .1231\, X_1 - .1418\, X_2 - .0939\, X_5$$
$$R^2 = .1185$$

Source	Sum of Squares	D of F	Mean Square	F Ratio
Total	12,121	1627		
Explained by X_1 and X_2	1,298	2		
Additional with X_5	138	1	138	21.0*
Unexplained by $X_1\, X_2\, X_5$	10,685	1624	6.58	

Model V. Regression of Fertility Upon Wife's Education, Wife's Age at Marriage and Husband's Age at Marriage

$$Y = 7.57 - .1235\, X_1 - .2057\, X_2 - .0009\, X_6$$
$$R^2 = .1071$$

Source	Sum of Squares	D of F	Mean Square	F Ratio
Total	12,121	1627		
Explained by X_1 and X_2	1,298	2		
Additional with X_6	0	1	0	0
Unexplained by $X_1\, X_2\, X_6$	10,823	1624	6.66	

* Significant by F test at .001 level.

Source:
    U. S., Bureau of the Census, Records of 1-in-1,000 Sample of 1960 Censuses.

jobs and high incomes married older and well-educated women, and these attributes of the wife affected the couple's childbearing. Educational attainment, however, on the part of either the husband or the wife, had the independent effect of reducing family size.

Chapter 8

THE USE OF BIRTH CONTROL

Introduction

American women who began their childbearing during the middle of the nineteenth century completed their families with an average of about five children, and more than one-quarter of these women had at least seven children.[1] This trend has changed and even the fertile women who began bearing children after World War II are going to complete their childbearing with an average of less than three and one-half children.[2] One of the major reasons for this demographic transition has been the widespread adoption of effective methods of birth control. Recent fertility studies in the United States have found that, at least among whites, more than 95 percent of the couples approve of fertility control, and that 90 percent of the couples intend to use a method of birth control at some point in their lives.[3]

As we noted in earlier chapters, there have been substantial long-run changes in family size among blacks. In this chapter, we shall first try to assess whether the past changes in Negro fertility

---

[1] U. S., Bureau of the Census, *Sixteenth Census of the United States: 1940*, Population, Differential Fertility: 1940 and 1910, Women by Number of Children Ever Born: Tables 4, 6, and 15.

[2] U. S., Bureau of the Census, "Changes in the Average Number of Children Ever Born to Women: 1960 to 1969," *Current Population Reports*, Series P–20, No. 178 (February 27, 1969), p. 2.

[3] Whelpton, Campbell and Patterson, *op. cit.*, Table 102 to 109; Charles F. Westoff and Norman B. Ryder, "Recent Trends in Attitudes Toward Fertility Control and in the Practice of Contraception in the United States," in *Fertility and Family Planning*, S. J. Behrman, Leslie Corsa, and Ronald Freedman (eds.) (Ann Arbor: University of Michigan Press, 1969), Tables 1 and 9.

rates were caused by changes in the use and effectiveness of birth control. Second, we shall describe what changes have occurred recently in the use of birth control by blacks and what implications they have for future fertility rates.

Studies of the Use of Birth Control before World War II

Walter Willcox analyzed data from the Census of 1900 and observed that black women who lived in the North, most of whom lived in cities, had unusually low fertility rates and the monograph which described Negroes, based on data from the Census of 1910, made a similar observation.[4] However, neither of these studies offered any explanation for the infrequent childbearing of urban blacks. Apparently, the first demographer to attempt explaining these fertility patterns was Warren Thompson in his monograph, *Ratio of Children to Women: 1920*.[5] He noted that, as of 1920, blacks in cities were not bearing enough children to replace themselves.[6] He contended that blacks, who were recent immigrants to cities, had not developed feelings of belonging to a community and, as a result, ties of family life were broken and most blacks lived in a disorganized environment. In Thompson's view, this disorganization itself, however, did not produce the low fertility rates. He believed that black women surveyed their position in society, assessed the difficulties their children would face and then decided to either limit the size of their family or had no children at all. In Thompson's words:

> . . . The motives leading to birth control are generally [more] concrete and have direct relation to the immediate personal advantage of having few or no children. Thus the desire for good clothes, for good food, for good living quarters, for gay night life, for freedom to flit hither and thither at will, for appearing well socially, for achieving the conventional successes of one's group, etc. are usually the immediate motives for the limitation of births among all classes. But may it not be that back of these concrete desires and intensifying their urge to a definite type of conduct lies, among the Negroes, an unconscious feeling of having but little chance to participate in the more important phases of the life of the

---

[4] Walter F. Willcox, "Negroes in the United States," pp. 67–68; U. S., Bureau of the Census, *Negroes in the United States: 1790–1915*, p. 290.

[5] Thompson, *op. cit.*, pp. 148–149.

[6] *Ibid.*, p. 152.

community or the age; hence, of the futility of self-sacrifice for the sake of children?[7]

Pearl's Study of Family Limitation

During the 1920s, there were no empirical studies investigating the use of birth control by blacks, so it is impossible to verify Thompson's assertion that many black women were controlling their fertility. The first large study of contraceptive use in this country was carried out in the early 1930s by Raymond Pearl. He observed that there was much heated discussion of birth control and that many protagonists made baseless claims about how many or few women were using birth control, but that no one really knew anything about the popularity of birth control or its consequences for the birth rate. Pearl designed a study which had two major aims: first, to determine what proportion of the married women in the United States used some method of contraception; second, to ascertain how effectively these women controlled their fertility.[8] He obtained information from women who delivered in the obstetrics wards of hospitals in or near major cities of the eastern United States. Eventually, the cooperation of 139 hospitals in 26 cities was secured, although no hospitals affiliated with the Catholic Church were contacted. The attending physician, resident or intern was instructed to obtain a reproductive history and an account of contraceptive use from each woman who had a child between July, 1931 and December, 1932. A total of 30,949 case histories was secured; 25,316 of these pertained to white women and 5,633 to Negro women.[9] At this time, about one-third of the births in the United States occurred in hospitals.

Relatively few black women reported they had ever used any form of contraception before delivery. Overall, only 16 percent

---

[7] *Ibid.*, p. 153.

[8] Raymond Pearl, "Preliminary Notes on a Cooperative Investigation of Family Limitation," *Milbank Memorial Fund Quarterly* XI, No. 1 (January, 1933), 37–59; "Second Progress Report on a Study of Family Limitation," *Milbank Memorial Fund Quarterly*, XIII, No. 3 (July, 1934), 258–284; "Third Progress Report on a Study of Family Limitation," *Milbank Memorial Fund Quarterly*, XIV, No. 3 (July, 1936), 363–407; "Fertility and Contraception in Urban Whites and Negroes," *Science* LXXXIII, No. 2160 (May 22, 1936), 503–506; "Fertility and Contraception in New York and Chicago," *Journal of the American Medical Association* CVIII, No. 17 (April 24, 1937), 1385–1390. *The Natural History of Population* (Oxford: University Press, 1939) Chap. iv.

[9] Pearl, "Third Progress Report on a Study of Family Limitation," pp. 259–260.

of the black women said they had used any technique to prevent themselves from becoming pregnant. The remaining five-sixths had done nothing to limit their fertility.[10] Douching and periodic abstinence were included as contraceptive techniques. Among white women, the practice of contraception was more widespread, for 43 percent of the women reported they had used some method of birth control.

To study the effectiveness with which women used birth control, Pearl isolated two groups of women. The first group included married-once women who had no detectable gynecological disease or difficulty and had never used birth control. The second group was composed of married-once women without gynecological disease who had practiced some form of contraception ". . . regularly and steadily without intermission . . ."[11] since the time of their marriage. This latter group included the women who claimed they had been using contraception throughout their marriage. Pregnancy rates per period of exposure were then computed for the two groups of women. Among whites, the age-specific pregnancy rates for users of birth control were 20 to 39 percent lower, depending upon the age group, than the pregnancy rates of women who had never attempted to limit their childbearing. Pearl assumed that this was a rough measure of the effectiveness of contraceptive use. Among blacks, the pregnancy rates for birth control users were almost exactly the same as the pregnancy rates of non-users. There was no measurable indication that the use of birth control had any effect on Negro fertility rates, and Pearl concluded that ". . . the general run of Negroes do not practice contraception effectively."[12]

Pearl's study strongly suggests that the use of birth control had no impact upon black fertility rates during the Depression decade when fertility rates were at an all-time low. However, we must ask if we can validly generalize from his study to the entire black population. His sample was highly selective. First, a woman had to bear a child to be included in the study. Sterile women and women who used contraception so effectively that they did not have a child, during 1931 or 1932, were not represented.

Second, Pearl's study was restricted to women who lived in or near an urban area, but in the early 1930s, the majority of

---

[10] *Ibid.*, p. 267.
[11] *Ibid.*, p. 278.
[12] Pearl, "Fertility and Contraception in Urban Whites and Negroes," p. 505.

blacks lived in rural areas.[13] We would assume that urban blacks were more aware of birth control and had greater access to health clinics than rural blacks. This implies that the use of birth control was more common in cities than in other areas and suggests that if Pearl's sample had included all black women, instead of just urban women, the proportion who had used birth control would have been even lower than 16 percent.

Third, the women in Pearl's study were over-representative of the upper educational attainment levels. Only 5 percent of the Negro women in his study reported they were illiterate, but the Census of 1930 found that 9 percent of the Negro women of the same age were unable to read and write.[14] Thirty percent of the black women in Pearl's sample had at least some high school education, but the Census of 1940 discovered that no more than 23 percent of the black women in the same age group had some high school education,[15] again indicating the selectivity of the sample. Recent fertility investigations have found that the use of contraception is directly linked to educational attainment among both whites and Negroes.[16] This evidence also implies that a national study of black women would have found a lower proportion using contraception than did Pearl's study.

Additional Studies

Two other very limited studies analyzed birth control use by blacks during the Depression decade. Regine Stix summarized findings pertaining to women who used three family planning and maternal health clinics.[17] One of these clinics, located in Spartan-burg, South Carolina, served blacks. A total of 455 Negro women in the area were referred to the clinic by doctors, welfare work-

---

[13] See Table 3–3.

[14] Pearl, "Third Progress Report on a Study of Family Limitation," pp. 273–278 and 280; U. S., Bureau of the Census, *Fifteenth Census of the United States: 1930*, Population, II, pp. 1226–1227.

[15] Pearl, *op. cit.*, p. 265; U. S., Bureau of the Census, *Sixteenth Census of the United States: 1940*, Population, IV, Part 1, Table 18.

[16] Norman B. Ryder and Charles F. Westoff, "Use of Oral Contraception in the United States; 1965," *Science* CLIII, No. 3741 (September 9, 1966), 1202.

[17] Regine K. Stix, "Contraceptive Service in Three Areas, Part I," *Milbank Memorial Fund Quarterly*, XIX, No. 2 (April, 1941), 171–188; "Contraceptive Service in Three Areas, Part II, The Effectiveness of Clinic Services," *Milbank Memorial Fund Quarterly* XIX, No. 3 (July, 1941), 304–326.

ers, and health nurses, in many cases because they needed assistance in preventing additional pregnancies. These women represented a poorly educated low-income population; however, they may have been typical of southern blacks at this period of time. The median annual family income of the urban black women who used this clinic was $400 and of the rural black women, $125, although 60 percent of the rural families received no cash income.[18]

These women were asked if they had ever used birth control before visiting the clinic and approximately 20 percent reported they had. Douching, an unreliable technique, was most frequently reported and accounted for one-half of all contraceptive use.[19] A few women indicated their husbands used condoms, but the cost of these limited their popularity. Questions were asked about induced abortions, and it was discovered that these were not widely used to control fertility. Stillbirths, however, occurred frequently to the Negro women and medical examinations revealed that diseases were the cause of these stillbirths. Stix concluded, "The Negro women in Spartanburg used very little contraception . . . and the contraception they used was not effective."[20]

In 1936, the National Committee on Maternal Health instituted a birth control clinic in Logan, West Virginia, with the intent of investigating how readily a rural non-farm population would accept birth control and which problems would develop in the operation of such a clinic.[21] Women who came to the center for birth control advice were asked about their age at marriage, childbearing, and their use of contraceptives. In addition to these women, an area sample of Logan County was drawn and women ages 15 to 44 who lived with a husband were interviewed. Almost all of these women were wives of coal miners.

The rates of contraceptive use among the two groups of women differed greatly. Among Negro women who came to the clinic seeking birth control, 32 percent reported they had, in the past, used some method of contraception, but among Negro women in the area sample, only 7 percent reported they had used contraceptives. The users of birth control were not very success-

---

[18] Stix, "Contraceptive Service in Three Areas, Part I," p. 173.

[19] Ibid., p. 175.

[20] Ibid., p. 188.

[21] Gilbert Wheeler Beebe, Contraception and Fertility in the Southern Appalachians (Baltimore: Williams & Wilkins, 1942); "Differential Fertility by Color for Coal Miners in Logan County, West Virginia," Milbank Memorial Fund Quarterly XIX, No. 2 (April, 1941), 189–195.

ful in preventing unwanted pregnancies for the major method they employed was the douche. The principal investigator, Gilbert Beebe, estimated that, for the black women, fertility rates during periods of contraceptive use were only seven percent below fertility rates for periods in which no contraceptives were used.[22] He concluded that the practice of contraception had very little impact upon the birth rates of blacks in Logan County.

It is impossible to draw any unqualified conclusions from these few studies of contraceptive use. However, two generalizations may be made. First, it is apparent that there was some use of birth control by black couples. In Pearl's study, although overall only 16 percent of the women had used birth control, 24 percent of the Negro women in New York City and 47 percent of the women in Chicago claimed they were users.[23] Upwards of one-quarter to one-third of the women who came to birth control clinics in Spartanburg or Logan County had done something to limit their fertility. Among the general black population, however, the proportion who had ever used birth control must have been much lower, perhaps closer to the 7 percent figure reported for the sample of rural women in Logan County.

Second, it is apparent from these studies that the practice of birth control did little to reduce fertility rates. Douching was consistently reported as the most popular method. Pearl's investigation found that fertility rates during periods in which contraceptives were used were similar to fertility rates during periods in which contraceptives were not used; and the findings of Stix and Beebe were similar. We can infer that, while the use of birth control may have affected the childbearing of some couples, the black fertility rates were lowest at a time when there was very little effective use of contraceptives.

Studies of Birth Control after World War II

There were no large studies of contraceptive use by blacks between the 1930s and 1960. During this period, there was an urbanization of blacks, an improvement in the average educational attainment level, and the opening of additional birth control clinics in some areas.[24] These changes may have led to greater birth

---

[22] Beebe, *Contraception and Fertility in the Southern Appalachians*, p. 107.

[23] Pearl, "Fertility and Contraception in New York and Chicago," p. 1387.

control use by Negroes, but it is unclear how rapidly contraception was adopted.

In 1960, Whelpton, Campbell, and Patterson selected a national sample of married women ages 18 to 39 who were living with their husbands.[25] This sample included a total of 270 non-white women, 256 of whom were blacks.[26] Information about age at marriage, lifetime childbearing, contraceptive use, and socioeconomic status was obtained from each woman. In discussing their findings, it is good to keep in mind the characteristics of their sample. *Married-spouse-present* women were the only women who were interviewed. The Census of 1960 found that no more than 73 percent of the ever-married non-white women ages 18 to 39 were *married-spouse-present*, so their data present no information about the contraceptive practices of ever-married women who were not living with a husband.[27] Their sample was representative of the national non-white female population with regard to age, number of children ever born and religious preference. However, it over-represented college-educated Negro women and women who lived in the North Central region. It was somewhat under-representative of women with less than a high school education and women who lived in the West.[28] The authors concluded that none of these differences were sufficiently large to affect their conclusions.

The principal findings of this 1960 study were the following: first, three-fifths of the non-white women reported they had ever used birth control, which was defined to include douching and abstinence. This is a much higher proportion than reported by the studies conducted in the 1930s, and implies that the use of contraception by blacks increased between the Depression and 1960. On the other hand, this study found that 81 percent of the white women had used birth control indicating that there was still a substantial racial difference in the use of contraception.[29]

Second, it was clear that most non-white women knew about birth control and planned to use it. Seventy-six percent of the non-white women either had used contraception or expected to

---

24 Myrdal, *op. cit.*, I, p. 178.

25 Whelpton, Campbell and Patterson, *op. cit.*, p. 3.

26 *Ibid.*, p. 335.

27 U. S., Bureau of the Census, *Census of Population: 1960*, PC(1)–1D, Table 176.

28 Whelpton, Campbell, and Patterson, *op. cit.*, pp. 408–410.

29 *Ibid.*, p. 358.

use it at some point in their married lives.[30] Of the non-white
women who did not intend to use birth control, three-fifths reported they had difficulties becoming pregnant, lessening their
need for contraceptives. There was no evidence of resistance to
birth control on the part of any large segment of the black population.

Third, non-white women frequently delayed using contraceptives until they had been married for some years and had borne
several children. Few non-white women used birth control to
space their first child or control their childbearing early in marriage.[31] A larger proportion of white women used birth control
early in their married lives.

Fourth, non-white women differed from white women in that
they often relied upon the less effective methods of preventing
pregnancy. Compared to whites, a relatively high proportion of
non-white women used the douche, jelly, and suppositories; few
used a diaphragm, a much more effective method.[32]

Fifth, as might be expected on the basis of the previous comments, non-white couples were typically less successful than white
couples in planning their families. In this study, families were
characterized as completely planned if pregnancies occurred only
after the couple stopped using contraception in order to have a
child. Only 7 percent of the non-white families were completely
planned in contrast to 21 percent of the white families.[33] The term
excess fertility was used to describe couples whose last child was
not desired by either the husband or the wife. Among non-whites,
31 percent were in this category; among whites, the proportion
classed as having excess fertility was 17 percent again indicating
the lack of success many blacks experienced in planning their
families.[34]

Finally, the use of birth control by non-white women was related to their place of residence and their socio-economic status.
Only one-third of the Negro women who lived on southern farms
had tried to limit their fertility, but more than three-quarters of
the women in the Northeast had.[35] Forty-two percent of the grade
school educated women had used contraceptives, but 86 percent
of the college educated women had.[36] Non-white women who were

---

[30] *Ibid.*, p. 358.
[31] *Ibid.*, p. 366.
[32] *Ibid.*, p. 360.
[33] *Ibid.*, p. 362.
[34] *Ibid.*
[35] *Ibid.*, pp. 354 and 358.
[36] *Ibid.*, p. 359.

not born in the rural South or who had more than a high school education limited their fertility almost as effectively as white women who had similar characteristics.[37]

In 1965, another national survey of fertility patterns and contraceptive practices was conducted, this one by Charles Westoff and Norman Ryder.[38] Once again, the study was restricted to married women who were living with their husbands at the time of the interview. To obtain more information about black respondents, the non-white population was double sampled which produced a total of 1039 interviews with non-white wives; 969 were with Negro women.[39] First, the period 1960 to 1965 witnessed an increase in the proportion of black women who used birth control. In 1965, 77 percent of the non-white wives reported they had used contraceptives compared to 59 percent five years earlier. The percentage who either had used or expected to use went up from 76 percent to 86 percent.[40] During this period, racial differences in the proportion ever using contraceptives declined as non-whites became more like whites in their use of birth control.

Second, the increases in the use of birth control were greatest among the groups of black women who used birth control the least in 1960. For instance, among Negro women whose husbands earned $6,000 or more in the year preceding the survey the pro-

---

[37] *Ibid.*, pp. 362, 364 and 365.

[38] Norman B. Ryder and Charles F. Westoff, "Use of Oral Contraception in the United States, 1965;" "The United States: The Pill and the Birth Rate, 1960–1965," *Studies in Family Planning*, No. 20 (June, 1967), 1–3; "Relationships Among Intended, Expected, Desired, and Ideal Family Size: United States, 1965;" "The Trend of Expected Parity in the United States: 1955, 1960, 1965," *Population Index* XXXIII, No. 2 (April–June, 1967), 153–168; Charles F. Westoff and Norman B. Ryder, "United States: Methods of Fertility Control, 1955, 1960, and 1965," *Studies in Family Planning*, No. 17 (February, 1967), 1–5; "Duration of Use of Oral Contraception in the United States: 1960–65," *Public Health Reports* LXXXIII, No. 4 (April, 1968), 277–287; "Experience with Oral Contraception in the United States, 1960–1965," *Clinical Obstetrics and Gynecology* XI, No. 3 (September, 1968), 734–752; "Recent Trends in Attitudes Toward Fertility Control and in the Practice of Contraception in the United States;" Charles F. Westoff, Emily C. Moore, and Norman B. Ryder, "The Structure of Attitudes Toward Abortion," *Milbank Memorial Fund Quarterly* XLVII, No. 1 (January, 1969) Part 1, 11–37; Charles F. Westoff, Larry Bumpass, and Norman B. Ryder, "Oral Contraception, Coital Frequency, and the Time Required to Conceive," *Social Biology* XVL, No. 1 (March, 1969), 1–10.

[39] Ryder and Westoff, "Oral Contraception in the United States, 1965," pp. 1199 and 1203.

[40] Westoff and Ryder, "Recent Trends in Attitudes Toward Fertility Control and in the Practice of Contraception in the United States," Table 15.

portion who had used birth control went up moderately from 76 percent in 1960 to 82 percent in 1965. However, among black women married to men who earned less than $4,000, the rise was much greater; from 56 percent to 71 percent.[41] It appears that during the first half of the 1960s, birth control became much more commonly employed by the lower socio-economic and rural groups of black women who reported very low rates of contraceptive use in 1960. As a result, regional and socio-economic differences in the use of birth control appear to have gradually diminished during this time span. Third, while studies of the effectiveness of birth control use have not been completed, there is some evidence of remaining racial differences in contraceptive practice. Oral contraceptives were first marketed in 1960. Five years later, in October of 1965, when this most recent fertility survey was conducted, 27 percent of the white respondents and 19 percent of the Negro said they had used the pills at some point.[42] The timing of the use of oral contraceptives and the purpose for which they were used differed:

> There is considerable evidence (here) for the view that Negroes are using oral contraception at a later stage in their marriage than whites, presumably to terminate fertility rather than to time births. Thus, by age, the percentages of women now using oral contraception are markedly different for whites and Negroes under 25, but the divergence is trivial for age groups 25–29 and 30–34. Similarly the percentages of women currently using oral contraception are much higher for whites than for Negroes for parities of 0 and 1, but the positions of the races are reversed at higher parities.[43]

With regard to educational attainment, however, there were smaller racial differences in use, although at each educational level, the proportion who had used oral contraception was lower among Negroes than among whites.

Conclusion

It appears that the trends in the use of birth control by blacks have generally moved in the opposite direction from trends in the

---

[41] *Ibid.*, Table 15.

[42] Ryder and Westoff, "Oral Contraception in the United States, 1965," p. 1203.

[43] *Ibid.*, p. 1202.

fertility rate, at least until recently. Before 1940, there must have been relatively few black women who effectively limited their fertility, but nevertheless, there had been a very long period, beginning in the late nineteenth century, during which the Negro birth rate declined. From 1940 to 1960, there was an increase in the use of birth control by black women and apparently a shift to more effective techniques. Yet, the fertility rate rose rapidly during this span. We can infer that the increase in the birth rate would have been even greater had not so many women begun using contraceptives.

Since 1960, the birth rate has declined and the use of birth control has become more common. As further tabulations from the 1965 National Fertility Study are published, it should become possible to further isolate and specify exactly what effects contraceptive use has had upon the recent changes in the birth rate.

From time to time, black writers, spokesmen, and orators have argued that whites were attempting to limit the growth of the black population or even exterminate Negroes. Marcus Garvey warned that unless blacks organized themselves, they might suffer the same fate at the hands of the white race as had the American Indians.[44] Recently, spokesmen for the Black Muslim movement, among others, have condemned the expansion of the government's efforts to provide birth control services in ghetto areas within the United States and to less developed nations in Africa and argued that this was a kind of genocide.[45] This opinion was not universally shared. Both W. E. B. DuBois and Martin Luther King observed the poverty of many blacks and health problems and expressed the view that the practice of birth control would allow many blacks to improve their lot and better care for their children.[46] The various surveys of contraceptive use have not asked black women about their ideological approval or disapproval of birth control. However, we can deduce that no more than a small share of the black population is completely opposed to the use of birth control, for the 1960 and 1965 surveys found that more than 90 percent of the fecund married black women either had used or intended to use contraception.

---

[44] Amy Jacques Garvey (compiler) *Philosophy and Opinions of Marcus Garvey,* reprint ed. (London: Frank Cass & Co. Ltd., 1967), Part I, pp. 46–49, XXXIII, No. 5.

[45] Lonnie Kashif, "New Birth Control," *Muhammad Speaks* (May 23, 1969), p. 27; "White Group Steps up 'Pill' Timetable," *Muhammad Speaks* (October 31, 1969), p. 9.

[46] W. E. B. DuBois, "Black Folk and Birth Control," *Birth Control Review* XVI, No. 6 (June, 1932), 166–167; Mary Smith, *loc. cit.*

In the future, it is probable that an even larger share of the black population will practice birth control because of the changing demographic composition of this population. Fewer women will come from rural backgrounds or live in rural areas, two factors which have in the past been associated with low rates of contraceptive use. Recent changes in educational attainment will probably foster the greater use of contraceptives. For instance, the percentage of black women ages 20 to 24 who were high school graduates went up from 44 percent to 60 percent in the eight years following 1960.[47]

Although contraceptive use by black women will probably increase, it is difficult to predict whether racial differences in the purposes for which birth control is used and the timing of use will diminish. This is because there appears to be a racial difference in the timing of family formation. At young ages, Negro childbearing rates are much higher than those of whites and, in recent years, the Negro-white difference in these fertility rates has grown wider.[48] Even after a decade of declining fertility rates, almost one-quarter of all black women bear a child prior to their eighteenth birthday. Many of the children born to these young women are reported as illegitimate. For instance, in 1967, 50 percent of the first births occurring to non-white women in the thirty-four states for which illegitimacy data are available were recorded as illegitimate births.[49] This implies that many black women become mothers prior to their marriage. Recent fertility studies in the United States suggest that older married Negro women and those who have already borne some children use contraceptives to almost as great an extent as similar white women. They tell us, however, very little about the use of contraceptives by unmarried women and racial differences in the use of birth control may possibly help to explain some of the differences in the fertility rates at these young ages.

Most, but not all, of the programs designed to encourage the use of birth control in the United States have restricted their activities to married women, often to women who have already become mothers. It may be that more than a few black teenage

---

[47] U. S. Bureau of the Census, *Census of Population: 1960*, PC(2)–1C, Table 19; "Educational Attainment: March, 1968," *Current Population Reports*, Series P-20, No. 182 (April 28, 1969), Table 1.

[48] U. S. National Center for Health Statistics, *Vital Statistics of the United States: 1967*, I, Table 1–15.

[49] *Ibid.*, Tables 1–50 and 1–57.

women premaritally bear children because they do not have access to contraceptive information and devices. If this continues into the future, we can expect that the proportion of women who use contraceptives to prevent unwanted additional children rather than to space their pregnancies will be greater among Negroes than among whites.

Chapter 9

THE EFFECTS OF CHANGES IN HEALTH CONDITIONS AND STANDARDS OF LIVING

Introduction

We have yet to explain why the fertility and growth rates of the black population fluctuated in the manner they did. Some possible explanations for changes in the birth rate have been ruled out. In Chapter 6 we indicated that there were only modest changes in the marital status of blacks, changes which were too inconsequential to account for the observed changes in fertility. In the last chapter, we indicated that it was unlikely that the use of contraceptives by black women explained the decrease in fertility and that after World War II both the use of birth control and fertility rates increased.

In this chapter, we examine one other factor which has apparently played an important role in determining the level of Negro fertility: changes in the ability of couples to bear children. Fecundity is a very difficult attribute to measure and there are very few studies, medical or otherwise, which attempt to assess the aggregate fecundity level of a population, or changes over time in fecundity. Nevertheless, there are certain indications, such as changes in some disease and death rates, and fluctuations in the proportion of married women who were childless, which suggest that prior to the Depression decade, fecundity problems and sterility may have been common among blacks.

This chapter begins by analyzing some general trends in black mortality rates, particularly maternal and infant death rates. Then it proceeds to describe trends with regard to two diseases: pellagra and venereal disease. Finally, changes in public health activities, medical facilities, and standards of living, which occurred between 1935 and the present, are described; changes which led to drastic reductions in mortality and morbidity rates among blacks. This, in turn, accounts for the post-Depression rise in childbearing rates.

Mortality Rates as Indicative of
Maternal and Child Health Conditions

In Chapter 3, we pointed out that the official life tables for Negroes computed from registered deaths in the Death Registration States showed that life expectation increased during the early decades of this century. However, life tables computed from census enumeration figures, rather than registered deaths, suggested that there was very little, if any, lengthening of the life span between the pre-Civil War period and the time of the Depression. In the late 1930s, Harold Dorn wrote a manuscript describing trends in Negro mortality for Gunnar Myrdal's study, *An American Dilemma*, and found much evidence that mortality rates among blacks had not declined during the early decades of this century.

Although it is impossible to state definitely the amount of change in the average length of life of the Negro population, the available data indicate that, except for the first few years of life, there has been very little improvement since the beginning of the century. The only series of data covering the entire period are for Negroes living in the original registration states of 1900. . . .

. . . the expectation of life among Negroes living in the North actually decreased during the first three decades of this century except for persons 20 years of age and younger. . . .

Better representation of the entire Negro population can be obtained by considering the trend of mortality in the death registration states of 1920. This group of states included about 65 percent of the Negro population in 1920 and nearly 70 percent in 1930. The trend of mortality among Negroes in these states presents an even more unfavorable picture than the trend in the original registration states. The expectation of life of Negro males decreased at every age including birth; the decrease among Negro females occurred at ages 20 and over. The only increase in expectation of life during the decade was for females under 20 years of age.

The trend in the expectation of life among Negroes in the general population agrees in general with that among the colored policy-holders of the Industrial Department of the Metropolitan Life Insurance Company. From 1921 to 1931, the expectation of life for both males and females from 10 to 60 years of age either decreased or failed to increase. However from 1911 to 1921 the expectation of life definitely increased at the same ages. Since 1931 the downward trend in the expectation of life has been stopped and slight increases have occurred at most ages. But even so, in 1938 the expectation of life for colored males was less than in 1921 at 40 years of age and over and among colored females it was at 50 years of age and over.[1]

Maternal Mortality

Trends in particular types of mortality rates which reflect maternal and child health conditions were analyzed to see if they fluctuated in the manner Dorn has described or in a different manner. The first to be examined is the maternal mortality rate which measures ". . . the risk of death from deliveries and complications of pregnancy, childbearing and the puerperium."[2] The maternal death rate was calculated by dividing the annual number of deaths attributed to maternal conditions by the annual number of live births.

Figure 9–1 shows the trend over time of the recorded maternal mortality rate for non-whites for the period 1920 to 1966. Between 1920 and 1933 states were added to the Death Registration Area and this may affect the comparability of the time series. However, the trend of maternal mortality in specific states for which information is available for all years from 1920 to 1933 is similar to that shown in Figure 9–1.[3]

It is clear that there was little real reduction in maternal mortality among non-whites until the 1930s. One study concluded that before the end of the 1920s ". . . the maternal mortality rate followed a desultory course not only in the expanding registration

---

[1] Myrdal, *op cit.*, I, p. cxxv.

[2] Robert D. Grove and Alice M. Hetzel, *Vital Statistics Rates in the United States: 1940–1960;* U. S., National Center for Health Statistics, (Washington: Government Printing Office, 1968), p. 33.

[3] Forrest E. Linder and Robert D. Grove, *Vital Statistics Rates in the United States: 1900–1940;* U.S., Bureau of the Census, *Sixteenth Census of the United States: 1940;* Table 36.

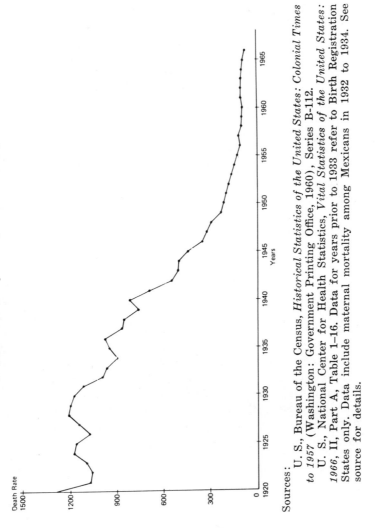

Figure 9–1

Maternal Mortality Rate for Non-whites

(Maternal Deaths per 100,000 Live Births)

Sources:

U. S., Bureau of the Census, *Historical Statistics of the United States: Colonial Times to 1957* (Washington: Government Printing Office, 1960), Series B-112.

U. S., National Center for Health Statistics, *Vital Statistics of the United States: 1966*, II, Part A, Table 1–16. Data for years prior to 1933 refer to Birth Registration States only. Data include maternal mortality among Mexicans in 1932 to 1934. See source for details.

area as a whole but in all geographic subdivisions."[4] Between the end of the 1920s and the late 1930s there were some indications of a modest reduction in maternal mortality; thereafter, the rate declined rapidly.

The trend over time in the maternal mortality rate among whites has been similar to that among non-whites but the racial difference in the rates has gradually widened for the white rate has decreased more rapidly. In the late 1930s, the white maternal mortality rate was approximately double that of Negroes, but in 1966, the non-white rate of 7 deaths per 100,000 live births was almost four times as great as the white rate.[5]

A number of factors explain why the maternal mortality rate dropped after the mid-1930s. Early in that decade, there was a growing awareness of the frequency of maternal deaths and how they might be prevented. The use of the sulfonamide drugs began in the late 1930s and this technological advance played a role in reducing the death rate.[6] Combined with these changes was an expansion of the publicly supported maternal health clinics and a trend toward the hospitalization of births, factors which are discussed later in this chapter.

Fetal Mortality

Fluctuations in the frequency of fetal deaths are indicative of changes in the health level of a population and changes in the ability of women to secure adequate pre-natal care. The index of fetal mortality trends used in this chapter is the fetal death ratio computed by dividing fetal deaths recorded in a year by the number of live births registered in that same year. This rate is influenced by state to state differences in the period of gestation required before the death of a fetus was registered as a fetal death. Fetal death rates, controlling for length of gestation, are available only for recent priods.[7]

Figure 9–2 shows the trend over time in the fetal death ratio among non-whites for the period 1922 to 1966, the years for which

---

[4] Sam Shapiro, Edward R. Schlesinger and Robert E. L. Nesbitt, Jr., *Infant, Perinatal, Maternal, and Childhood Mortality in the United States* (Cambridge: Harvard University Press, 1968), p. 144.

[5] U. S., National Center for Health Statistics, *Vital Statistics of the United States: 1966*, I, Table 1–51; II, Part A, Table 1–24.

[6] Shapiro, Schlesinger and Nesbitt, *Infant, Perinatal, Maternal and Childhood Mortality in the United States*, p. 146.

[7] Grove and Hetzel, *op. cit.*, Tables 30–33.

211

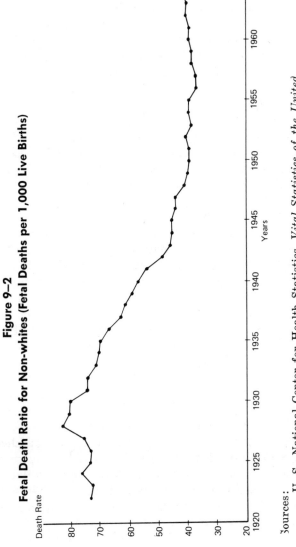

Figure 9–2
Fetal Death Ratio for Non-whites (Fetal Deaths per 1,000 Live Births)

Sources:

U. S., National Center for Health Statistics, *Vital Statistics of the United States: 1966*, II, Part A, Table 3–2. Data for years prior to 1933 refer to Birth Registration States only. Data include fetal mortality among Mexicans for years 1932 to 1934.

data are available. There was no downward trend in this rate before the mid-1930s but, between the late 1930s and the early 1950s, the fetal death ratio was cut in half. Since that time, there has been little change in the fetal death ratio. At each date, the fetal death ratio among whites was approximately one-half as large as that for non-whites but there is no evidence of either a widening or narrowing of the racial difference.

Infant Mortality Rates

The infant mortality rate, that is, deaths of children under one in a year divided by recorded live births for that year, has frequently been employed as an index of health levels. Figure 9–3 shows the trend in the non-white infant mortality rate for the period 1920 to 1966.

Infant mortality trends may differ from trends in maternal and fetal death for much evidence indicates that, at least in cities, infant mortality among blacks declined early this century. For instance, in the Death Registration States of 1900, the infant mortality for non-whites was around 275 deaths per 1,000 births at the turn of the century.[8] One decade later, in the identical states, it declined to 235 and by 1920, to 190. During the 1920s, infant mortality apparently fell more rapidly, reaching a level of about 120 in 1930.[9] These rates were estimated from data concerning registered infant deaths and the population under one year of age enumerated by the census. Thus the level of these infant mortality rates and some of their fluctuations may be attributable to changes in census coverage.

To surmount these problems, health statisticians encouraged the registration of births so that they could be more confident of the infant mortality level. Infant mortality rates, computed from data pertaining to registered births and deaths, are available for certain states and cities beginning about 1916 and they demonstrate that there was a decline in the infant death rate in cities of both the North and South. For instance, in New York City, the non-white infant mortality rate fell from 176 in 1917 to 105 in 1930; in Boston, from 167 to 90; in Philadelphia, from 193 to 100; in Richmond, from 219 to 119; and in Louisville, from 166 to 96.[10]

---

[8] Linder and Grove, op. cit., Table 7.
[9] Ibid., Table 7.
[10] Holmes, op. cit., Table XXV.

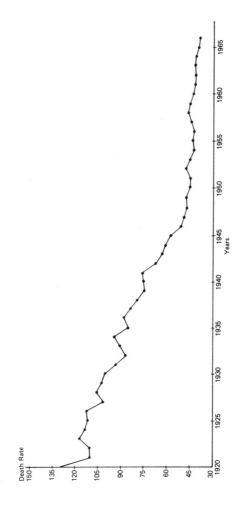

Figure 9-3

Infant Mortality Rate for Non-whites (Infant Deaths per 1,000 Live Births)

Sources:

U.S., Bureau of the Census, *Historical Statistics of the United States: Colonial Times to 1957*, Series B-109. U.S., National Center for Health Statistics, *Vital Statistics of the United States: 1966*, II, Part A, Table 2–1. Data for years prior to 1933 refer to Birth Registration States only. Data include infant mortality among Mexicans for years 1932 to 1934.

We cannot be certain that improvements in infant health characterized the entire black population at this time. There are two reasons for this. First, most, but not all, studies of Negro infant mortality conducted early this century found that rural infant mortality rates were about one-half as large as those of urban areas.[11] There was a gradual urbanization of blacks during this period, that is, a shift from areas of apparently low infant mortality to areas of higher death rates.[12] This may have offset improvements in urban infant mortality rates. Second, prior to 1930, infant death rates in cities fell more rapidly than those in rural areas. For instance, in North Carolina and Virginia, states with large rural black populations, the non-white infant mortality rates declined less rapidly than in Massachusetts and New York, states in which most blacks lived in cities; in Maryland, the rural infant death rate fell slowly, compared to the urban.[13] The increasing poverty of rural blacks and the absence of specific programs to reduce infant deaths in rural areas, may explain the lack of change in rural infant mortality rates.

It is uncertain, then, which course the national infant death rates among blacks followed prior to the mid-1930s. As the authors of one study noted, possible errors in the registration system and the census make it difficult to know much about infant mortality trends.[14]

Between 1935 and 1950, there was a pronounced decline in the infant mortality rate, averaging about 5 percent each year.[15] Upwards of one half of this decrease was attributable to lower death rates from pneumonia, influenza and other infectious and parasitic diseases.[16] Hospitalization for delivery, expanded programs of pre-natal care, and improved techniques of care for the newborn assisted in reducing infant mortality.

In 1935, the non-white infant mortality rate was about 60 percent greater than that of whites.[17] Between that date and 1950,

---

[11] *Ibid.*, Chap. vi.

[12] See Table 3–2.

[13] Holmes, *op. cit.*, Table XXV.

[14] Shapiro, Schlesinger and Nesbitt, *Infant and Perinatal Mortality in the United States*, p. 2.

[15] Mary A. McCarthy, *Infant, Fetal, and Maternal Mortality, United States: 1963;* U.S., National Center for Health Statistics, Data from the National Vital Statistics System, Series 20, No. 3 (September, 1966), p. 6.

[16] Shapiro, Schlesinger and Nesbitt, *Infant and Perinatal Mortality in the United States*, p. 9.

[17] Grove and Hetzel, *op. cit.*, Table 38.

the infant mortality rates of both races declined at about the same rate.[18] Since 1950, the decline among whites has been faster than the decline among non-whites. As a result, in 1966, the infant mortality rate among non-whites was about 90 percent greater than that among whites.[19]

Figure 9–4 shows the non-white infant mortality rate for deaths caused by syphilis. This rate was computed by dividing the number of infant deaths, attributed to syphilis, by the number of births registered in that year. If an infant dies of syphilis, it is very likely that his mother was not examined during her pregnancy to see if she had any venereal diseases. This death rate, then, may be indicative of the medical care and treatment which was available to pregnant black women.

In the early 1920s there were about 300 infant deaths from syphilis per 100,000 non-white births. This did not decline until the late 1930s; in fact, the infant death rate from syphilis may have increased during the 1920s and early 1930s. A very sharp decline in infant deaths from syphilis began around 1938 and by the mid-1950s this rate was reduced to about 3 per 100,000 births.

We can summarize this section by noting that these death rates, which reflect maternal and infant health conditions, declined very little, if at all, before the mid-1930s but then, for a score of years, they fell very rapidly. In general, these rates reached low levels during the mid-1950s and since that time there has been very little fluctuation.

Trends in Disease Rates among Blacks

In this section, we discuss trends in two diseases which afflicted many blacks in the past. First, pellagra is described, for changes in the prevalence of this ailment are indicative of changes in the living standards of Negroes in rural areas and small towns of the South. In addition, one of the side effects of this disease was a reduction in fecundity. Second, changes in the incidence and effects of venereal diseases are described because one of the venereal diseases, gonorrhea, can produce sterility and another, syphilis, reduces the likelihood that a woman will bear a live child if she has conceived.

---

[18] McCarthy, op. cit., p. 6.
[19] U.S., National Center for Health Statistics, Vital Statistics of the United States: 1966, II, Part A, Table 2–1.

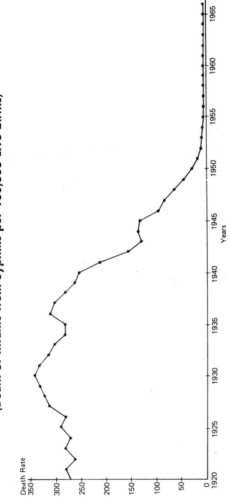

Figure 9–4
Infant Mortality from Syphilis among Non-whites
(Death of Infants from Syphilis per 100,000 Live Births)

Sources:

Forrest E. Linder and Robert D. Grove, *Vital Statistics Rates in the United States: 1900–1940,* U. S., Bureau of the Census, Sixteenth Census of the United States: 1940, Table 32.

U.S., National Office of Vital Statistics, *Vital Statistics of the United States,* 1945 through 1958, Various Tables.

U.S., National Center for Health Statistics, *Vital Statistics of the United States,* 1959 through 1966, Various Tables.

Data for years prior to 1933 refer to Birth Registration States only. Data include infant mortality among Mexicans for years 1932 to 1934.

Pellagra

Pellagra is a dietary deficiency disease caused by lack of intake of nicotinic acid. It affects the skin, the alimentary tract and the central nervous system. It is easily recognized by the numerous skin lesions it produces and by swelling of the tongue. Besides these symptoms, pellagra victims typically report irritations of the skin and mouth, inability to digest food, diarrhea, general weakness, and loss of energy.[20] It is not a contagious disease and generally is not a fatal disease although about 7,000 deaths were attributed to pellagra each year during the 1920s; it must have been a contributing factor in many other deaths.[21]

It is difficult to determine if pellagra has any direct consequences upon fertility. Skin lesions, particularly excoriations of the genitals, are one of its consequences; thus, both males and females who suffer from pellagra are quite susceptible to venereal diseases.[22] One of the early manifestations of this disease in females is irregularity of menstruation and, in cases of severe pellagra, there is continual amenorrhea.[23] Pellagra during pregnancy apparently leads to complication and fetal deaths. It appears, then, that pellagra may have an effect on fertility.

During the nineteenth and early twentieth centuries, many different theories were propounded to explain pellagra in Europe. This disease was not commonly reported in the United States until 1907 but after that date a growing number of investigations reported that it was endemic in the South.[24] Gradually, a public awareness of the disease emerged and, in 1914, the Public Health Service assigned one of its epidemiologists, Joseph Goldberger, to the study of pellagra.[25] He observed that it was common among the inmates of institutions but absent among staff members, more common in rural areas than in cities, and almost exclusively a disease of the impoverished. He rapidly came to the view that it was a dietary deficiency ailment, rather than an infectious dis-

---

[20] Oliver S. Ormsby and Hamilton Montgomery, *Diseases of the Skin,* eighth ed. (Philadelphia: Lea and Felger, 1954), pp. 470–473; Seale Harris, *Clinical Pellagra* (St. Louis: C. V. Mosby, 1941), Chap. xviii.

[21] Linder and Grove, *op. cit.,* Tables 15 and VIII.

[22] Harris, *op. cit.,* pp. 121 and 316.

[23] Joseph Gillman and Theodore Gillman, *Perspectives in Human Malnutrition* (New York: Grune and Stratton, 1951), P. 421; Harris, *op. cit.,* p. 128.

[24] Harris, *op. cit.,* p. 34.

[25] Milton Terris, "Introduction" in *Goldberger on Pellagra,* Milton Terris (ed.) (Baton Rouge: Louisiana State University Press, 1964), p. 10.

ease. Shortly thereafter, he demonstrated that he could either induce or cure the disease among institutional populations by changes in diet.[26] Poverty in rural areas and the reluctance of state authorities to spend large sums for inmate care meant that fresh meat, poultry, fresh vegetables, milk and eggs were often absent from the diet for long periods of time. Many individuals had to survive on a diet of corn meal, sorghum, and salt pork; consequently, they developed pellagra. In rural areas, tenant farmers and sharecroppers frequently did not keep a cow or raise vegetables, partly because of poverty and ignorance and partly because landowners believed that all arable land should be devoted to cotton.[27]

Many studies pointed out the relationship of pellagra to income, and showed that variations in income were matched by variation in this disease.[28] Studies of consumer income and food expenditures in South Carolina mill towns indicated that families who had higher incomes were able to purchase fresh meat and milk and thereby avoided pellagra, but poor families could afford only an unvaried diet which led to pellagra.[29] In 1914, the price farmers received for cotton fell to about seven cents per pound compared to about eleven cents in the preceding period.[30] The next year, 1915, there was a great increase in pellagra reflecting the shortage of income in rural areas. The cotton crop of 1915 brought more favorable prices and pellagra decreased. The post-World War I deflation and decline in cotton prices brought about a rise in pellagra.[31]

Most medical studies did not assess the prevalence of pellagra, rather they typically focused upon the symptoms, care and

---

[26] Joseph Goldberger, "The Cause and Prevention of Pellagra"; Joseph Goldberger, C. H. Waring, and David G. Willets, "The Prevention of Pellagra: A Test of Diet Among Institutional Inmates"; Joseph Goldberger and G. A. Wheeler, "The Experimental Production of Pellagra in Human Subjects by Means of Diet," in *Goldberger on Pellagra.*

[27] Joseph Goldberger and Edgar Sydenstricker, "Pellagra in the Mississippi Flood Area," in *Goldberger on Pellagra*, p. 279; Thomas Jackson Woofter, Jr., *Negro Migration* (New York: W. D. Gray, 1920), p. 87.

[28] Rupert B. Vance, *Human Factors in Cotton Culture* (Chapel Hill: University of North Carolina Press, 1929), p. 248.

[29] Joseph Goldberger, G. A. Wheeler, and Edgar Sydenstricker, "A Study of the Relationship of Family Income and Other Economic Factors to Pellagra in Seven Cotton Mill Villages of South Carolina in 1916," in *Goldberger on Pellagra*, pp. 225–267.

[30] U.S., Department of Agriculture, *Agricultural Statistics: 1967*, Table 85.

[31] Joseph Goldberger, "Pellagra: Its Nature and Prevention," in *Goldberger on Pellagra*, p. 376.

treatment of individuals who already had the disease. A few sample surveys were carried out in rural areas and they suggested that, at any point in time, between 2 and 25 percent of the population suffered from this disease.[32] Descriptions of rural life indicate that pellagra was endemic—very many people must have had, at least temporarily, minor cases which were cured by improvements in their diet.[33]

There is evidence indicating that the disease became more common throughout the South between 1900 and 1930. One investigation of trends in income and the cost of living concluded that living standards declined in southern cities between the turn of the century and World War I, causing poorer diets and a rise in pellagra.[34] Another study suggested there was a general rise in pellagra during the 1920s due, in part, to deteriorations in income from cotton. Goldberger estimated that pellagra cases in Alabama, Louisiana, Mississippi and Tennessee in 1927 were about two and one-half times as numerous as in 1924.[35]

Pellagra, except for pellagra in alcoholics, was almost exclusively a southern disease. In seven southern states, it is possible to put together a time series on pellagra mortality among nonwhites beginning in 1920. These death rates are shown in Figure 9–5. In five of these states, the pellagra mortality rate in 1930 was higher than a decade earlier.

Pellagra gradually declined during the 1930s. This did not reflect improved economic conditions in rural areas. Rather, dietary changes to eliminate the disease became well known, state and county health agencies became more numerous and active, the Red Cross supplied yeast to rural areas, and private philanthropists such as John Rockefeller and the Rosenwald Fund began supporting rural health projects.[36]

The increase in pellagra before the Depression suggests that rural health and economic conditions were getting worse. There is much additional evidence which supports this view. First, statistics indicating land ownership might be considered since own-

---

[32] Goldberger and Sydenstricker, *loc. cit.*, p. 273–274; Johnson, *op. cit.*, p. 188.

[33] Myrdal, *op. cit.*, I, 174; Stix, *loc. cit.*, p. 176; Johnson, *op. cit.*; Thomas J. Woofter and Ellen Winston, *Seven Lean Years* (Chapel Hill: University of North Carolina Press, 1939), p. 124.

[34] Edgar Sydenstricker, "The Prevalence of Pellagra, Its Possible Relation to the Rise of the Cost of Food," in *Goldberger on Pellagra*, pp. 113–127.

[35] Goldberger and Sydenstricker, *op. cit.*, p. 275.

[36] Harris, *op. cit.*, pp. 42–46; Johnson, *op. cit.*, p. 102.

220

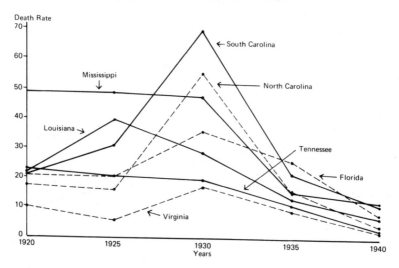

Figure 9–5
Pellagra Deaths per 100,000 Population,
Non-whites in Southern States

Source:
Linder and Grove, *op. cit.*, Table 20.

ing land indicates some financial ability. For some decades after
the Civil War, landholdings by rural blacks increased; by 1900,
one-quarter of the Negro farmers owned their land. After 1900,
the proportion who owned land declined; after 1910, the actual
number of black landowners decreased.[37] Both Myrdal and Frazier viewed this drop in farm ownership as indicative of growing
poverty among rural blacks.[38]

Second, beginning about 1890, there were a series of developments which adversely affected the productivity and income of
southern agriculture. Between 1890 and the 1920s, boll weevil infestation gradually spread eastward from the Rio Grande Valley
to the Atlantic seaboard. The immediate effect of this disease was
a destruction of the cotton crop.[39] After four or five years, there
was a partial recovery in most areas but meanwhile banks failed,
landlords went bankrupt, and merchants went out of business.

[37] U. S., Bureau of the Census, *Historical Statistics of the United
States: Colonial Times to 1957*, Series K 8–52.
[38] Myrdal, *op. cit.*, I, pp. 231–235; Frazier, *The Negro Family in the
United States*, p. 191.
[39] Vance, *op. cit.*, Chap. iv.

Farmers were forced to sell whatever items might bring cash, so there was a decrease in the ownership of animals, a change which would help explain the spread of pellagra.

Rupert Vance described in detail the economic collapse which occurred in Georgia and South Carolina as the boll weevil moved through these parts of the Cotton Belt in the 1920's.[40] He observed that although crops of both white and Negro farmers were equally affected by the insect, many white farmers found employment in nearby expanding southern industries; the displaced black farmers became refugees who had to depend upon their kin for support.[41]

Despite the devastation wrought by the boll weevil, the price for cotton received by the farmers who were able to grow the crop, did not consistently go up during the early decades of this century. Except for a prosperous period centered around World War I, a general depression afflicted southern agriculture for most of this period. Gross income per southern farm worker in 1927 was only 58 percent as great as in 1919.[42] From the 1860s to the 1930s, the amount of land devoted to farms in the Southeast actually declined, and productivity per acre for the two most important crops, cotton and tobacco, changed very little during this period.[43] Yet, the number of male agricultural workers increased from 1.2 million to 2.1 million.[44] In Myrdal's view, this was a classic example of over-population.[45]

During the 1930s, cotton prices fell to record lows and farm income continued to decline. In addition, the Agricultural Adjustment Act of 1933 further impoverished rural blacks. In the South, this act was administered by, and often to the advantage of, large landowners.[46] This law called for drastic reductions in the acreage devoted to cotton; by 1938, cotton acreage was little more than 60 percent as great as in 1933.[47] Later, the law pro-

---

[40] Rupert B. Vance, "The Old Cotton Belt," in *Migration and Economic Opportunity*, Carter Goodrich et al. (eds.) (Philadelphia: University of Pennsylvania Press, 1936), pp. 124–163.

[41] *Ibid.*, p. 133.

[42] Clarence Heer, *Income and Wages in the South* (Chapel Hill: University of North Carolina Press, 1930), p. 18.

[43] U. S., Department of Agriculture, *op. cit.*, Tables 85 and 150; Myrdal, *op cit.* I, 231; Woofter and Winston, *op cit.*, p. 123.

[44] T. J. Woofter, Jr., *Landlord and Tenant on the Cotton Plantation* (Washington: Works Administration, 1936), pp. 11, 15 and 16.

[45] Myrdal, *op. cit.*, p. 231.

[46] *Ibid.*, pp. 255–270.

[47] U.S., Department of Agriculture, *op. cit.*, Table 85.

vided benefits to landowners who would reduce the number of tenants or mechanize production. This had the effect of forcing sharecroppers and tenants to leave farms although there were often no jobs available in cities. At least in the early years of its operation, the Agricultural Adjustment Act benefited the landowners almost exclusively.[48]

Venereal Diseases

Gonorrhea and syphilis are two of the more common venereal diseases, and both have effects on the fertility rate of a population. Gonorrhea, if untreated, produces pelvic infections in women including salpingitis which may eventually close the Fallopian tubes, causing sterility.[49] While syphilis does not have the direct consequence of producing sterility, a syphilitic woman whose disease is untreated quite likely may experience a stillbirth or spontaneous abortion if she does become pregnant. Various investigations suggest that 30 to 50 percent of the pregnancies occurring in syphilitic women who receive no care, end in fetal deaths; upwards of twenty percent of the infants born to such women die from congenital syphilis shortly after birth.[50] One investigator concluded "A syphilitic woman, untreated, has only one chance in six of bearing a healthy live infant as compared with a normal woman's three chances in four."[51]

Venereal diseases have been diagnosed and described for a very long time, however scientific investigations of their prevalence among blacks are not numerous. Early in this century, groups of black hospital patients were given Wasserman tests; such studies suggested that 25 to 30 percent of the adult hospital patients had syphilis.[52] In the 1920s, officials of the Julius Rosen-

---

[48] Charles S. Johnson, Edwin R. Embree and W. W. Alexander, *The Collapse of Cotton Tenancy* (Chapel Hill: University of North Carolina Press, 1935), pp. 60–61.

[49] Nels A. Nelson and Gladys L. Crain, *Syphilis, Gonorrhea and the Public Health* (New York: Macmillan Co., 1938), p. 107; R. R. Wilcox, *Textbook of Venereal Disease and Treponematoses* (Springfield, Ill.: Charles C. Thomas, 1964), p. 79.

[50] Richard S. Weiss and Herbert L. Joseph, *Syphilis* (New York: Thomas Nelson & Sons, 1951), p. 136; Rudolph H. Kampmeier, *Essentials of Syphilology* (Philadelphia: J. B. Lippincott, 1943), p. 406.

[51] Joseph E. Moore, *The Modern Treatment of Syphilis* (Springfield, Ill.: Charles C. Thomas, 1941), p. 474.

[52] H. H. Hazen, "Syphilis in the American Negro," *American Journal of Syphilis, Gonorrhea and Venereal Disease*, XX, No. 5 (September, 1936), 531, 537; H. L. McNeil, "Syphilis in the Southern Negro," *Journal of the American Medical Association*, LXVII, No. 14 (September 30, 1916), 1003.

wald Fund observed the very high infant and maternal mortality rates among rural blacks and the absence of medical care in such areas. They believed that syphilis played an important role in keeping death rates high; thus, they initiated a program to determine the prevalence of syphilis among rural blacks and then demonstrated therapeutic methods. The assistance of the Public Health Service and state health agencies was secured, and six counties in six southern states were selected. Blacks were encouraged to come for serologic tests and were provided with treatment if they had syphilis. A total of 33,200 tests were given and 21 percent of the adults were found to have syphilis. The prevalence of this disease ranged from a high of 40 percent in Macon County, Alabama to a low of 9 percent in Albemarle County, Virginia.[53] Infection rates were higher among women than among men and higher among the population of childbearing age than among the older population.[54] Later, in the 1930s, other investigations were conducted both of rural black populations and of blacks who used medical facilities in cities. One author reviewed and summarized the many studies of syphilis among blacks and concluded that, during the 1930s, about 20 percent of the adult black population suffered from venereal disease, and that because of ignorance, poverty, and lack of medical facilities, Negroes received very little treatment for this disease.[55] Clark described the findings of the survey sponsored by the Rosenwald Fund, and estimated that for every southern black who received any treatment for syphilis, there were twenty-five who had the disease but were not treated.[56]

Fewer studies have investigated the prevalence of gonorrhea since its effects are seldom fatal. Medical descriptions suggest that gonorrhea is much more common than syphilis—from two to four times as common.[57] Empirical studies and health statistics bear our this contention.[58] For instance, in 1967, the reported number of new cases of gonorrhea was greater than four times the reported number of new cases of syphilis.[59] In addition, it is very likely that many women had undetected gonorrhea, for it

---

[53] Taliaferro Clark, *The Control of Syphilis in Southern Rural Areas* (Chicago: Julius Rosenwald Fund, 1932), p. 6.

[54] *Ibid.*, Johnson, *op. cit.*, pp. 188–189.

[55] Hazen, *loc. cit.*, p. 553.

[56] *Ibid.*

[57] Nelson and Crain, *op. cit.*, p. 204.

[58] Lida J. Usilton, "Prevalence of Venereal Disease in the United States," *Venereal Disease Information*, XI, No. 12 (December 20, 1930), 556.

[59] *VD Fact Sheet—1968*, Vol. XXV, Table 6.

224

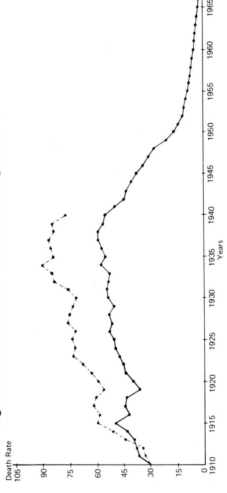

Figure 9-6

Deaths from Syphilis per 100,000 Non-whites, Death Registration States of 1910 and All Death Registration States

Source:

Linder and Grove, *op. cit.*, Tables 16 and 18.

Robert D. Grove and Alice M. Hetzel, *Vital Statistics Rates in the United States: 1940–1960*, Government Printing Office, 1968), Table 63.

U.S., National Center for Health Statistics, *Vital Statistics of the United States 1961 through 1966*, Vol. II, Part A, Tables 1–9 or 1–10. Deaths of Mexicans were included with deaths of non-whites for years 1932 to 1934.

does not necessarily cause pain or produce obvious manifestations. It is likely that gonorrhea was common in the rural South. These studies indicate that venereal diseases were quite prevalent among blacks during the Depression decade; they undoubtedly had the effect of reducing fertility rates. However, the birth rate among blacks fell for many decades beginning in the late nineteenth century. We must ask if there was a corresponding rise in venereal disease which would explain the long run trend toward lower fertility rates.

There are certain indications that syphilis may have become more common among blacks. There are some historians and writers who described health conditions of slaves and believed that syphilis, although known, was not very common. They conjectured that the isolation of slaves on plantations inhibited the spread of venereal disease.[60] Frequently, the accounts of slave health fail to mention syphilis but go into much greater detail when describing yellow fever, cholera, and tuberculosis.[61] Unfortunately, none of these descriptions provides anything more than impressionistic reports of morbidity and mortality among slaves.

The mortality rate from syphilis is one index of the prevalence of venereal disease and the availability of medical care, but it is an imprecise indicator since many people who die of syphilis may have contacted the disease many years, even decades, prior to their death. Table 9–6 shows the trend over time in the annual death rate of non-whites from syphilis.[62] For years between 1910 and 1940, two mortality rates are shown. One set of rates refers to the Death Registration States of 1910 (a group of twenty states and the District of Columbia).[63] Only one of these states, Maryland, was a southern state. The second set of rates refers to the entire Death Registration Area which grew to include the national population in 1933.

In both the Death Registration States of 1910 and in all registration states, the mortality rate from syphilis increased during

---

60 Stampp, *op. cit.*, p. 303.

61 O. W. Taylor, *op. cit.*; J. G. Taylor, *op. cit.*; Sydnor, *op. cit.*; Phillips, *op. cit.*

62 There were changes in 1929 and 1939 in the types of deaths of aneurysms which were classified as deaths caused by syphilis. Linder and Grove, *op. cit.*, pp. 18–25 and 282.

63 The Death Registration States of 1910 were: California, Colorado, Connecticut, Indiana, Maine, Maryland, Massachusetts, Michigan, Minnesota, New Hampshire, New York, Ohio, Pennsylvania, Rhode Island, Utah, Vermont, Washington, Wisconsin, and the District of Columbia.

the 1920s and 1930s and then reached a peak toward the end of that decade. Thereafter, this death rate fell, slowly at first and then more rapidly during the late 1940s.

Most blacks who lived in the Death Registration States of 1910 lived in cities. Since the death rate in this fixed area was higher than the syphilis death rate for the entire Death Registration Area, we have an indication that mortality from this cause was more common in cities than in rural areas and that, within cities, this mortality rate increased after 1910.

The military has collected health statistics for a long time; these suggest that fertility-inhibiting diseases may have increased among Negroes. During World War I, 6.5 percent of the colored recruits given physical examinations had positive reactions to a test for syphilis.[64] Among the first two million males selected for service in World War II, 27 percent of the blacks had syphilis.[65] This suggests that the prevalence of syphilis increased, but it must be remembered that these were not random samples of the population. Changing recruitment procedures, as well as changes in medical technology, may have influenced these rates.

Changes in childlessness among black women are consistent with the hypothesis that health conditions deteriorated and that venereal diseases became more common. We noted in Chapter 4 that apparently no more than 10 percent of the Negro women born 1835 to 1844 reached menopause without becoming mothers. Childlessness increased from one birth cohort to the next; among the women born 1905 to 1909, approximately one-third did not bear a child. In Chapter 8, we indicated that relatively few Negro women used birth control effectively prior to World War II implying that these fluctuations in childlessness reflect changes in fecundity rather than intentional changes in planned family size.

Improvements in Health Conditions

After the middle of the Depression decade, Negro mortality rates declined rapidly. In this section, we describe two of the changes which brought about the lower death and disease rates. First, there was an expansion of public health facilities, and also tech-

---

[64] Maurice R. Davie, *Negroes in American Society* (New York: McGraw-Hill, 1949), p. 240.

[65] R. A. Vonderlehr and Lida J. Usilton, "Syphilis Among Men of Draft Age in the United States," *Journal of the American Medical Association*, CXXX, No. 17 (December 26, 1942), p. 1370.

nological improvements which led to the control of diseases and mitigation of their effects. Second, there was a rapid rise in the typical standard of living of blacks which brought better diets and improved housing conditions.

Maternal Health and Welfare Programs

Early this century, concern developed about the high infant and maternal death rates which prevailed in this country. As the birth and death registration systems became more complete, they demonstrated the frequency of these deaths.[66] In 1920, the maternal mortality rate for the Birth Registration Area of the United States was approximately twice as large as the maternal mortality rate in England and three times as large as the rates in Scandinavian lands.[67] In 1921, Congress enacted the Sheppard-Towner Law. This legislation provided federal monies which could be appropriated to the states if they undertook programs to reduce infant and maternal mortality. One and one-quarter million dollars was dispensed annually to the forty-seven states which participated in this program.[68] The American Medical Association and other groups opposed this law, believing it to be a prelude to socialized medicine, and these appropriations were stopped in 1929.[69] Immediately thereafter, thirty-five states cut their spending in this field and nine states eliminated maternal and child health programs.[70] Paul Douglas estimated that total government spending for maternal and child health decreased from 3.4 million dollars in 1929 to 1.2 million in 1934.[71]

The Federal Social Security Act was passed by Congress in 1935. The major provisions of this law provided assistance for the elderly, established unemployment insurance programs and initiated a national system of old age insurance. However, two titles of this law had direct consequences for health conditions, and indirectly they influenced the fertility rate of blacks. Title V of the Social Security Law appropriated money ". . . for promoting the

---

[66] Shapiro, Schlesinger and Nesbitt, *Infant, Perinatal, Maternal and Childhood Mortality in the United States*, p. 223.

[67] Paul H. Douglas, *Social Security in the United States* (New York: McGraw-Hill, 1936), p. 196.

[68] *Ibid.;* John J. Hanlon, *Principles of Public Health Administration*, fourth ed. (St. Louis: C. V. Mosby, 1964), p. 63.

[69] Hanlon, *op. cit.*, p. 62.

[70] *Ibid.*, p. 63.

[71] Douglas, *op. cit.*, p. 198.

health of mothers and children, especially in rural areas and in areas suffering from severe economic distress."[72] The Children's Bureau spent about four million dollars annually for these purposes. Each state received certain funds regardless of its ability to match federal monies but other sums were allocated on the basis of each state's needs.[73] Within one year of this act's passage 51 states and territories sought federal funds and programs were approved and funded.[74] Within four years of passage, six hundred new pre-natal clinics were established and the operations of existing pre-natal clinics were strengthened or expanded.[75]

In 1939, Congress appropriated additional funds through the Social Security Act for maternal and child health; during the 1940s, the government's activities in this field grew more extensive. An important development was the passage, in 1943, of a law which provided infant and maternity benefits to the wives and children of enlisted men in the lower four pay-grades. This act supported complete prenatal, delivery and postnatal care of the mother and total care of the infant until he attained his first birthday.[76] During the latter years of World War II, approximately one-seventh of the infants born in the United States benefited from this program.[77]

In 1946, Congress passed the Hill-Burton Act which provided support for the construction of general hospitals and required that states develop plans for hospital utilization.[78] This had the effect of encouraging hospitalization for birth, particularly in rural areas where hospital care had been difficult or impossible to obtain.

Hospitalization of blacks for delivery was one of the consequences of the expanded maternal health programs. This may have had an effect upon the aggregate fecundity of blacks. Presumably, pregnant women who deliver in hospitals are less likely to contact contagious diseases or suffer injuries in childbirth than

---

[72] *Ibid.*, p. 453.

[73] *Ibid.*, p. 198.

[74] U. S., Social Security Board, *First Annual Report of the Social Security Board: 1936*, p. 53.

[75] Katherine R. Lenroot, "Child Welfare: 1930–1940," *The Annals of the American Academy of Political and Social Science* CCXII (November, 1940), 2.

[76] Arthur J. Altmeyer, *The Formative Years of Social Security* (Madison: University of Wisconsin Press, 1966), p. 146.

[77] *Ibid.*

[78] Shapiro, Schlesinger and Nesbitt, *Infant, Perinatal, Maternal and Childhood Mortality in the United States*, p. 226.

women who deliver at home or who use the services of a mid-wife. In addition, physicians should be better able to recognize and treat venereal diseases. Shown below are proportions of non-white births occurring in hospitals for the period 1935 to 1965.[79]

Date	Percent of Hospital Births
1935	17.3%
1940	26.7
1945	40.2
1950	57.9
1955	76.0
1960	85.0
1965	89.8

We do not know when the trend toward the hospital birth of blacks began, however, we can be certain that prior to 1940 relatively few Negro births occurred in hospitals. The figures shown above probably overestimate the number of hospital births since they refer only to registered births. Births occurring outside of hospitals; they were much less likely to be registered than those occuring in hospitals.[80] It was only during and after World War II, when blacks migrated to cities and when maternal health services grew, that the hospitalization of blacks became common.

Public Health Programs

Government activities or expenditures for controlling contagious disease or for curing those who suffered from disease expanded very slowly in the United States. Predecessors of the Public Health Service can be traced back to 1798, but for many decades the chief interest was the health of seamen and the quarantine of ships carrying diseased crewmen or passengers.[81] In 1842, the Chadwick Report described the very unsanitary living conditions in England which fostered the spread of contagious diseases and high infant death rates. Seven years later, the Shat-

---

[79] Elizabeth C. Tandy, *Infant and Maternal Mortality Among Negroes*, U. S. Department of Labor, Bureau Publication No. 243 (1937), p. 7; U. S. National Center for Health Statistics, *Vital Statistics of the United States: 1966*, Vol. I, Table 1–23.

[80] U. S. National Office of Vital Statistics, *Vital Statistics of the United States: 1950*, Vol. I, Table 6.43.

[81] Hanlon, *op. cit.*, p. 55.

tuck Report described similar conditions in Massachusetts.[82] This eventually led to the founding of the first state department of public health in Massachusetts in 1869, although five port cities, Baltimore, Charleston, Philadelphia, Providence, and Cambridge, had established city public health services before the Civil War.[83] Fifty years elapsed between the time Massachusetts set up a public health department and the time when each state had such a department.[84]

During the early twentieth century new efforts were made to arouse interest in public health programs. In 1909, President Roosevelt convened a conference, "Report on National Vitality: Its Waste and Conservation," which linked good health among the population to problems of conservation and preservation of natural resources.[85] In 1911, the first county departments of public health came into existence and during World War I, the activities of the Public Health Service were modestly expanded.[86] In 1930, President Hoover called a conference on child health and protection which pointed out the nation's extensive public health needs.[87] Five years later, President Roosevelt's Committee on Economic Security attempted to measure the economic and social cost involved in poor health, and then claimed that existing knowledge in the field of health could cure or prevent many diseases if facilities and personnel were increased.[88]

These efforts came to fruition in 1935 when the Social Security Act was passed. Title VI of that act appropriated money ". . . for the purpose of assisting states, counties, health districts and other political subdivisions of the states in establishing and maintaining adequate public health service, including the training of personnel for state and local health work."[89] Each year, the Public Health Service was to spend two million dollars for research on public health and to allocate eight million dollars to states, a sum which was later increased by Congress.[90] This act was innovative for it meant that for the first time large sums of

---

[82] *Ibid.*, pp. 52–53.
[83] *Ibid.*
[84] *Ibid.*, p. 52.
[85] Wilson S. Smillie, *Public Health Administration in the United States* (New York: Macmillan, 1940), p. 501.
[86] Hanlon, *op. cit.*, p. 58.
[87] Smillie, *op. cit.*, p. 501.
[88] *Ibid.*
[89] Quoted in Douglas, *op. cit.*, p. 462.
[90] Smillie, *op. cit.*, p. 505.

federal monies were supplied to states to finance their public health programs.

These funds were given to the states, not so much on the basis of their ability to match federal funds, but rather on the basis of their special health problems and needs.[91] The major aim was to assist and expand the service provided by the state public health agencies and to aid state agencies in promoting city and local health activities. After these funds became available, the major problem was finding sufficiently trained personnel, a problem which was remedied by instituting short-run training sessions.[92]

This title of the Social Security Act was of great assistance to public health during the late 1930s and had an impact in many rural areas which previously lacked health services.[93] Between 1934 and 1938, federal spending for health purposes trebled and state and local expenditures increased by 50 percent.[94] Within one year after passage of the Social Security Act, almost all states had used federal funds to strengthen their public health nursing programs. In addition:

33 states expanded their public health engineering staffs
27 states added new laboratory facilities
24 states strengthened their preventable disease programs
19 states added personnel to their vital statistics programs
13 states set up tuberculosis control programs
11 states set up programs to detect and cure syphilis
11 states added units to promote industrial hygiene.[95]

Throughout the 1940s, government support for health activities became more widespread. New laws provided direct and indirect federal assistance for health and medical care in new and different ways such as the school lunch program and the Hill-Burton hospital construction act. During the 1950s, there were modest annual increases in government spending for health and the iniation of new programs. Then, during the mid-1960s there were much sharper annual rises in government spending as many

91 *Ibid.*
92 *Ibid.*, p. 509.
93 Wilson Gee, *The Social Economics of Agriculture* (New York: Macmillan, 1942), p. 468.
94 U. S. Bureau of the Census, *Historical Statistics of the United States: Colonial Times to 1957*, Series Y 484–516 and Series Y 547–574.
95 Hanlon, *op. cit.*, p. 58.
96 U. S. Department of Health, Education, and Welfare, *Health, Education and Welfare Trends: 1966–1967*, p. s-44.

new programs came into existence.[96] For example, in 1963 the National Institute of Child Health and Human Development was established and the Social Security Act was amended to appropriate more money for maternal and child health care.[97] The following year, 1964, the anti-poverty program was set up which provided federal monies for community health centers in poverty neighborhoods.[98] The 1965 amendments to the Social Security Act provided, in addition to a new program of medical care and hospitalization insurance for the elderly, a new funding arrangement whereby the federal government provided three-quarters of the cost of child health programs established in impoverished areas.[99] These changes may have the consequence of improving the delivery of health services to people who otherwise would find it difficult to obtain adequate medical care. In the four-year span from 1964 to 1968, the death rate of non-white children under one year of age declined more than in the preceding nine-year period reflecting, in part, the results of the new programs.[100]

In brief, prior to the 1930s, effective public health programs were operative in only some areas of the country, chiefly the older and larger cities and some progressive states. Changes in federal spending during the Roosevelt era permitted many more cities and states to develop public health programs. This reduced the prevalence of contagious disease, aroused greater interest in health care, and played a part in cutting infant mortality among non-whites and increasing life expectancy.

The Control of Venereal Disease

The examination of selectees for World War I revealed that a surprisingly large number had venereal diseases. As a result, in 1918, Congress passed the Chamberlain-Kahn Act which created a Division of Venereal Disease within the Public Health Service and appropriated one million dollars annually to this Division, part of which could be dispersed to states if they undertook venereal disease control programs. Forty-seven states participated in this program.[101] After World War I, interest in controlling vene-

---

[97] Shapiro, Schlesinger and Nesbitt, *Infant, Perinatal, Maternal and Childhood Mortality in the United States*, pp. 228–229.

[98] *Ibid.*, p. 229.

[99] *Ibid.*, pp. 230–231.

[100] Grove and Hetzel, *op. cit.*, Table 56; U. S. National Center for Health Statistics, *Monthly Vital Statistics Report*, "Annual Summary for the United States, 1968," Vol. 17 (August 15, 1969), Table 5.

[101] R. A. Vonderlehr and J. J. Heller, *The Control of Venereal Disease* (New York: Reynal and Hitchcock, 1946), p. 6.

real diseases waned. The program of allocating funds to states ended in 1921, and the budget of the Division of Venereal Disease was reduced.[102]

Various studies, such as those we described earlier in this chapter, found that venereal diseases were common in the United States during the 1920s and 1930s. Expenditures for the detection and control of venereal disease were the second largest single type of spending supported by the public health title of the Social Security Law. More money was expended for venereal disease than for any other single disease.[103] As these efforts were made, the magnitude of the national venereal disease problem was more widely recognized. Consequently, Congress made special appropriations for venereal disease research and control, such as the LaFollette-Bullwinkle bill, enacted in 1938.[104] The testing of recruits for World War II again revealed the prevalence of syphilis and gonorrhea; in both 1941 and 1942 Congress amended the LaFollette-Bullwinkle Act to provide more funds for the eradication of venereal diseases.[105] In 1942, as a wartime emergency measure, the Public Health Service established rapid treatment centers throughout the country to curb the spread of venereal diseases.[106] Then, in 1945, the Public Health Service assumed responsibility for administering a nationwide program.[107]

Expenditures and facilities for the elimination of venereal diseases increased after 1935. Also, there were advances in the methods used to treat these diseases. In 1907, Ehrlich developed Salvarsan which was the first effective chemotherapy for syphilis. However, treatment with Salvarsan required intake of the drug over long periods of time, 12 to 18 months, and many patients terminated treatment before they were fully cured.[108] During the 1920s and 1930s, new methods for administering massive dosages of the arsenical drugs were developed. These gradually reduced the treatment period so that by the late 1930s a cure could be effected by a hospital stay of two weeks or less. During the early

---

[102] *Ibid.*, p. 8; Monroe Lerner and Odin W. Anderson, *Health Progress in the United States: 1900–1960* (Chicago: University of Chicago Press, 1963), p. 178.

[103] U.S., Social Security Board, *Second Annual Report of the Social Security Board: 1937*, p. 83.

[104] U.S., Public Health Service, *Milestones in Venereal Disease Control*, Public Health Service Publication, No. 515 (1958), p. 5.

[105] Vonderlehr and Usilton, *loc. cit.*, p. 1368.

[106] Vonderlehr and Heller, *op. cit.*, p. 153.

[107] U.S., Public Health Service, *op. cit.*, p. 6.

[108] Henry S. Mustard, *An Introduction to Public Health* (New York: Macmillan, 1958), p. 144.

Figure 9–7

Primary and Secondary Syphilis Cases per 100,000 Non-whites

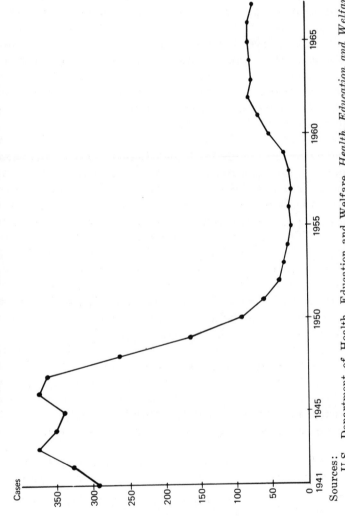

Sources:
U.S., Department of Health, Education and Welfare, *Health, Education and Welfare Trends: 1962*, p. 18; *Health, Education and Welfare Trends: 1966–67*, p. S-28; U.S., National Communicable Disease Center, *VD Fact Sheet—1968*, p. 12.

years of World War II, even more rapid treatment programs were initiated.[109] In 1943, the most significant singular advance in the treatment of venereal disease occurred. It was discovered that injections of penicillin were effective in curing both syphilis and gonorrhea.[110] Within a very short time, penicillin therapy became the preferred mode of treatment.[111] This greatly reduced the cost of controlling venereal disease for a hospital stay was no longer necessary. In addition, physicians in private practice could easily treat this disease.

Figure 9–3 showed that the death rate of non-white infants from syphilis began to decline during the late 1930s. Thus, a reduction in infant mortality was one consequence of the expanded programs for control of venereal disease. It is difficult to know what effect these programs had upon the fecundity of the non-white population, but we do know that the reported incidence of venereal disease, among both whites and non-whites, reached a peak during World War II and then declined very rapidly sinking to a minimum in the late 1950s. Such a change would have the effect, *ceteris paribus*, of increasing fertility. Figure 9–7 shows the reported incidence of primary and secondary syphilis per 100,000 non-whites for the period 1941 to 1967. Unfortunately, there are no statistics indicating the long-run trends in gonorrhea among blacks. The available figures suggest that gonorrhea has been much more common than syphilis and that, changes in the incidence of gonorrhea have been similar to changes in the incidence of syphilis.[112] Most of the venereal disease control programs were directed at both syphilis and gonorrhea so there may have been a rapid decline in gonorrhea during the 1940s and 1950s.

In summary, the period after 1935 was one in which many public health agencies made efforts to control venereal disease and the success of these efforts lessened sterility and reduced problems of subfecundity among Negroes.

Changes in the Standard of Living

Poverty and ignorance help to explain the prevalence of disease among blacks prior to World War II. Between the late 1930s

---

[109] *Ibid.*; Vonderlehr and Heller, *op. cit.*, p. 49.

[110] U.S., Public Health Service, *op. cit.*

[111] Ambrose King, *Recent Advances in Venereology* (Boston: Little-Brown, 1964), pp. 70 and 238.

[112] U. S., Public Health Service, *VD Fact Sheet—1968*, Tables 3 and 8.

and 1960s, there were improvements in the standard of living among blacks, a change which, along with the expansion of medical facilities, lessened the impact of many diseases.

We have noted some of these changes in socio-economic status previously. For instance, after the Depression, the income of blacks went up. The median income of male non-white workers was less than $500 for the year of 1939. But by 1950, the median income of male workers increased to $1800, by 1960 to $3100, and by 1967 to $4400. Table 9-1 contains these figures and shows that there were similar increases in the income of black families and full-time year-round workers.

Someone might argue that while income has gone up, prices have also risen and the present status of blacks may be no better than it was during the late 1930s. To accurately compare the present economic status of blacks to their pre-war position would be a very extensive project. However, we can be certain that the income of non-whites has risen much more rapidly than have consumer prices. Between 1939 and 1950, the consumer price index rose by 73 percent but the median income of male non-white workers quadrupled. Since 1950, the same pattern of change has occurred. Prices have increased but the income of non-whites has increased more rapidly. Table 9-1 contains consumer price indices.

The statistical measurement of poverty dates only from the late 1950s.[113] This involves not only surveying income, but establishing minimum income levels. For instance, in 1967, an urban family of four was classified as impoverished only if the family income was less than $3335 for the year.[114] The time series concerning poverty which has been developed for the period 1959 to 1967 suggests, first, that considerable progress has been made in reducing poverty and, second, that poverty has been and still is extremely common among blacks. For example, the proportion of all non-whites living in poverty declined from 55 percent in 1959 to 35 percent in 1967. Among non-white children under 18 years of age, 64 percent lived in impoverished households in 1959, and 43 percent in 1967.[115] Table 9-1 indicates that the income position

---

[113] U. S., Bureau of the Census, "The Extent of Poverty in the United States: 1959 to 1966," *Current Population Reports*, Series P-60, No. 54 (May 31, 1968).

[114] U. S., Bureau of the Census, "Family Income Advances, Poverty Reduced in 1967," *Current Population Reports*, Series P-60, No. 55 (August 5, 1968).

[115] *Ibid.*, Table 2.

TABLE 9–1
Trend in Non-white Income and Consumer Prices: 1939–1967

Year	Trends in Median Income			Indices of Income (1939 = 100)			Index of Consumer Prices (1939 = 100)
	Families and Unrelated Individuals	Male Workers		Families and Unrelated Individuals	Male Workers		
		All	Year-round Full-time		All	Year-round Full-time	
1939	$ 489	$ 460	$ 639	100	100	100	100
1947	1,448	1,279	—	296	278	—	161
1948	1,486	1,615	—	304	351	—	173
1949	1,533	1,367	—	318	297	—	171
1950	1,671	1,828	—	342	397	—	173
1951	1,943	2,060	—	397	448	—	187
1952	1,987	2,038	—	406	443	—	191
1953	2,357	2,233	—	482	485	—	193

Table 9–1 (Cont'd)

Year							
1954	2,333	2,131	—	477	463	—	193
1955	2,418	2,342	2,831	494	509	—	193
1956	2,429	2,396	2,912	497	521	443	196
1957	2,536	2,436	3,137	519	530	456	202
1958	2,437	2,652	3,368	498	577	491	208
1959	2,672	2,844	3,339	546	618	527	210
1960	3,058	3,075	3,789	625	669	523	213
1961	2,908	3,883	3,883	595	655	593	215
1962	3,088	3,023	3,799	631	657	608	218
1963	3,268	3,217	4,104	668	699	595	220
1964	3,675	3,426	4,285	752	745	642	223
1965	3,808	3,432	4,277	779	746	671	227
1966	4,344	3,864	4,528	888	840	709	231
1967	4,750	4,369	5,069	971	950	793	238

Sources:

Herman P. Miller, *Rich Man, Poor Man* (New York: Thomas Y. Crowell, 1964), pp. 42–43.
U.S., Bureau of the Census, *Historical Statistics of the United States: Colonial Times to 1957*, Series G 149 and 170, E 113; *Statistical Abstracts of the United States: 1967*, p. 355; *Current Population Reports*, Series P-60, "Consumer Income," No. 6, Table 2; No. 15, Tables 17 and 33; No. 53, Tables 17 and 33; No. 59, Table 23; No. 60, Table 17.

of non-whites in 1959 was far superior to what it was in 1939. We can infer that poverty was even more common in 1939 than twenty years later when it was first measured.

In describing income statistics, we should note that non-white income has always been very far below that of whites. While rigorous comparisons are difficult to make, the median income of families and unrelated individuals might be considered. In 1939, the non-white median for this group was about 37 percent as large as the white median. By the early 1950s, this improved to a little over 50 percent, probably reflecting the changes in labor market conditions during World War II. There was little change during the later 1950s, but, beginning in the 1960s, there was an apparent narrowing of the racial gap in income. By 1966, the non-white median was about sixty percent as large as that of whites.[116]

In addition to changes in income, there have been advances in the educational attainment of blacks since 1940. These are indicated in Table 9–2 which shows the years of schooling completed by Negroes age 25 and over for dates between 1940 and 1968. These figures have been standardized for age. Among both males and females, the proportion with a complete high school education increased from about 7 percent in 1940 to about 30 percent in 1968. These improvements in educational attainment are likely to continue, for there has been a rise in the proportion of young blacks who are attending school.[117] The cohorts of blacks born after 1937 will be the first cohorts in which more than one-half of the individuals will graduate from secondary school.[118]

There has also been an upgrading of the occupational level of the Negro labor force and a reduction in the proportion who are out of work. Figures in Table 9–3 are pertinent to this topic for they show the occupations of employed workers and the proportion of the labor force which was unemployed for dates be-

---

[116] U.S., Bureau of the Census, "Income in 1966 of Families and Persons in the United States," *Current Population Reports*, Series P-60, No. 53 (December 28, 1967), Tables G and 17; Mary F. Hanson, *Trends in Income of Families and Persons in the United States: 1947–1964*, Bureau of the Census, Technical Paper 17 (Washington: Government Printing Office, 1967).

[117] U. S. Bureau of the Census, *Census of Population: 1960*, PC(1)–1D, Table 167; "School Enrollment: October, 1965," *Current Population Reports*, Series P-20, No. 162 (March 24, 1967), Table 3.

[118] U. S. Bureau of the Census, "Educational Attainment: March, 1968," *Current Population Reports*, Series P-20, No. 182 (April 28, 1969), Table 1

TABLE 9–2
Educational Attainment of Negroes 25 and Over; 1940–1968*

	1940	1950	1960	1964	1968
Males					
Years of School Completed:					
College 4 or more	1%	2%	3%	5%	4%
1–3	2	3	4	4	6
High School 4	4	7	11	15	20
1–3	7	12	17	21	21
Elementary 5–8	38	38	36	33	29
1–4	35	30	22	17	(20)
No Years Completed	13	8	7	5	
Total	100%	100%	100%	100%	100%
Females					
Years of School Completed:					
College 4 or more	1%	2%	3%	3%	5%
1–3	2	3	4	5	5
High School 4	5	9	14	20	22
1–3	9	14	21	23	24
Elementary 5–8	42	42	38	34	30
1–4	30	24	16	12	(14)
No Years Completed	11	6	4	3	
Total	100%	100%	100%	100%	100%

* Figures for 1940 and 1950 refer to non-whites. These data have been standardized for age using the age distribution of the Negro population in 1960 as the standard.

Sources:

U. S. Bureau of the Census, *Sixteenth Census of the United States: 1940*, Population, Vol. IV, Part 1, Table 18; *Census of Population: 1950*, P-C1; Table 115; *Census of Population: 1960*, PC(2)–1C, Tables 1 and 19; *Current Population Reports*, "Negro Population: March, 1964," Series P-20, No. 142 (October 11, 1965) Table 6, "Educational Attainment: March, 1968," Series P-20, No. 182 (April 28, 1969) Table 1.

tween 1940 and 1966. During World War II, unemployment was cut sharply. Since the end of that war, there have been only slight reductions in unemployment but there has been an increase in the proportion of blacks who work at higher paying, white collar jobs and a decrease in the proportion who hold lower paying jobs on farms or as domestic servants. Investigations of occupational and industrial changes since 1960 indicate there has been a rapid rise in the employment of blacks in professional, clerical, and craftsmen jobs but that blacks are still under-represented at these occupational levels.[119]

---

[119] U. S. Department of Labor, *The Negroes in the United States*, Bulletin No. 1511 (June, 1966), Chap. ii; U. S. Bureau of the Census, *Current Population Reports*, "Social and Economic Conditions of Negroes in the

TABLE 9–3
Employment Status of Negroes: 1940–1966*

	1940	1950	1960	1966
Males				
Occupation of Employed Workers:				
Professional, Technical	2%	2%	3%	4%
Managers, Officials	1	2	2	3
Clerical, Sales	2	4	7	8
Craftsmen	4	8	11	10
Operatives	13	21	27	31
Service Workers	15	15	16	15
Laborers	22	24	22	22
Farmers, Farm Laborers	41	24	12	7
Total	100%	100%	100%	100%
Percent of Labor Force Unemployed	18	8	9	7
Females				
Occupation of Employed Workers:				
Professional, Technical	4%	5%	8%	9%
Managers, Officials	1	1	1	1
Clerical, Sales	2	5	9	13
Craftsmen	–	1	1	1
Operatives	6	15	14	15
Service Workers	70	62	62	58
Laborers	1	2	1	1
Farmers, Farm Laborers	16	9	4	2
Total	100%	100%	100%	100%
Percent of Labor Force Unemployed	15	8	9	7

* Figures for 1966 refer to labor force age 18 and over.

Sources:
U. S. Bureau of the Census, Sixteenth Census of the United States: 1940, Population, Non-White Population by Race, Tables 7 and 8; Census of Population: 1950, P-E, No. 3B, Table 9; Census of Population: 1960, PC(2)–1C, Table 32; Current Population Reports, "Negro Population: March, 1966," Current Population Reports, Series P-20, No. 168, (December 22, 1967) Tables 15 and 16.

Two consequences of the changes in socio-economic position of blacks were a rise in food consumption and improvements in housing conditions. Figures showing per capita food consumption by non-whites are unavailable, but, for the national population, per capita food consumption in 1950 was 6 percent greater than in 1939; in 1962, it was 11 percent greater than in 1939.[120]

United States," Series P-23, No. 24 (October, 1967), pp. 27–42; "Recent Trends in Social and Economic Conditions of Negroes in the United States," Series P-23, No. 26 (July, 1968), pp. 11–17.

[120] U. S. Bureau of the Census, Historical Statistics of the United States: Colonial Times to 1957, Series G 545; Historical Statistics of the United States: Continuation to 1962 and Revision, Series G 545.

The proportion of non-white occupied homes which were owner occupied, went up from 24 percent in 1940 to 38 percent in 1960.[121] Overcrowding in non-white occupied homes declined during this same period. In 1940, 40 percent of the homes contained more than one person per room, but, by 1960, this decreased to 28 percent.[122] There were also improvements in the physical conditions and facilities of homes lived in by blacks, for there was an increase in the proportion of homes with flush toilets and indoor piped water. By 1960, about 70 percent of the non-white occupied houses had exclusive use of flush toilets and 80 percent had a piped water supply.[123] Between 1960 and 1966, there were further improvements in the conditions and facilities of homes for non-whites, although the quality of non-white occupied homes remains far below that of white occupied housing.[124] The changes in housing characteristics, which have occurred since 1940, are not simply a function of the urbanization of blacks. Rather, there has been a rise in home ownership and an improvement in the physical facilities of homes in both urban and rural areas.

Summary

The theory of demographic transition has been frequently employed to describe the demographic changes which many populations have experienced.[125] Supposedly, for decades, even centuries, generally high birth rates and widely fluctuating mortality rates have prevailed. Over the long run, growth rates have been near zero, because changes in mortality such as those produced by epidemics, droughts, and floods, offset the high fertility. During the second stage, fertility rates remain high but death rates begin to fall as technological improvements lead to increases in agricultural output and medical innovations are introduced. As a result, the population begins to grow consistently. During the third stage, the fall in mortality is accelerated as technological develop-

---

[121] U. S. Bureau of the Census, *Census of Housing: 1950*, Vol. I, Part 1, Table 3; *Census of Housing: 1960*, HC(1)–1, Table 9.

[122] U. S. Bureau of the Census, *Sixteenth Census of the United States: 1940, Housing*, Vol. II, Part I, Table 53; *Census of Housing: 1960*, HC(1), Table 25.

[123] U. S. Bureau of the Census, *Census of Housing: 1950*, Vol. 1, Part 1, Table 8; *Census of Housing: 1960*, HC(1)–1, Table 24.

[124] U. S. Bureau of the Census, "Social and Economic Conditions of Negroes in the United States," pp. 53–56.

[125] C. P. Blacker, "Stages in Population Growth," *The Eugenics Review*, XXXIX (October, 1947), pp. 89–97.

ments become more numerous, and contagious diseases are controlled. This has the effect of increasing the growth rate. The fertility may begin to decline during this stage; as the population becomes urbanized, educational levels will go up and parents may elect to have smaller families. During the fourth stage, the mortality rate is stabilized at a fairly low level; and the birth rate declines to a low level which has the consequence of slowing population growth.

The black population of the United States experienced a demographic transition but in a manner very different from that described in the previous paragraph. During the early nineteenth century, death rates among blacks were very high but fertility rates were even higher and the population annually grew at a rate of 2 percent or more. Beginning in the latter part of the nineteenth century, the birth rate declined; the decline continued until the late 1930s and affected all social classes in both urban and rural areas. As far as we can detect, this decrease was chiefly brought about, not by changes in marital patterns or by the increased use of contraceptives, but by alterations in health conditions which were unfavorable to fecundity. During this same period, there were only modest improvements in mortality. Certain contagious diseases, such as yellow fever, cholera, malaria, and typhoid fever—once major causes of death—gradually disappeared as ecological changes occurred and technologies for eliminating carriers of these diseases improved.[126] However, as we pointed out in this chapter, living conditions in southern rural areas may have deteriorated and life expectancy among blacks was probably only a little greater in 1930 than seventy years earlier. Thus, the black population differs from many others since fertility rates declined more rapidly than mortality rates for an extended period of time. During the Depression decade, the population increased at an annual rate of well under one percent.

Beginning in 1935, major efforts were made to improve health standards and during World War II, income went up rapidly among blacks. In the twenty year span from 1935 to 1955, death rates were substantially reduced and life expectancy increased. Negroes rapidly moved into urban areas and their socioeconomic position improved. One might predict that this would lead to a continuation of the low fertility rates of the Depression

---

126 Carl C. Dauer, Robert F. Korns, and Leonard M. Schuman, *Infectious Diseases* (Cambridge: Harvard University Press, 1968), Chap. i.

era. This did not happen. Instead, fertility rates began to climb around 1940 and continued to increase for about twenty years. By the late 1950s, the black population was growing at about 2.5 percent each year or approximately as fast as in the pre-Civil War period. This increase in fertility resulted from improved health conditions and the minimization of fertility-impairing diseases. During the 1940s and 1950s, some women began using effective contraceptives but, as the fertility studies demonstrate, many black women delayed using birth control or used ineffective methods and consequently excess childbearing occurred frequently.

Birth rates have fallen since the late 1950s, and this is an important component of the demographic transition. The further urbanization of blacks and continued improvements in educational attainment have led more couples to be aware of the possibilities and advantages of limited numbers of children. Since 1960, new contraceptive methods—the estrogen-progestin pills and the intrauterine devices—have become popular. These technological innovations have fostered a more widespread and effective use of birth control. Thus, the contemporary decline in Negro fertility differs from the decline which occurred prior to the Depression for it results from the deliberate control of childbearing.

The evidence presented in this monograph does not permit us to predict whether racial differences in fertility will someday be nonexistent or whether the fertility of blacks may be persistently higher or lower than that of whites. We do observe that the long-run trends in white and Negro fertility have been quite similar, although we have not examined how the fertility of subgroups of the white population such as foreign born whites compares to that of Negroes. In addition, the patterns of rural-urban and socio-economic differentials in fertility are the same among whites and blacks and, apparently, this has been the case for a long time. The studies of fertility desires and expectations which have been conducted recently, suggest there is very little racial difference in the number of children couples wish to have. However, a look at vital statistics data for any recent year finds that black fertility rates are substantially higher than those of whites. We believe there are two major reasons for this. First, among women in rural areas and among those with the characteristics of low economic status, black fertility rates exceed those of whites by a wide margin. Second, as indicated in the last chapter, fertility rates at young ages, particularly during the teen years, are much higher among blacks than among whites. The changing characteristics of the black population and the growing use of birth control will probably lead to lower fertility rates but it is impossible to know whether this will have the consequence of eliminating racial differences in family size.

Chapter 10

APPENDIX: THE CONSTRUCTION
OF NEGRO COHORT FERTILITY RATES

Estimating Negro Births: 1935 to 1964

Development of the Birth Registration System

In Chapter 4, we outlined the techniques used to calculate Negro cohort fertility rates. In this chapter, we will describe these methods in detail as well as the assumptions which were made in computing these rates. The first step in the process of computing cohort fertility rates was to determine how many Negroes were born each year. The registration of births and deaths has a very long history in this country. As early as 1632, Virginia required an annual listing of births and marriages, and by the end of the seventeenth century, each of the colonies had laws which required the registration of births.[1] These laws apparently had little impact, for there was no regular compilation of vital events by any of the colonies. Massachusetts, in 1841, became the first state to establish a modern registration system and to publish annual vital statistics.[2] After the Civil War, other New England states followed the lead of Massachusetts, but the primary concern of vital statisticians in the nineteenth century was the recording of deaths and causes of death.[3]

---

[1] Sam Shapiro, "Development of Birth Registration and Birth Statistics in the United States," *Population Studies*, IV (June, 1950), 86; John Shaw Billings, "The Registration of Vital Statistics," *American Journal of Medical Sciences*, CLXIX (January, 1883), 36.

[2] Shapiro, *loc. cit.*, p. 87.

[3] Walter F. Willcox, *Introduction to the Vital Statistics of the United States: 1900 to 1930* (Washington: Government Printing Office, 1933), p. 13.

When the Bureau of the Census became a permanent agency in 1902, Congress delegated the responsibility for collecting birth statistics to it. The Census Bureau quickly established minimum standards for a birth registration system, and Pennsylvania, in 1905, enacted the first birth registration law which satisfied the Bureau's criteria. Efforts were made to establish a Birth Registration Area, in 1908, but work for the Thirteenth Census interfered. Finally, with the help of the American Public Health Association and the Children's Bureau, a Birth Registration Area came into existence in 1915. Ten states and the District of Columbia were included.[4] One of the major motivations for a registration system was to learn more about the frequency and causes of infant mortality.

The Birth Registration Area expanded slowly and blacks were not well represented until large southern states were admitted during the 1920s. Finally, in 1933, when Texas entered the Birth Registration Area coverage became nationwide.

Early Tests of Birth Registration Completeness

If the birth registration system recorded every Negro birth, we could compute fertility rates directly from the published tabulations. Unfortunately, each registration system misses some vital events which makes it necessary to determine the extent of under-registration.

In order to be admitted to the Birth Registration Area, a state had to demonstrate that 90 percent of the births occurring within the state were registered. Tests of the completeness of registration were conducted, but they were not always rigorous. For instance, a list of children might have been obtained from a local school and then these names checked to determine what proportion had birth certificates. In other areas, double post cards were mailed to a sample of residences. Householders were instructed to return the post card if a birth had occurred within the last year. An attempt was then made to find birth certificates for these infants.[5] These tests provided no information about registration completeness at the national level and furnished accurate esti-

---

[4] *Ibid.*

[5] A. W. Reidrich, J. Collinson, and F. D. Rhodes, *Comparison of Birth Tests by Several Methods in Georgia and Maryland*, U. S., Public Health Service, Special Report Series, VII, No. 60 (November 10, 1939).

mates for local areas only if the lists of children were unbiased samples of all births—a criterion these tests probably did not satisfy.

Improved methods for estimating the completeness of registration involved the use of census data. Each census enumerates how many people are under one year of age. Using this figure, and making an allowance for infant mortality, estimates can be derived of the number of births which occurred in the one year period preceding the census. These estimates of births can then be compared to the number of recorded births to ascertain the completeness of registration.

Elbertie Foudray, in constructing life tables for 1920, employed a variant of this approach. First, she assumed that all births occurring within the District of Columbia, in 1919, were registered. Then, she took the number of registered births, made an allowance for infant deaths, and obtained an estimate of the population under one as of January 1, 1920—the date of the Fourteenth Census. She compared these estimates of the population under one to the number enumerated by the census. This comparison revealed that the census missed 9 percent of the white infants and 25 percent of the non-white infants in the District of Columbia. She then assumed that in every other city and state, census coverage of the population under one was similar to coverage in Washington. That is, she inflated the census counts of population under one in each area by the undercount rates she calculated for Washington, producing what were believed to be estimates of the "correct" population under one in each area. Her next step, was to adjust the "correct" population in each area for infant deaths to obtain an estimate of how many births occurred in that area in the one year period preceding the Census of 1920. Finally, she compared registered births to her estimates of births to ascertain the completeness of registration. She found that the registration of non-white births ranged from a high of 91 percent, in a group of northern cities, to a low of 74 percent in southern states.[6]

Pascal Whelpton used a refined version of this same method to determine how completely births were registered during 1929. He discovered that the registration of non-white births ranged

---

[6] U. S., Bureau of the Census, *United States Abridged Life Tables: 1919–20* (Washington: Government Printing Office, 1923).

from a high of 104 percent in Delaware, to a low of 40 percent in Oklahoma.[7]

While the Foudray and Whelpton studies were among the first to rigorously assess the completeness of birth registration, they did not provide national estimates of births, since not all states were included in the Birth Registration Area at these times. Furthermore, these tests hinged upon the assumption that, within one or more areas, all births were registered. Subsequent investigations demonstrated that this was not a valid assumption.

The Birth Registration Tests of 1940 and 1950

The first national test of the completeness of birth registration was carried out in conjunction with the Census of 1940. Census enumerators filled out special infant cards for all children born between December 1, 1939 and March 31, 1940. Vital registrars in every state were required to prepare special copies of all birth certificates issued during this December to March period. An extensive effort was then made to match each infant enumeration card with the appropriate birth certificate. Matching was attempted, using the infant's name, the mother's maiden name, and the father's name. A form letter was dispatched requesting more information from the parents of all children whose infant card remained unmatched after three searches. If no reply was received, a second form letter was mailed, and if still there was no response, unmatched infant cards were forwarded to local registrars who attempted to match infant cards with birth certificates. Infant cards unmatched after this final search were assumed to represent unregistered births. The completeness of registration was computed by dividing the number of matched infant cards by the total number of infant cards obtained by census enumerators.[8]

This test found that 82 percent of the non-white births occurring during the designated period were registered. In New England, registration was nearly complete, while in Arizona and

---

[7] Pascal K. Whelpton, "The Completeness of Birth Registration in the United States," *Journal of the American Statistical Association* XXIX, (June, 1934), pp. 128–129.

[8] Robert D. Grove, *Studies in the Completeness of Birth Registration*, U. S. Public Health Service, Special Report Series, XVII, No. 18 (April 20, 1943), pp. 224–230.

New Mexico fewer than half the non-white births were registered. Among whites, 94 percent of the births were registered.[9]

Since the results of the birth registration test served as a base for the estimates of black births and population described in Chapter 4, it is necessary to be certain that the test determined accurately the completeness of registration. Let us consider, first, the possibility that the birth registration test over-estimated the completeness of birth registration. This might have occurred in two ways: infant cards from the census may have been improperly matched to birth certificates, thus over-estimating the number of registered births, or, the events of being registered and being enumerated may not have been independent but related, so as to affect the estimated completeness of registration.

It is unlikely that the registration test overstated the degree of matching, for each infant card was assumed unmatched until proved otherwise. Clerical errors and chance agreements between names on birth certificates and infant cards may have resulted in some mistakes, but Shapiro investigated this problem and found no serious errors.[10]

A more important cause of error may have been a relationship between being registered and being enumerated. Shown below, for the total population, are results from the 1940 test of birth registration completeness.[11]

	Registration		
	R	R̄	Total
Enumeration E	636,076	55,381	687,457
Ē	101,331		
Total	737,407		

The estimate of registration completeness, $P(R)$, was computed by dividing 636,076 by 687,457; $P(R) = 92.5$ percent. If the probability of being enumerated by the census is independent of the probability of being registered, the birth registration test gives an unbiased estimate of the completeness of birth registration. It is important to bear in mind that an unbiased estimate is obtained even if the census failed to enumerate a substantial pro-

---

9 *Ibid.*

10 Shapiro, *loc. cit.*, p. 87.

11 The figures in this table refer to the total population. Data showing non-white births by month, although used in the previously cited source, were not publicly available.

portion of infants, so long as registration and enumeration were independent.

On the other hand, if the probability of being enumerated is greater for infants who were registered than for those who were not registered, the birth registration test will give a biased estimate of birth registration completeness. It may be that the likelihood of an infant's being enumerated was greater if his birth were registered than if it were not registered. Unregistered births may occur in out of the way areas which are also poorly enumerated.

Chandrasekar and Deming have indicated the extent of bias which is introduced if the two events, enumeration and registration, are related.[12] The following table may be considered. The values along the left hand column indicate the estimates of under-registration, $P(\bar{R})$, on the assumption that enumeration and registration are independent. The values along the top indicate the ratio of the probability of an infant's being enumerated if he was registered, that is $P(E|R)$, to the probability of being enumerated if his birth was not registered, that is $P(E|\bar{R})$. The numbers in the body of the table show by what amount the first estimate of under-registration must be increased to compensate for the lack of independence. For example, if the first estimate of under-registration is 18 percent and if subsequent investigation demonstrates that registered births were 1.1 times as likely to be enumerated as unregistered births, the estimate of under-registration should be raised to 19.6 percent.

$P(\bar{R})$	Ratio of $P(E|R)$ to $P(E|\bar{R})$				
	1.10	1.25	1.50	1.75	2.00
.120	.011	.024	.040	.051	.060
.150	.014	.030	.050	.064	.075
.180	.016	.036	.060	.077	.090
.210	.019	.042	.070	.090	.105

This table shows that as long as $P(E|R)$ does not greatly exceed $P(E|\bar{R})$, the error introduced by assuming independence will be small. Although we know the census contains errors, by definition it enumerates everyone. It is difficult to believe that registered infants were very much more likely to be enumerated

12 C. Chandrasekar and W. E. Deming, "On a Method of Estimating Birth and Death Rates and the Extent of Registration," *Journal of the American Statistical Association*, XLIV (March, 1949), 101–116.

than unregistered births. For instance, to get a ratio of $P(E|R)$ to $P(E|\bar{R})$ as large as 1.50, the probability of a non-registered infant's being enumerated would have to be .67 or less. This seems to be a very low probability of being enumerated in a national census.

Considering the small size of these possible errors and considering that enumeration and registration were carried out by separate agencies with separate staffs, at different times and in different places, it is likely the assumption of independence of registration and enumeration does not introduce serious error. We conclude from this analysis that the birth registration test of 1940 did not overestimate the registration of black births.

Second, we must consider the possibility that the birth registration test underestimated the completeness of birth registration. This may have happened because many infant cards which should have been matched were not matched or because the events of enumeration and registration were related in such a manner as to understate registration completeness.

It is unlikely that either of these occurred. We have already described the care taken to assure proper matching. The only possible way in which the lack of independence of enumeration and registration would produce underestimates of registration is if unregistered infants were more likely to be enumerated than registered infants; that is if $P(E|\vec{R})$ exceeded $P(E|R)$. It seems very improbable that infants whose births were not registered would be more completely counted by the census than infants whose births were registered.

This investigation and an examination of the data for internal consistency confirm the accuracy of the birth registration test of 1940.

The birth registration test conducted in 1950 used procedures which were very similar to those used in 1940. The time span was shortened to three months, but because of rising fertility rates, the number of births involved in the 1950 test exceeded those in the 1940 test.

The registration of non-white births improved after 1940. The 1950 test found that 94 percent of all non-white births were registered, a substantial improvement over the 82 percent figure of a decade earlier. A major reason for this improvement was the increase in hospitalization of non-whites for birth. As indicated in the last chapter, in 1940, only 27 percent of the births occurred in hospitals, but in 1950, 58 percent of the births were in hospitals.

However, the registration of both hospitalized and non-hospitalized non-white births improved in the decade between 1940 and 1950.[13]

Estimates of the Completeness of Registration for Years other than 1940 and 1950

The birth registration tests provided estimates of under-registration for only two dates but the results of these tests have been used to generate under-registration rates for each year since 1935. To estimate births in the 1935 to 1940 period, it was assumed that the registration rates indicated by the 1940 test applied to the entire period, 1935 to 1940. Results from the 1940 test were employed to calculate registration rates specific for state, color, and place of occurrence (hospitalized or non-hospitalized). That is, for each state: four under-registration rates were computed; one for hospitalized white births, one for hospitalized non-white births, one for non-hospitalized white births, and one for non-hospitalized non-white births. The number of registered births in each of these categories was determined and then inflated by the appropriate under-registration rates. Summing these figures for all states, produced national estimates of births and under-registration for the years 1935 to 1940.[14]

To estimate registration completeness for years between 1940 and 1950, the under-registration rates for 1940 and 1950, specific for state, color and place of occurrence, were compared. It was assumed that there was a linear change in the completeness of registration between 1940 and 1950. This produced four under-registration rates for each state for each year. The number of registered births in each category was then increased by the appropriate under-registration rate and the results for states were summed to obtain national estimates.

Rates from the birth registration test of 1950 have been used for the period after 1950. Each year, the number of recorded births, specific for state, color, and place of occurrence, have been increased by the under-registration rates computed from the 1950 test. This procedure implies there has been no improvement in the registration of births within the specific categories, an as-

---

[13] U. S., National Office of Vital Statistics, *Vital Statistics of the United States: 1950*, I, Table 6.43.

[14] *Ibid.*

sumption that some might question. However, the 1950 study found that virtually all (99.5 percent among whites and 98.2 percent among non-whites) hospitalized births were registered. It is difficult to improve upon these high rates of registration completeness. As non-hospitalized births have become rarer and rarer, the completeness of birth registration has increased. In 1966, 99.4

TABLE 10–1
Total Negro Births, Percent of Births Unregistered and Number of Native Female Negroes Attaining Age 14 Each Year: 1920–1964

Year	Total Negro Births	Percent of Births Unregistered	Number of Women Attaining Age 14
1920	366,173		131,122
1921	351,610		132,292
1922	360,359		130,614
1923	355,614		139,240
1924	357,650		155,240
1925	349,937		142,338
1926	335,266		146,920
1927	333,979		139,376
1928	321,454		141,574
1929	329,101		139,820
1930	327,352		135,135
1931	312,567		136,838
1932	327,816		144,940
1933	316,244		156,460
1934	315,908		152,979
1935	319,255	20.1%	147,350
1936	312,332	19.8	151.883
1937	327,452	19.6	150,311
1938	331,934	19.2	153,753
1939	334,550	18.9	151.364
1940	340,854	18.7	145,426
1941	358,519	17.4	144,662
1942	369,966	16.2	140,424
1943	374,444	15.0	144,955
1944	375,856	13.7	142,405
1945	367,634	12.4	141,925
1946	411,408	10.8	139,488
1947	445,370	9.4	141,043
1948	468,826	8.2	141,382
1949	486,111	7.2	142,904
1950	502,719	6.4	140,407
1951	516,080	5.9	147,482
1952	525,420	5.6	150,740
1953	545,582	5.2	150,781
1954	570,751	4.9	154,117

Table 10–1 (Cont'd)

Year	Total Negro Births	Percent of Births Unregistered	Number of Women Attaining Age 14
1955	589,712	4.5	161,419
1956	605,520	4.2	168,473
1957	616,998	4.0	170,878
1958	623,549	3.9	173,068
1959	628,004	3.8	170,673
1960	624,245	3.6	190,487
1961	629,955	3.4	207,568
1962	623,889	3.4	218,363
1963	619,443	3.2	227,484
1964	625,491	3.1	235,228
1965	599,121	3.1	242,111
1966	573,969	2.8	248,545

Sources:
    See text.

percent of the white and 97.2 percent of the non-white births were registered according to these estimates.[15]

This discussion has described the under-registration of non-white births, but this monograph has focused upon Negro population growth. The procedures described above determined what percentage of the non-white births were not registered each year from 1935 to 1966. The number of registered black births was then increased by the under-registration rate for non-whites to produce annual estimates of Negro births. These are shown in Table 10–1 along with the estimated proportion of births which were not registered. These figures refer to births occurring within the conterminous United States.

In 1962 and 1963, New Jersey did not tabulate births by race. Distributions of New Jersey births by race, for 1961 and 1964, were used to estimate the number of blacks born within New Jersey in 1962 and 1963.

Estimating Census Undercount of Black Women

The previous section described the methodology employed to estimate black births for the period since 1935. To construct cohort fertility rates, additional data were needed; namely, births for

---

[15] U. S., National Center for Health Statistics, *Vital Statistics of the United States: 1966*, I, Table 1–20.

the years before 1935 and estimates of the number of women eligible to bear children each year. As a first step in computing these figures, it was necessary to determine how many native black women were alive in the United States in 1960. This information should have been available from the Census of 1960, but, as we mentioned in Chapter 2, census counts are not always accurate. For this reason, we first studied the degree of census undercount and then corrected census data for these ommissions.

Many different methods have been used to correct census data for its deficiencies. To adjust for the undercount of blacks in the censuses of 1870 and 1890, the Census Bureau made assumptions about the similarity of decennial growth rates and concluded that the Census of 1870 missed 9 percent of the blacks and the Census of 1890, 4 percent.[16] Although this provides some information about particular censuses, other techniques are needed to estimate undercount more accurately. One method which has been used from time to time is that of post-census investigations or re-enumerations. Following the Census of 1870, officials from New York and Philadelphia clamored that their cities had been seriously undercounted, and President Grant ordered the Census Office to re-enumerate these places. These recounts found that the original enumerations had underestimated the population by about 2 percent.[17] After the Census of 1900, a county just outside Washington was re-enumerated and, on the basis of this study, Walter Willcox concluded that nationally the white population was undercounted by 1.5 percent and the Negro population by 2.5 percent.[18] Following the Census of 1950, a number of sample areas were re-enumerated to determine census coverage. This study found the white population was undercounted by about 1 percent and the non-white by about 3 percent.[19] Recent studies suggest that post-census re-enumerations are not very efficient in estimating census undercount, perhaps, because both the census and the post-census study are carried on in rather similar fashion and people missed by one may likely be missed by the other.

---

[16] U. S., Bureau of the Census, *Negro Population in the United States: 1790–1915*, pp. 25–29.

[17] U. S., Secretary of the Interior, *Ninth Census of the United States: 1870*, I., p. xx.

[18] Walter F. Willcox, *Negroes in the United States*, U. S., Bureau of the Census, Bulletin 8 (Washington: Government Printing Office, 1904), p. 189.

[19] U. S., Bureau of the Census, *The Post Enumeration Survey: 1950*, Technical Paper No. 4 (Washington: Bureau of the Census, 1960), Table 1.

The development of a birth registration system and tests of birth registration completeness permit a more thorough investigation of census omissions. Annual births can be survived to census dates to determine how completely the census enumerated the population. The following section describes use of this technique.

Estimating the Census Undercount of Black
Women Born During and After 1935

This investigation was begun by ascertaining errors in the count of females who were 0 to 24 years old in 1960, that is, women who were born 1935 and after. The first step was to determine how many black females were born each year from 1935 to 1960. These figures were obtained by dividing the total black births which occurred in a year (shown in Table 10–1) by the percentage of registered births which were female.

Decennial censuses are taken as of April 1. The second step was to determine how many births occurred between April 1 of one year and March 31 of the next so that birth statistics would be compatible with census data. Figures showing registered births by month of occurrence were employed to do this.

The third step involved surviving each birth cohort from its year of birth to dates of subsequent censuses. Consider black females born in the United States between April 1, 1938 and March 31, 1939. The survivors of this cohort, as of April 1, 1940—the date of the Census of 1940—composed the female Negro population at age one. Ten years later, survivors of this same birth cohort should have been enumerated at age eleven by the Census of 1950; a decade later, the Census of 1960 should have counted survivors of the same cohort at age 21.

Each cohort born after April 1, 1935 was survived to the dates of the 1940, 1950 and 1960 censuses. This technique yielded estimates of the native female Negro population ages 0 to 4 in 1940, 0 to 14 in 1950, and 0 to 24 in 1960.

Survival rates for this procedure came from United States life tables for Negroes or non-white females for the periods 1939–41, 1949–51 and 1959–61.[20] It was assumed that the mortal-

20 Thomas N. E. Greville, *United States Life Tables and Actuarial Tables: 1939–41*, U. S., Bureau of the Census, *Sixteenth Census of the United States: 1940*, Table 9; U. S., National Office of Vital Statistics, *United*

ity rates of a given life table were operative for a ten year period centered upon the census year. For instance, women born in the twelve month span following April 1, 1939 were survived from 1938 to 1945, according to the mortality rates from the life table for 1939–41; from 1945 to 1955, according to rates from the life table for 1949–51; and for the period after 1955, mortality rates from the 1959–61 life table were used. During this time, infant mortality rates changed more rapidly than death rates at older ages. A trend line was fitted and the infant mortality rate was assumed to change annually.

No correction was made for the out-migration of native Negro women from the United States. For fiscal years 1946 through 1958, the Immigration and Naturalization Service tabulated the number of citizens who emigrated.[21] During this thirteen year period, a total of only 2,048 Negro women departed. The Census of 1960 enumerated Americans who were living abroad and found there were only 20,000 Negro females residing outside the country compared to about ten million in the United States.[22] Both pieces of information suggest that there has been very little out-migration of female blacks.

The fourth step was to ascertain the extent of census undercount. This was done by comparing the estimated number of survivors at each census date to the number at the same age enumerated by the census. The difference between these two numbers represented net census undercount. Table 10–2 shows the estimated number of survivors, the enumerated populations and the rates of undercount. These computations were made for single years of age but Table 10–2 shows the data for five-year age groups.

Estimates of the Undercount of
Negro Women Born before 1935

To estimate the census undercount of women born before 1935, an iterative technique was employed.[23] We might consider

---

States Life Tables: 1949–51, Vital Statistics Special Reports, XLI, No. 1 (November 23, 1954), Table 9; U. S., National Center for Health Statistics, *Life Tables: 1959–61*, I., No. 1 (December, 1964), Table 9.

[21] U. S., Department of Justice, *Annual Report of the Immigration and Naturalization Service*, 1946 through 1958, Table 13A (through 1951) and Table 14 (after 1951).

[22] U. S., Bureau of the Census, *Census of Population: 1960*, PC(3)–1C, Table 2.

[23] Coale, *loc. cit.*

TABLE 10-2
Net Census Undercount of Native Negro Females Born Since 1935

	Census of 1940			Census of 1950			Census of 1960		
	Survivors of Births	Census Count	Net Census Undercount	Survivors of Births	Census Count	Net Census Undercount	Survivors of Births	Census Count	Net Census Undercount
0– 4	746,883	627,352	−16.01%	1,039,988	942,254	−9.40%	1,459,510	1,357,161	− 7.02%
5– 9				838,088	767,812	−8.39	1,263,909	1,193,264	− 5.59
10–14				733,949	676,666	−7.81	1,028,637	981,377	− 4.59
15–19							832,810	753,861	− 9.48
20–24							725,684	638,619	−12.00

Sources:

U. S., Bureau of the Census, Census of Population: 1960; PC(1)–1D, Table 158; PC(2), Tables 1 and 8.

U. S., Bureau of the Census, Census of Population: 1950; II, Part 1, Table 97; PE-No. 3B, Tables 2 and 26.

U. S., Bureau of the Census, Sixteenth Census of the United States: 1940, Population Characteristics of the Non-white Population by Race, Table 3.

the group of native female Negroes who were 10 to 14 years old in 1950. Table 10–2 indicates the census missed about eight percent of the women in this age group. The Censuses of 1940 and 1950 were taken at the same time of year. The enumeration forms and the procedures used in the two censuses were similar, therefore, the assumption was made that the undercount patterns in 1940 were similar to those in 1950. Specifically, we assumed that Negro females ages 10 to 14, in 1940, were under-enumerated to the same extent as Negro females ages 10 to 14 in 1950, that is, by 8 percent. The 1940 census count of this age group was then inflated by this undercount rate to derive a corrected estimate of the 1940 population. In 1940, the census enumerated 669,000 native black females ages 10 to 14.[24] The correction for undercount raised this figure to 726,000.

The corrected 1940 population figures were then survived for a decade according to the mortality schedules of the previously mentioned life table. This produced estimates of the population, in 1950, corrected for census undercount. These corrected estimates of population were compared to the population enumerated in 1950, to ascertain net census undercount at ages over 14 years.

For example, consider the women ages 10 to 14 in 1940. We determined there were 726,000 native black females in this age group in 1940. The survival rates indicated that 708,000 of these women lived to be 20 to 24 years old, in 1950, but the Census of 1950 enumerated 664,000 native black women aged 20 to 24.[25] The estimated and enumerated populations were compared to determine census undercount. This comparison indicated the Census of 1950 failed to enumerate 6 percent of the Negro women ages 20 to 24.

This iterative process was used sequentially. The undercount rate for ages 20 to 24, in 1950—6 percent in this example—was applied to the 1940 census count of female Negroes aged 20 to 24 years which produced a corrected estimate of the 1940 population in this age group. The corrected 1940 population was then survived for a decade to determine the 1950 population, ages 30 to 34, corrected for census undercount. This figure was compared to the enumerated population to ascertain the undercount rate.

---

[24] U. S., Bureau of the Census, *Sixteenth Census of the United States: 1940*, Population, Characteristics of the Non-white Population by Race, Table 3.

[25] U. S., Bureau of the Census, *Census of Population: 1950*, Vol. II, Part 1, Table 97; P-E No. 3B, Tables 2 and 26.

TABLE 10–3
Net Census Undercount of Native Negro Females: 1940–1960

	1940	1950	1960
0– 4	−16.1%	−9.4%	− 7.0%
5– 9	− 8.4	−8.4	− 5.6
10–14	− 7.8	−7.8	− 4.6
15–19	− 9.7	−9.7	− 9.5
20–24	− 6.2	−6.2	−12.0
25–29	− 7.1	−7.1	− 9.0
30–34	− 9.8	−9.8	− 4.5
35–39		−2.6	− 6.3
40–44		−6.2	− 7.3
45–49			− 8.0
50–54			− 7.4

Source:
    See text for methodology used to compute these rates.

This iterative technique produced estimates of the net census undercount of native Negro women in the age range 15 to 44, in 1950. As a by-product, estimates of the undercount at ages 5 to 34, in 1940, were derived. The estimates of native female Negroes ages 15 to 44, in 1950, were survived ten years, again using the previously mentioned life tables to determine the number of native female Negroes 25 to 54, in 1960. Table 10–3 shows net census undercount rates for 1940, 1950, and 1960. The undercount rates for women born 1935 and after come from the comparison of survivors of annual births to census figures, while the undercount rates for older women were derived by the iterative technique.

We may ask why the iterative procedure was performed with data from the Censuses of 1940 and 1950, rather than from the more recent Census of 1960. For instance, we might have assumed that undercount rates in 1950 were similar to undercount rates in 1960, or that undercount rates in 1940 were an average of the undercount rates observed in 1950 and 1960.[26]

Data from the Census of 1960 were not used because the age question asked in 1960 differed from the age question asked in 1940 or 1950. In the earlier years respondents were asked how old

---

[26] Estimates of the net census undercount of non-whites calculated in this fashion have been published. U. S., Bureau of the Census, "Estimates of the Population of the United States and Components of Change, by Age, Color, and Sex," *Current Population Reports*, Series P-25, No. 310 (June 30, 1965), Table C-2.

they were. As a result, there was much age heaping, because many Negroes claimed to be at ages ending in the digits 0 or 5. In 1960, respondents were asked their year of birth and, as a result, the reporting of age by non-whites was more accurate in 1960 than in earlier years. The Myers "blended" index provides a concise measure of the accuracy of age reporting.[27] This index takes on values from 0 to 180. If many people misstate their age; that is, if many people claim to be at ages ending in particular digits, the Myers index takes on a high value. On the other hand, a low value suggests that age is accurately reported. Shown below are Myers indices for non-white for the period 1890 to 1960.

Census Date Non-whites	Myers Index
1890	26.8
1900	20.5
1910	18.3
1920	15.7
1930	18.8
1940	11.9
1950	8.2
1960	3.4
Whites—1960	1.0

These Myers indices show the general improvement in the reporting of age by non-whites and indicate that the 1940 and 1950 censuses were more similar in accuracy of age reporting than the censuses of 1950 and 1960.

Melvin Zelnik has argued that change in the format of the age question, in 1960, substantially altered the pattern of census undercount by age.[28] He held that the 1940 and 1950 undercount patterns were similar because these censuses asked similar age questions, but that the 1960 pattern was different. For this reason the iterative procedure did not make use of data from the Census of 1960.

---

[27] Paul J. Myers, "Errors and Bias in the Reporting of Ages in Census Data," *Transactions of the Actuarial Society of America*, XLI, Part 2, No. 104 (October, 1940), 411–415.

[28] Melvin Zelnik, "An Examination of Alternative Estimates of Net Census Undercount by Age, Sex, and Color: 1950 and 1960," Paper presented at the 1966 meeting of the Population Association of America, New York, April, 1966.

Estimating Annual Births: 1920 to 1934, Estimating the Number of Black Women Who Attained Age 14 Each Year: 1920 to 1966

The methodology outlined in the previous section produced estimates of the 1960 native female black population, 0 to 54 years, by five-year age groups. These five-year age groups were separated into single-year-of-age figures using the age distribution reported in 1960 as a guide. The 1960 age distribution was used since this census suffered least from problems of age heaping.

Estimates of Negro Births: 1920 to 1934

Women who were at each single-year-of-age, in 1960, are survivors of a larger number of women who were born in a particular year. For instance, women enumerated at age 29 by the Census of 1960 are survivors of the cohort born between April 1, 1930 and March 31, 1931. If mortality rates for the intervening period are known, a revival technique can be employed to estimate how many births occurred many years before the census of 1960. We can begin with the women alive at age 29 in 1960, make an allowance for those who died, and obtain an estimate of how many women were born between April, 1930 and March, 1931.[29]

This revival technique was used to estimate female births for each twelve month period beginning with April 1, 1920. Adjustments were then made to convert the estimates to calendar year estimates. Finally, we proceeded from estimates of female births to estimates of total births by using data indicating what proportion of registered births were female in each year. Table 10–1 shows these estimates of annual births for the period 1920 to 1934.

For the years after 1935, mortality rates were obtained from the three previously described life tables. A national life table for female Negroes for 1929–31 was used for the span 1925 to 1934.[30] No national life table for Negroes in 1920 was published since the Death Registration Area included only thirty-four states at that

---

[29] For a further discussion of this revival technique see: Ansley J. Coale and Melvin Zelnik, *New Estimates of Fertility and Population in the United States* (Princeton: Princeton University Press, 1963), Chap. viii.

[30] U. S., Bureau of the Census, *United States Life Tables: 1930* (Washington: Government Printing Office, 1936), Table I–D.

time. However, there was a 1919–21 life table for Negroes who lived in the 1920 Death Registration Area and there were two 1929–31 life tables for Negroes.[31] One showed the mortality experience of Negroes who lived in the Death Registration Area as it was defined in 1920 and the other showed the mortality experience of the national Negro population. The two 1929–31 life tables for female blacks were compared and the ratios of their age-specific mortality rates were computed. These ratios were then used with the 1919–21 life table for Negroes in the 1920 Death Registration Area to compute a 1919–21 life table for the national Negro population. This life table was then used in the revival procedure.

The most serious problem in estimating births which occurred before 1935 is incomplete knowledge of mortality rates. As we indicated in Chapter 3, there is reason for thinking that the life tables for blacks in the 1920s and 1930s, computed from registered deaths, underestimated the true mortality rates, although it is impossible to ascertain exactly what the mortality rates were. If the mortality rates were higher than those indicated in the life tables derived from vital statistics data, our estimated numbers of births are too low. Much further research concerning the mortality level of blacks before 1935 is needed in order to explore possible errors in the estimates of births occurring before that date.

One previous estimate of births, in the pre-1935 period, was developed. During the late 1940s, Whelpton derived some new estimates of birth registration completeness for 1920 and 1930. He made assumptions about the number of births occurring in non-registration states and then estimated annual non-white births. We can infer an estimate of Negro births from his figures. For the period 1930 to 1934, his estimates are almost identical to those used in this monograph. His estimates for the 1920s exceed those of this monograph by about 4 percent.[32]

Estimates of Women Attaining Age 14: 1920 to 1966

To compute cohort fertility rates, it is necessary to know the number of women who reached age 14 each year, for this was as-

---

[31] *Ibid.*, Tables I–D, IV–D, and V–D.

[32] P. K. Whelpton, *Births and Birth Rates in the Entire United States: 1909 to 1948*, U. S., National Office of Vital Statistics, Vital Statistics, Special Reports, Selected Studies, Vol. XXXIII, No. 8 (September 29, 1950).

sumed to be the minimum age for childbearing. To determine these numbers, the estimates of native female Negroes, in 1960, were again utilized. Revival procedures were employed to estimate how many women became 14 each year from 1920 to 1959. For instance, women at age 54, in 1960, are survivors of the group of women who became 14 years old in 1920.

To determine the number of women who reached age 14 after 1960, the appropriate age groups were survived forward from the 1960 census date. Women at age 12 in 1960, for example, were survived two years to ascertain how many women became 14 in 1962. Table 10–1 shows how many native Negro females attained age 14 each year.

There is an important advantage in using the methodology described in this chapter to construct cohort fertility rates. The data are internally consistent. That is, all estimates of births and of the number of potential mothers were derived from one estimate of the 1960 female Negro population. Previous methodologies which have been used to construct cohort fertility rates, such as those described by Whelpton, did not use internally consistent figures.[33] Rather, estimates of births and estimates of potential mothers came from different sources.

One might ask why the procedures presented in this chapter were not used to estimate black births in the pre-1920 period. Three reasons discouraged the analysis of fertility rates for the period before 1920. First, cohorts born before 1906 were 55 years old or over in 1960. It is difficult to use iterative techniques to ascertain the census undercount of the older population, for there are major problems of age misstatement among these older groups, and these errors seriously affect the estimates of census undercount at older ages.[34]

Second, estimating births in the pre-1920 era presumes knowledge of mortality trends for this period. However, there are no national life tables for this time, and those which do exist, report the mortality experience of blacks who lived in urban areas. Most Negroes lived in rural areas and probably had life expectations which were longer than those of urban Negroes. In addition, mortality rates apparently fluctuated widely in the years

---

[33] Whelpton, *Cohort Fertility*, Chap. iii.

[34] Coale, *loc. cit.*, pp. 41–43; U. S., Bureau of the Census, "Accuracy of Data on Population Characteristics as Measured by Reinterviews," *Evaluation and Research Program of the U. S., Censuses of Population and Housing: 1960*, Series ER–60, No. 4, Table 24.

which followed World War I.[35] Consequently, there appears to be no reliable way to construct accurate national life tables for the Negro population in the pre-1920 period.

Third, to construct cohort fertility rates, we need to know about year to year changes in the age of women who bear children and the order (e.g. first, second, third, etc.) of the children. However, the birth registration statistics provide little information for Negroes during the pre-1920 period. For these reasons, the fertility analysis began with the cohort of women who reached childbearing age in 1920.

Determining Births by Cohort

Births by Age of Mother and Order for Calendar Years

The previous sections of this chapter described how the basic data were obtained. These data had to be adjusted and subdivided before cohort fertility rates could be computed. We began by dividing annual births according to age of mother.

The annual vital statistics publications showing tabulations of Negro or non-white births by age of mother were used in this procedure. However, the birth registration tests of both 1940 and 1950 indicated that the completeness of birth registration varied with the age of the mother. Generally, the younger the mother, the more likely her child was to have a birth certificate.[36] This meant that it was necessary to divide the number of births occurring each year into two components; one component representing registered births and the other representing unregistered births. Registered births were apportioned by single-year-of-age of mother according to the figures shown in the annual vital statistics volumes. A different procedure was used for the unregistered births. Data from the 1940 and 1950 birth registration tests, as well as information about year to year fluctuations in the age-specific birth rates of Negroes, were used to apportion unregistered births by age of mother. As a final step, the age-of-mother distributions of registered and unregistered births were added together to produce annual distributions of black births by single-year-of-age of mother.

---

[35] Coale and Zelnik, *op. cit.*, p. 141.
[36] U. S., National Office of Vital Statistics, *Vital Statistics of the United States: 1950*, I, Table 6–51.

It was assumed that no women younger than 14 years or older than 49 years, bore children. Reported births at younger or older ages were allocated to either age 14 or 49.

Vital statistics volumes, for most years, contained tables showing registered Negro or non-white births by age of mother and order of child. The 1950 test of birth registration completeness found that, after controls were made for age of mother, there were no substantial differences in the registration of non-white births by order of birth.[37] Children of one order were just about as likely to be registered as children of any other order. Consequently, no adjustment was made for differences in registration completeness by order of birth; rather the published tabulations were used as a guide to subdivide annual births by order.

The National Office of Vital Statistics did not tabulate non-white births by age of mother and "order" for the years 1939 through 1945 or before 1924. The distribution of births by order for 1938 was used as a guide for the years 1939, 1940, and 1941 while the 1946 tabulation served for the years 1942 through 1945. The distribution for 1924 was used for the years 1920 to 1923.

These procedures and computations resulted in tables showing births by single-year-of-age of mother and order of child for calendar years from 1920 to 1966.

Births for Cohorts

To construct cohort fertility rates, births must be related to the women who are eligible to bear children at a specified age in a given year. Consider the black women born between January 1 and December 31, 1941. Survivors of this cohort became 14 during 1955. They may have borne children at age 14 during either 1955 or 1956. A woman might have celebrated her fourteenth birthday January 1, 1955 and given birth to a youngster the next morning. Another woman in the same birth cohort may have been born December 31, 1941; become 14 on December 31, 1955 and given birth to an infant on December 30, 1956; just one day before celebrating her fifteenth birthday. This makes it necessary to separate births occurring to 14 year-old-women in 1955 into two parts; one component is attributable to women born during

---

[37] *Ibid.*, Table 6–53.

TABLE 10-4

Births by Age of Mother and Order Occurring to Negro Women Born in 1941; Births by Order

Age of Mother	Total	First	Second	Third	Fourth	Fifth	Sixth	Seventh	Eighth and Higher
14	3,957	3,957							
15	8,627	7,625	1,002						
16	16,976	13,379	3,187	410					
17	25,630	16,652	7,260	1,506	212				
18	34,542	18,209	11,471	3,915	816	130			
19	39,963	17,044	13,470	6,793	2,148	416	92		
20	42,070	14,085	13,497	8,918	3,970	1,242	281	75	
21	43,017	11,566	12,697	9,919	5,671	2,280	687	148	47
22	40,906	8,806	10,918	9,534	6,468	3,380	1,277	386	136
23	37,718	6,609	8,725	8,480	6,772	4,153	1,974	712	293
24	31,732	4,885	6,622	6,634	5,694	4,150	2,304	1,004	439

Source:
See text for methods of calculation.

1941; the other component is attributable to women born in 1940. Similarly, births at age 14, in 1956, must be separated into two components. To determine the total number of births occurring at age 14 to women who were born in 1941, we must add births occurring in 1955 to those which occurred in 1956.

As a separation factor, the value one-half was used. That is, it was assumed that one-half of the births at age 14, in 1955, were attributable to the cohort born in 1940 and one-half attributable to women born in 1941. This separation factor was used to divide births, specific for age of mother and order, for each calendar year. Then, the separated births were added together to obtain the total which occurred to each cohort at each age. The value one-half is not valid for all ages and it may be quite deficient for youthful ages. Nevertheless, Whelpton's elaborate investigation demonstrated that the use of one-half as a separation factor introduced very little bias.[38]

Table 10–4 shows births by age of mother and order for the Negro women born in 1941. Similar tables were calculated for each cohort born between 1906 and 1951. It was assumed that fourteen-year-old women could only bear first children, fifteen-year-old women could only bear first or second children and so forth.

The Calculation of Cohort Fertility Rates

Determining Parity Distributions for Each Cohort

We have described how we obtained the number of black women who reached age 14 for each year. To construct cohort fertility rates, we also needed to know how many women survived from age 14 to age 15, from 15 to 16 and to each higher age. To derive these figures, we began with the women who attained age 14 in a given year and survived them year by year according to the survival rates specified by the previously mentioned life tables. Estimates of births and of women were then employed to calculate distributions of Negro women by number of children ever born.

We might consider the Negro women who became 14 in 1955. Between ages 14 and 15, a few women died, others bore a first child, and a very small number both bore a child and died. By relating the number of births and the death rates, we determined

---

[38] Whelpton, *Cohort Fertility*, pp. 392–399.

TABLE 10–5
Parity Distribution by Age of the Negro Women Born in 1941

Age	Year Age Attained	Total Women	Women by Number of Children Ever Born							
			None	One	Two	Three	Four	Five	Six	Seven or More
14	1955	161,419	161,419							
15	1956	161,332	157,378	3,955						
16	1957	161,232	149,660	10,571	1,001					
17	1958	161,113	136,178	20,749	3,776	410				
18	1959	160,979	119,424	30,117	9,523	1,703	212			
19	1960	160,826	101,116	36,820	17,065	4,798	897	130		
20	1961	160,658	83,979	40,351	23,720	9,435	2,627	454	92	
21	1962	160,473	69,810	40,891	28,267	14,369	5,350	1,413	298	75
22	1963	160,268	58,165	39,707	31,006	18,595	8,732	3,004	836	223
23	1964	160,042	49,285	37,540	32,345	21,632	11,806	5,101	1,725	608
24	1965	159,803	42,519	35,399	32,563	23,324	14,417	7,275	2,986	1,321
25	1966	159,547	37,566	33,606	32,498	24,227	15,938	9,109	4,281	2,323

Source:
See text for a description of the methods of calculation.

what number of women at age 15 had no children and what number had one child. The number of women who had one child at age 15—first parity women—was equal to the number of women who bore a child at age 14 minus those who both bore a child and died between age 14 and 15. The number of zero parity women at age 15 was equal to the number of zero parity women at age 14 minus those who had a first child and minus those who died but did not bear a child.

Between ages 15 and 16, some of the zero parity women had a first child, some of the first parity women had a second child, some women died, and a very few women both had a child and died. Again, information about births and death rates was used to determine the distribution of sixteen-year-old women by number of children ever born.

Table 10–5 shows the parity distribution of black women born in 1941. Similar tables were computed for each birth cohort. These distributions refer to exact ages. This means that the distribution for age 15 includes all childbearing which occurred while these women were 14, but includes no childbearing at age 15. Similarly, the data for age 16 refer to all childbearing which occurred prior to age 16.

Measures of Childbearing Derived from Cohort Fertility Tables

Cumulative Parity Distributions

Parity distributions answer some questions about fertility performance. However, additional measures are needed if childbearing patterns are to be concisely summarized. For example, we must determine the average number of children born to a cohort of women by a certain age. Also, we need to ask what proportion of the women at a given age had no children, and what proportion have had one, two, or three children.

To answer these questions, cumulative parity distributions were calculated for each cohort. These distributions show the average number of children ever born per 1000 women, who attained a given age and also indicate what proportion of the women have borne a specified number of offspring. These proportions are cumulative; that is, they show the proportion of women who have had one or more, two or more, or three or more children. Table 10–6 contains the cumulative parity distribution for the cohort of Negro women born in 1941.

TABLE 10–6
Cumulative Parity Distribution for Negro Women Born in 1941

Age	Year Age Attained	Women Attaining Age	Cumulative Births to Women	Births per 1000 Women	None	Cumulative Parity Distribution per 1,000 Women						
						One or More	Two or More	Three or More	Four or More	Five or More	Six or More	Seven or More
14	1955	161,419	0	0	1,000							
15	1956	161,332	3,955	25	975	25						
16	1957	161,232	12,574	78	928	72	6					
17	1958	161,113	29,531	183	845	155	26	3				
18	1959	160,979	55,119	342	742	258	71	12	1			
19	1960	160,826	89,584	557	629	371	142	36	6	1		
20	1961	160,658	129,425	806	523	477	226	78	20	3	1	
21	1962	160,473	171,311	1,068	435	565	310	134	44	11	2	
22	1963	160,268	214,073	1,336	363	637	389	196	80	25	7	1
23	1964	160,042	254,644	1,591	308	692	457	255	120	46	15	4
24	1965	159,803	292,173	1,828	266	734	512	309	163	72	27	8
25	1966	159,547	323,437	2,027	235	765	554	350	198	98	41	15

Source: See text for a description of the methods of calculation.

TABLE 10–7
Parity Progression Ratios for Negro Women Born in 1941

Age	Year Age Attained	Progression Ratios per 100 Women[a]						
		0 to 1	1 to 2	2 to 3	3 to 4	4 to 5	5 to 6	6 to 7
14	1955	0						
15	1956	3						
16	1957	7	9					
17	1958	16	17	10				
18	1959	26	28	17	b			
19	1960	37	38	25	18	b		
20	1961	48	47	35	25	b	b	
21	1962	57	55	43	33	25	b	b
22	1963	64	61	50	41	32	26	b
23	1964	69	65	56	47	39	31	26
24	1965	73	70	60	53	45	37	31
25	1966	77	73	63	57	50	42	35

[a] The first column of progression ratios indicates the proportion of women who had at least one child by each age. The other columns indicate what proportion of women, at a given parity level, progressed to the next higher parity level by each age. The number 9 in the second column, for example, indicates that out of every 100 women who had at least one child by age 16, 9 of them also had a second child.

[b] These progression ratios were not computed because the denominator included fewer than 100 women.

Source:
  See text for a description of the methods of calculation.

Parity Progression Ratios

Another measure which was valuable for describing fertility changes was the parity progression ratio. These ratios indicate what proportion of the women at a given parity progressed to the next higher parity; that is, what proportion had at least one additional child. As indicated in Chapter 4, parity progression ratios permit analysis of change over time in family formation and are of particular assistance in determining first, how rapidly women bore children, and second, at what parity women terminated their childbearing.[39]

Table 10–7 shows parity progression ratios for the cohort born in 1941. Similar tables were constructed for the other cohorts of black women.

---

[39] For a discussion of the usefulness of parity progression ratios see: Grabill, Kiser and Whelpton, op. cit., pp. 352–355.

Probability of Birth Data

A further comparison of the fertility of different cohorts can be made if probabilities of childbearing are analyzed. We might ask about the probability that a woman of a given age would bear a child or, whether the probability of bearing a child at this age has been pretty much the same for all cohorts." A further refinement is to ask about the probability that women of a given age and at a specified parity level would bear an additional child. To answer these questions, probability of birth matrices were computed for each cohort using data about births by age of mother and order of child and the distributions of women by parity. Table 10–8 shows probabilities of childbearing for the Negro women born in 1941.

Comparison of Census and Cohort Measures of Fertility

The Census of 1960 asked married women how many children they had borne and distributions of women by age and by num-

TABLE 10–8
Probabilities of Childbearing by Age and Parity for Negro Women Born in 1941

Age	Year Age Attained	All Women[a]	First to Zero[b]	Second to First[b]	Third to Second[b]	Fourth to Third[b]	Fifth to Fourth[b]	Sixth to Fifth[b]	Seventh to Sixth[b]
14	1955	.02	.02						
15	1956	.05	.05	.25					
16	1957	.11	.09	.30	.41				
17	1958	.16	.12	.35	.40	c.			
18	1959	.21	.15	.38	.41	.48	c.		
19	1960	.25	.17	.37	.40	.45	c.	c.	
20	1961	.26	.17	.33	.38	.42	.47	c.	c.
21	1962	.27	.17	.31	.35	.39	.43	.49	c.
22	1963	.26	.15	.28	.31	.35	.39	.43	c.
23	1964	.24	.13	.23	.26	.31	.35	.39	.41
24	1965	.20	.11	.19	.20	.24	.29	.32	.34

[a] This column shows the probability that any woman in this cohort would bear a child at the specified age.

[b] These columns show the probabilities that a first birth would occur to zero parity women, that a second birth would occur to first parity women and so forth.

[c] Probabilities were not calculated when the denominator included fewer than 1000 women.

Source:
See text for a description of the methods of calculation.

TABLE 10–9
Comparison of Census and Cohort Estimates of Children Ever Born per 1,000 Women

Age in 1960	Cohort	Census	Ratio of Cohort to Census
16	75	71	106
17	178	148	120
18	335	285	118
19	557	531	105
20	839	773	108
21	1109	1024	108
22	1359	1304	104
23	1633	1550	105
24	1973	1793	110
25	2195	1992	110
26	2395	2191	109
27	2555	2397	107
28	2744	2478	111
29	2823	2601	109
30	2980	2696	111
31	3032	2773	109
32	3181	2962	107
33	3195	2941	109
34	3232	2890	112
35	3141	2857	110
36	3080	2972	104
37	3102	2944	105
38	3009	2850	106
39	3052	2887	106
40	2929	2878	102
41	2762	2787	99
42	2818	2807	100
43	2881	2810	103
44	2843	2656	107

Sources:
Census Data: U. S., Bureau of the Census, *Census of Population: 1960*, PC(2)–3A, Table 5.
Cohort Data: See text for description of methods of calculation.

ber of children were tabulated. These census data may be compared to the fertility rates derived by the cohort analysis. Table 10–9 shows the average number of children ever born per 1000 women, ages 15 to 44, as indicated by the two sources. A final column in this table shows the ratio of cohort based on cumulative fertility rate to that obtained from the 1960 Census data.

The census fertility rates should be corrected in two ways before they are compared to the cohort data. The census estimates refer to population at average ages. For instance, the age group, 16, includes some women who just became 16 years old and some women who were nearly 17. On the average, these women were 16 and 1/2 years old. Thus, the census fertility rates for this age group include some childbearing which occurred at age 16. The cohort based rates refer to exact ages. The cohort based rate for age 16, for example, includes all childbearing which occurred prior to age 16 but no childbearing at age 16. If the census rates were corrected to match cohort data, they would be reduced slightly.

Cohort rates refer to the fertility of Negro women in the coterminous United States, while the census fertility rates were tabulated for the non-whites. Non-Negro, non-whites—Indians and Orientals—tend, in the aggregate, to have lower fertility rates than Negroes. The fertility of these groups, at most ages, is more like that of whites than Negroes. Shown below are numbers of children ever born per 1000 women as indicated by the Census of 1960.[40]

Age of Women	Children Ever Born per 1,000 Women		
	Whites	Non-Negro Non-whites	Negroes
15–19	117	131	208
20–24	993	902	1320
25–29	1960	1848	2383
30–34	2398	2562	2882
35–39	2471	2872	2905
44–44	2362	3271	2758

A second adjustment should then be made to the census fertility rates to exclude the childbearing of non-Negro non-whites. If such a correction were made, the census rates for ages under 35 would be increased by a small amount.

It is impossible to make these adjustments to the census rates. It may be that the second correction would offset the first and that the net effect of the correction would be nil. If this is the case, we can assume that the cohort based rates yield estimates of fertility which are about 5 to 10 percent higher than those obtained from census data. Why should there be this dis-

---

[40] U. S., Bureau of the Census, *Census of Population: 1960*, PC(2)–3A, Tables 1 and 8.

crepancy? The chief reason is probably an assumption which is implicit in the census inquiries. Only women who reported they had been married were asked about their childbearing, while all never-married women were assumed to have no children. The results of this assumption are most obvious at ages 17 and 18 where the cohort fertility figures are about 20 percent higher than those from the census. The cohort rates probably reflect the numerous illegitimate children borne by these women. At the older ages the cohort rates exceed the census by only about 7 percent.

Census and cohort distributions of women by number of children ever borne are compared in Table 10–10. Data are shown for seven specific age groups of women. The largest differences in the distributions are in estimates of the proportion of women

TABLE 10–10
Comparison of Census and Cohort Distributions
of Women by Number of Children Ever Born: 1960

Age	Source of Data	Total	None	One	Two	Three	Four	Five or Six	Seven or More
					Women by Number of Children				
18	Census[a]	100.0%	82.6	9.9	5.4	1.6	.3	.1	.1
	Cohort	100.0	74.8	18.2	5.8	1.1	.1		
22	Census	100.0	44.9	16.7	7.4	11.1	5.7	3.8	.4
	Cohort	100.0	36.1	23.9	19.7	12.1	5.6	2.4	.2
26	Census	100.0	29.0	15.0	16.4	14.3	10.7	11.6	3.0
	Cohort	100.0	20.0	17.4	19.3	16.4	11.8	12.2	2.9
30	Census	100.0	25.1	13.8	15.5	13.2	9.7	14.0	8.7
	Cohort	100.0	18.9	13.2	16.1	14.6	11.5	16.2	9.5
34	Census	100.0	23.2	14.6	15.5	12.1	9.9	13.7	11.0
	Cohort	100.0	16.8	15.1	15.9	13.2	10.4	15.0	13.6
38	Census	100.0	26.2	16.3	14.5	10.4	9.1	10.8	12.7
	Cohort	100.0	18.8	22.2	15.2	10.4	8.1	11.5	13.8
42	Census	100.0	28.6	16.5	13.5	9.9	8.4	10.6	12.5
	Cohort	100.0	26.7	19.2	14.1	10.0	7.1	9.4	13.5

[a] Census based rates refer to non-white women. Single women were assumed to have no children.

Source:
U. S., Bureau of the Census, *Census of Population: 1960*, PC(2)–3A, Table 5.

who have had no children or only one child. Census estimates at
each age indicate there are more childless women than do the
cohort estimates. The cohort figures, on the other hand, indicate
there are more first parity women than do census estimates. As
we noted, the census assumes that never-married women are
childless, and this probably explains the larger proportions childless as indicated by census data. At the higher parity levels, there
are only small differences between the census and cohort estimates of fertility.

Subject Index

Adams, John Q., Census of 1840 critique, 26

Africa, birth control programs, 203; colonization, 31; origin of slavery, 15, 16, 21

African Colonization Society, 31

Age at marriage, differentials, 167–187; effect on fertility, 167–191; trends, 138–141

Age heaping, 262

Agricultural Adjustment Program, 48, 221, 222

Aid-to-dependent children, 133

Alabama, census enumeration, 24; Mobile mortality rates, 60; out-migration of blacks, 45; pellagra, 219

Alaska, black population, 28

Albemarle County, Virginia, venereal diseases, 224

American Indians, difficulty of enslaving, 15; identification in census, 27; treatment of by whites, 203

American Medical Association, 228

American Public Health Association, 247

Antibiotics, 73

Arizona, birth registration, 249

Arsenical drugs, 234

Atlanta, race riot, 46

Baltimore, infant mortality, 70, 71; life table, 61; public health department, 231

Birth control, methods, 195, 197–200, 202, 224, 244; trends, 10, 11

Birth Registration Area, 228, 246, 247, 249–251

Birth registration system, 25, 78, 79, 246–255

Black laws in the Midwest, 41

Black Muslims' views of birth control, 203

Boll weevil, 11, 46, 48, 71, 131, 220, 221

Boston, black population, 16, 44; infant mortality, 212

California, black population, 28

Cambridge, Mass., public health department, 231

Canada: destination of fugitive slaves, 31

Cancer, 74

Carpetbaggers, influence upon Census of 1870, 24

Catholic Church influence, 21

Census enumeration, possible errors, 23–29, 66, 78, 255–262

Chadwick Report, 230

Chamberlain-Kahn Act, 233

Charleston, as early colony, 15; as port of entry, 30; as port for export, 18; black population, 19; mortality rate, 60; occupation of blacks, 129; public health department, 231

Charles Town. See Charleston

Chesapeake Bay Area slave population, 19

Chicago, birth control use by black women, 198; black population, 46, 47, 75

Childlessness, as indication of health conditions, 109–112; differentials, 110, 115–123, 163, 164; trends, 3, 56, 57, 94–96

Children's Bureau, and birth registration system, 247; health activities, 229

Cholera, 38, 58, 225, 243

Cincinnati, black population, 42, 44

Cirrhosis, 74

Cohort fertility rates, calculation, 246–277; trends, 77–100

Columbus, Ohio, black population, 42

Components of difference between two rates methodology, 112, 114, 150

Connecticut, as part of Death Registration Area, 61; black population, 17

Consumer Price Index trends, 236, 238, 239

Cotton farming, 11, 29, 30, 45, 46, 48, 73, 130, 131, 218, 221

Death Registration Area, development, 208; mortality rates, 6, 61, 62, 71, 225, 227, 264

Delaware, registration of births, 249

Demographic Transition, 14, 242

Department of Labor. See Moynihan, Daniel Patrick

Desertion, effect on fertility, 159–164; rural-urban differences, 148–150; trends, 143, 145, 157–159

Detroit, black population, 42

Diabetes, 74

Diarrhea, as cause of death, 70, 72; associated with pellagra, 217

Diet trends, 36, 37, 72, 215–222, 241

Division of Veneral Disease, 233, 234

Divorce, as a reported marital status, 137, 138, 143, 145, 148; effect on fertility, 162; socio-economic differences, 154, 155

Education, effect on age at marriage, 166–187; effect on female fertility, 120–123, 166–187; effect on male fertility, 124, 125, 188–191; effect on marital status, 152–155; trends, 235–240

Emancipation Proclamation, effect on slaves, 49; related to family system, 128, 129

Emphysema, 74

England, comparative mortality in, 36, 228; public health, 230

European immigration, 17

Fertility, regional differentials, 6, 104–106, 112–117; region-of-birth differences, 114–117, 167–187; rural-urban differentials, 6, 106–109, 112–114; socio-economic differen-

tials, 4, 117–123, 167–191; trends, 2–6, 13, 14, 20, 21, 31–35, 51–58, 76–126

Fetal mortality rate trends, 210, 212, 222

Freedman's Bureau, 49, 59, 130

Genocide, black, 203

Georgia, black population, 19; census enumeration, 24; cotton production, 29, 221

Gonorrhea, effect on fertility, 12, 215, 222; Prevalence, 224, 225, 234, 235

Grant, President Ulysses S., 256

Growth of American Families Study, 108, 123

Hawaii, black population, 28

Hayes, President Rutherford B., 45

Heart disease, 74

Hill-Burton Act, 229, 232

Hoffman, Frederick, 60

Home ownership trends, 210, 229, 230, 252

Hoover, President Herbert H., 231

Hudson Valley, 16

Illegitimacy trends, 130, 131, 133, 146, 160, 173, 204

Illinois, ban on black immigration, 41; migration of blacks to, 46

Immigration and Naturalization Service estimates of out-migration, 258

Indentured servants, 15

Indiana, as part of Death Registration Area, 46; ban on black immigration, 41

Indigo, 19, 29

Infant mortality trends, 70, 212–215, 222–235

Influenza, as cause of death, 74; effect on infant mortality, 214; epidemic of 1918, 71

Kansas, migration of blacks, 45

LaFollett-Bullwinkle Act, 234

Land ownership, 219

Legal marriage among slaves, 129

Logan, West Virginia, 197, 198
Louisiana, black population, 28, 30; out-migration of blacks, 45; pellagra, 219
Louisiana Purchase, 30
Louisville infant mortality rate, 212

Macon County, Alabama, health conditions, 224
Maine, as part of Death Registration Area, 61
Malaria, 18, 38, 70, 243
Marital status of blacks, effect on fertility, 8–10, 159–165, 166–187; rural-urban differences, 142, 143, 147–151; socio-economic differences, 151–159; trends in, 8–10, 127–165
Marriage Registration Area, 139
"Marriage squeeze," 86, 98, 141
Maryland, black population, 19; infant mortality, 214; mortality trend, 225; tobacco growing, 18
Massachusetts, abolition of slavery, 18; as part of Death Registration Area, 61; black population, 17; infant mortality, 214; life table, 36; sanitary conditions, 231; vital statistics, 246
Maternal mortality trends, 208–212, 224, 228
Metropolitan Life Insurance Company mortality records, 71, 72, 208
Michigan, as part of Death Registration Area, 61; black population, 42, 44
Middle passage, mixing of slaves, 128; mortality, 21
Miscegenation, 21
Mississippi, pellagra, 219; post-reconstruction government, 45
Mobile, Alabama, 60
Mortality trends, 6–8, 20, 21, 35–39, 58–74, 206–235; fetal, 210–212
Mulatto, Census definition, 26, 129
Myers Blended Index, 262

National Committee on Maternal Health, 197
National Fertility Study, 203

National Institutes of Child Health and Human Development, 233
National Office of Vital Statistics, birth tabulations, 267
New Amsterdam, black population, 16; early settlement, 15
New England, trade, 16; vital registration in, 246, 249
New Hampshire, as part of Death Registration Area, 61
New Jersey, as part of the Death Registration Area, 61; tabulations of birth by race, 255
New Mexico, registration of births, 250
New Orleans, free black population, 129; life tables, 61; mortality trends, 60
Newport, Rhode Island, early settlement, 15
New York City, birth control use, 198; black population, 17, 44–46, 75; Census enumeration in 1870, 256; infant mortality, 70, 212; rioting, 17
New York State, as part of Death Registration Area, 61; black population, 17; mortality trends, 214. See also New York City
Nicotinic acid in relation to pellagra, 217
North Carolina, infant mortality trends, 214; out-migration of blacks, 45
Northwest Ordinance, 41

Octoroon, Census definition, 26, 27
Ohio, admission to union, 28; ban on black immigration, 41
Oklahoma birth registration, 249
Oral contraceptives, 202, 244
Orientals, Census identification, 27

Parity progression ratios, 89–92, 273
Pellagra, 11, 215, 217–222
Penicillin, 235
Pennsylvania, birth registration, 247; black population, 17. See also Pittsburgh; Philadelphia
Pennsylvania Railroad, use of black workers, 47

Philadelphia, black population, 44, 46; census enumeration of 1870, 256; discrimination, 185; early settlement, 15; free blacks, 129; infant mortality, 71, 212; public health activities, 231
Pittsburgh, black population, 45; riots, 44
Pneumonia, as cause of death, 70, 74; in relation to infant mortality, 214
Portsmouth, Ohio, black population, 42
Princeton Fertility Study, 187
Providence, Rhode Island, health department, 231
Prudential Insurance Company, comments of Frederick Hoffman, 60
Public Health Service, development, 230–234; fight against disease, 12, 217, 224

Quadroon, Census definition, 26, 27
Quakers, assistance to blacks in Michigan, 44; opposition to slavery in Pennsylvania, 17

Red Cross, fight against pellagra, 219
Region-of-birth, effects of fertility on family status, 171–187
Rhode Island, as part of Death Registration Area, 61; black population, 17
Richmond, Virginia, infant mortality rates, 212; out-migration of blacks, 45
Rio Grande Valley boll weevil infestation, 220
Rockefeller Foundation, 219
Roosevelt, President Franklin Delano, 231
Roosevelt, President Theodore, 231
Rosenwald Fund, 219, 220
Royal African Company, slave trading, 16

Salpingitis, 222
Salvarsan as treatment for venereal diseases, 234
Savannah, Georgia, mortality, 60

Scalawags, effect on Census of 1870, 24
Serologic tests for venereal diseases, 224
Shattuck Report, 230
Sheppard-Towner Act, 228
Slave breeding study, 35
Slave trade, reasons for, 1, 15–21; volume, 29–31
Smallpox, 58
Social Darwinism, 59
Social Security Act, effect on public health activities, 12, 228–234
South Carolina, agricultural productivity, 18, 29, 30, 221; black population, 19; census enumeration, 24; pellagra, 218
South Dakota, admission to the Union, 28
Spartanburg, birth control use, 196–198
Sulfa drugs, 73, 210
Syphilis, control, 233–235; prevalence, 12, 74, 215, 222–227

Tennessee, black population, 19; mortality trends, 72; pellagra, 219
Tetanus as cause of death, 39
Texas, birth registration, 247; black population, 28; boll weevil infestation, 131
Tidewater Area black population, 19
Tobacco, 18, 30, 48, 221
Treaty of Paris, 17
Tuberculosis, 38, 59, 70, 72, 74, 225
Tuskegee, Alabama, health conditions, 72, 73
Typhoid Fever, 70, 72

Unemployment trends, 240
Urbanization, effect on fertility, 112–114; effect on marital status, 147–151; trends, 44–51

Venereal diseases. See Syphilis; Gonorrhea
Vermont as part of Death Registration Area, 61
Virginia, black population, 19; infant mortality, 214; tobacco growing, 18; vital registration, 246

Washington, D.C., as part of Death
   Registration Area, 61; black pop-
   ulation, 185; infant mortality, 70;
   life expectation, 6
Wasserman test, 222
West Indies, marriage, 21; trade,
   15, 16, 18
Widowhood, effect on childbearing,

159–164; rural-urban differences,
   142, 143; socio-economic differences, 152–155; trends, 137–138,
   145–149, 183
Wilmington, N.C., riot, 46

Yellow Fever, 38, 45, 225, 243

Author Index

Alexander, W. W., 222
Allen, James E., 16
Altmeyer, Arthur J., 229
Anderson, Odin W., 234

Back, Kurt W., 159
Baker, Ray S., 46
Bancroft, Frederic, 30, 35
Beebe, Gilbert, 197, 198
Behrman, S. J., 192
Bentley, George R., 58, 59
Billings, John S., 61, 69, 246
Blacker, C. P., 242
Bogue, Donald, v
Bontemps, Anna, 45, 46
Borgatta, Edgar F., 177
Bridenbaugh, Carl, 15, 16, 18, 19
Bumpass, Larry, 109, 201

Campbell, Arthur, v, 89, 97, 108, 109,
   111, 120, 123, 167, 185, 192, 199
Chandrasekar, C., 251
Chicago Committee on Race Rela-
   tions, 46, 47, 70
Chitwood, Oliver P., 16, 19
Cho, Lee Jay, 54
Clague, Alice J., 160
Clark, Taliaferro, 224
Coale, Ansley J., 25, 32, 33, 54, 55,
   63, 66, 68, 78, 136, 258, 263, 265
Collinson, J., 247
Conroy, Jack, 45, 46
Cooks, Edmond, 34
Corsa, Leslie, 192
Cowley, Malcom, 30
Crain, Gladys L., 222, 224

Daniels, John, 44
Dauer, Carl C., 243
Davie, Maurice R., 227
Davis, John P., 47
DeBow, J. D. B., 28
Demeny, Paul, 32, 33, 63, 67, 68
Deming, W. E., 251

Donald, Henderson H., 60
Dorn, Harold F., 104, 207, 208
Douglas, Paul, 228, 231
Dow, George F., 30
Dublin, Louis I., 20, 36, 38, 62, 68,
   70–72
DuBois, W. E. B., 18, 29, 30, 44, 46,
   59, 69, 70, 71, 185, 203
Duncan, Beverly, 168
Duncan, O. Dudley, v, 114, 177, 188

Ehrlich, Paul, 234
Elkins, Stanley M., 35
Embree, Edwin R., 222
Eversley, D. E. C., 20

Farley, Reynolds, 32, 49
Folger, John K., 168
Foudray, Elbertie, 248, 249
Frank, Myrna E., 120
Franklin, John H., 16, 17, 47, 59
Frazier, Franklin, 9, 17, 35, 128–133,
   142, 145, 157, 185, 220
Freedman, Ronald, v, 109, 111, 120,
   123, 167, 192
Freeman, Bettie, 104
Fuller, George N., 42–44

Garvey, Amy J., 203
Garvey, Marcus, 203
Gee, Wilson, 232
Gillman, Joseph, 217
Gillman, Theodore, 217
Gingrich, Paul, 67, 68
Glass, David V., 20
Glick, Paul, v
Goldberg, David, v, 109, 114
Goldberger, Joseph, 217–219
Goodrich, Carter, 221
Gover, Mary, 72
Grabill, Wilson H., v, 54, 89, 92, 96,
   97, 103, 104, 106, 119, 120, 123,
   167, 273
Graunt, John, 106

Green, Constance M., 49, 59, 70
Greene, Evarts B., 17, 19–21
Greene, Lorenzo J., 16
Greville, Thomas N. E., 67, 69, 257
Grove, Robert D., 208, 210, 212, 214, 216, 217, 220, 223, 225, 233, 249

Hanlon, John J., 73, 228, 230–232
Hanson, Mary F., 237
Harlan, Louis R., 186
Harrington, Virginia, 17, 19–21
Harris, Abram L., 44–46, 158
Harris, Seale, 217, 219
Harter, Carl L., 185
Hauser, Philip, v
Hayse, George E., 44
Hazen, H. H., 222, 224
Heer, Clarence, 73, 221
Heer, David M., 25
Heise, David R., 177
Heller, J. J., 233–235
Hermalin, Albert I., v
Heskovitz, Melvin J., 29
Hesslink, George K., 42, 44
Hetzel, Alice M., 208, 210, 214, 233
Hodge, William, v
Hoffman, Frederick, 60
Holmes, S. J., 71, 72, 212, 213
Hutchinson, E. P., 34

Jacobs, Philip P., 74
Jarvis, Edward, 26
Jernegan, Marcus W., 15
Johnson, Charles S., 72, 73, 214, 219, 222
Jordan, Winthrop, 21, 31, 38
Joseph, Herbert L., 222

Kampmeier, Rudolph H., 222
Karpinos, Bernard D., 54
Kashif, Lonnie, 203
Kellogg, Paul U., 45
Kennedy, Louise, 72
Keyfitz, Nathan, v
King, Ambrose, 235
King, Martin L., 203
Kiser, Clyde V., 89, 92, 96, 97, 103, 104, 106, 119, 120, 123, 167, 273
Klebba, A. Joan, 74
Klein, Herbert S., 18, 21, 35
Korns, Robert F., 243

Lenroot, Katherine R., 229
Lerner, Monroe, 234
Liebow, Elliot, 185
Linder, Forrest E., 208, 212, 216, 217, 220, 223, 225
Litwack, Leon F., 42, 44
Lopez, Alvaro, 32
Lotka, Alfred J., 31, 36, 62, 70–72

Mannix, Daniel P., 30
Manus, Edgar J., 16
Matras, Judah, v
McCarthy, Mary A., 214, 215
McDowell, Arthur J., 104
McKee, Samuel, 15
McKie, Thomas J., 59
McNeil, H. L., 222
McPherson, James M., 49, 59
Meier, August, 45, 50
Miller, Herman P., 74, 137, 239
Miller, Kelly, 25
Montgomery, Hamilton, 217
Moore, Emily, 201
Moore, George H., 15
Moore, Joseph E., 222
Moore, Wilbert E., 168
Moriyama, Iwao M., 73–74
Mott, Frederic D., 73
Moynihan, Daniel P., 132, 133, 145, 157
Mustard, Henry S., 234
Myers, Paul J., 262
Myrdal, Gunnar, 48, 74, 158, 186, 199, 207, 208, 219–221

Nam, Charles B., 168
Nelson, Nels A., 222, 224
Nesbitt, Robert E., 74, 210, 214, 228, 229, 233
Nettels, Curtis P., 19

Okun, Bernard, 52, 111
Olmstead, Frederic, 24
Ormsby, Oliver S., 217
Osofsky, Gilbert, 46

Palmore, James A., v
Patterson, John, 108, 109, 111, 120, 185, 192, 199
Pearl, Raymond, 194–196, 198

Phillips, Ulrich B., 17–19, 29–31, 35, 36, 225
Postell, William D., 36–39
Potter, J., 20
Potter, Robert, 187
Powell, Theophilus O., 59

Quarles, Benjamin, 31
Quillin, Frank U., 42

Rainwater, Lee, 132
Reidrich, A. W., 247
Reiss, Albert J., Jr., 188
Rhodes, F. D., 247
Roemer, Milton, I., 73
Rossiter, William, 20
Rudwick, Elliot M., 47
Ryder, Norman B., 185, 187, 192, 196, 201, 202

Sagi, Philip, 174, 187
Schlesinger, Edward R., 74, 210, 214, 228, 229, 233
Schuman, Leonard M., 243
Sellers, James B., 37
Shapiro, Sam, 74, 210, 214, 228–229, 233, 246, 250
Sheldon, Eleanor B., 168
Shorter, Frederic, 32, 33, 63, 68
Sibley, Elbridge, 72
Siegel, Jacob S., 25, 66
Smillie, Wilson S., 231
Smith, Abbot E., 16
Smith, Mary, 203
Spencer, Herbert, 120
Spear, Allen H., 46
Spero, Sterling D., 44, 45, 158
Spiegelman, Mortimer, 36, 62, 68, 70–72
Stampp, Kenneth M., 34–39, 225
Stanton, William, 26
Staudenraus, Philip J., 31
Stix, Regine, 196, 198, 219
Stycos, J. M., 159
Sutherland, Stella H., 20
Sydenstricker, E., 218, 219
Sydnor, Charles S., 37, 39, 225

Taeuber, Alma F., 47

Taeuber, Conrad, 47, 48, 138
Taeuber, Irene B., 47, 48, 138
Taeuber, Karl F., v, 47
Tandy, Elizabeth C., 230
Taylor, Joe Gray, 28, 37, 38, 225
Taylor, Orville W., 36, 38, 39, 225
Terris, Milton, 217
Thompson, Warren S., 58, 107, 193, 194
Truesdell, Leon E., 140
Tucker, George, 28
Turner, Edward R., 44

Usilton, Lida J., 224, 227, 234, 235

Vance, R. B., 218, 220, 221
Ventura, Stephanie J., 160
Visaria, Pravin M., 63
Vonderlehr, R. A., 227, 233–235

Wade, Richard C., 37, 42, 44, 49
Walker, Francis, 24
Waring, C. H., 218
Warner, Sam Bass, 44
Weiss, Richard S., 222
Westoff, Charles F., 174, 201, 202, 185, 187, 192, 196
Wharton, Vernon L., 45, 59
Wheeler, G. A., 218
Whelpton, Pascal K., 77, 89, 92, 96, 97, 104, 106, 108, 109, 111, 119, 120, 123, 167, 185, 192, 199, 248, 249, 264, 265, 269, 273
Wilcox, R. R., 222
Willcox, Walter F., 58, 66, 104, 193, 246, 256
Willets, David G., 218
Winsborough, Hal, v
Winston, Ellen, 219, 221
Woodson, Carter, 72
Woodward, C. Vann, 45, 46
Woofter, T. J., 218, 219, 221
Wright, Carroll D., 26
Wright, R. R., Jr., 45

Yancey, William, 132

Zelnik, Melvin, 25, 32, 33, 68, 262, 263, 265

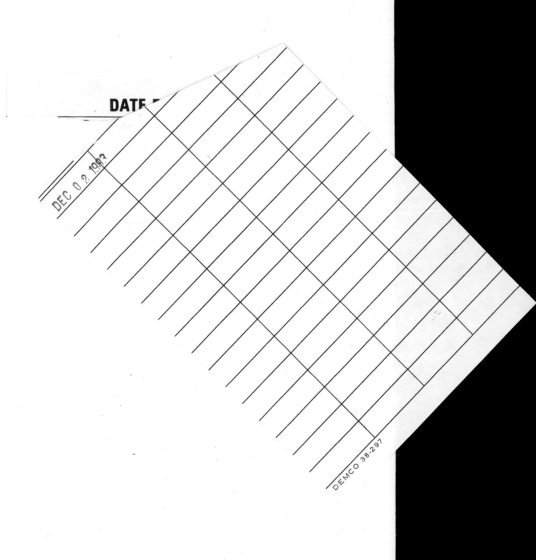

DATE

DEC 0 2 1993

DEMCO 38-297